OUTSTANDING IN
THEIR FIELD

OUTSTANDING IN THEIR FIELD

HOW WOMEN CORPORATE DIRECTORS SUCCEED

Elizabeth Ghaffari

Foreword by Toni Rembe

PRAEGER
An Imprint of ABC-CLIO, LLC

A B C CLIO

Santa Barbara, California • Denver, Colorado • Oxford, England

Library of Congress Cataloging-in-Publication Data

Ghaffari, Elizabeth.
  Outstanding in their field : how women corporate directors succeed / Elizabeth Ghaffari ; foreword by Toni Rembe.
    p. cm.
  Includes bibliographical references and index.
  ISBN 978-0-313-37584-2 (hard copy : alk. paper) — ISBN 978-0-313-37585-9 (ebook)
  1. Women executives.   2. Boards of directors.   3. Corporate governance.
4. Leadership in women.   I. Title.
HD6054.3.G43   2009
658.4'22082—dc22   2009009966

13   12   11   10   09   1   2   3   4   5

This book is also available on the World Wide Web as an eBook.
Visit www.abc-clio.com for details.

ABC-CLIO, LLC
130 Cremona Drive, P.O. Box 1911
Santa Barbara, California 93116-1911

This book is printed on acid-free paper ∞

Manufactured in the United States of America

To
my mother,
the first outstanding woman in my life,
with thanks for all the times she read to me

Contents

FOREWORD

Corporations are viewed by many as faceless and rigid. But they are fascinating organizations in which human beings bring goods and products to the marketplace and thrive among the plethora of human relationships that involve customers, employees, investors, lenders, innovators, suppliers, government and community representatives, and countless others. In our fast-moving global environment with its rapidly changing economic times, an enlightened Chief Executive Officer realizes the need for an outside group of smart, thoughtful, and dedicated directors who meet periodically with top management to oversee matters of the corporation's business strategy, operations, and governance: a group of men and women from different backgrounds who are interested in the long-term viability and profitability of the corporation and are not afraid to challenge conventional wisdom, hazard unsolicited advice, and ask tough questions.

It is clear that none of the outstanding women interviewed by Ms. Ghaffari sat down at age 19 or 20 and planned her career around becoming a director of a *Fortune* 1000 company. Rather, as Ms. Ghaffari's prescient book demonstrates, corporate directorships are usually the by-product of success in another field, not a job someone aspires to as an end in itself. The interviews themselves illuminate some of the character traits and personal attributes that contributed to the successful careers of these exceptional directors—careers in which they developed the expertise, experience, and recognition that raised their visibility and desirability as potential corporate directors. Most had a passion for their chosen field, an intellectual curiosity, an interest in building a business or an organization, and the time and willingness for board service when the opportunity arose.

Some of the women interviewed started their careers in the teaching profession, confirming the theory that skills in communication, organization, and group psychology gleaned from the classroom often translate into success in business and other endeavors, including the boardroom. Many contributed in a meaningful way to community and charitable organizations where they were noted by other leaders and recommended for corporate board service. All of them, regardless of background, demonstrated a passion for their chosen fields, an intellectual curiosity, an interest in business- or organization-building, and the time and willingness for board service.

The interviews show how networking can add visibility to potential director candidates and how the board itself can be a resource that extends the corporation's network. They also show how serving on a board with such a group of interesting and talented people can be a learning experience in itself, and even fun. Of course the type of team assembled for any board will depend on the industry and the particular corporation involved: health services, consumer products, entertainment, engineering, communications, transportation, natural resources—the list and sublists are endless. The company may be vertically or horizontally integrated or a conglomerate of unrelated enterprises. It may be primarily local, far-flung and international, expanding into new regions, or downsizing.

In all cases, an effective board will be a resource for keeping the company on target, drawn from people who have demonstrated success and knowledge in areas impacting the corporation and who understand the basic business and value drivers and the environments in which the company operates. Such a board would include people who are able to work through the noise on Wall Street and the daily gyrations of the company's stock, who know that, in the media, management will be heroes one day and villains the next, and that a large company cannot consistently grow annual sales and profits at a fixed percentage into infinity. They know that blindly following the latest business mantra, such as "pay for performance," can cause stock-based executive compensation to get out of hand and that a company focused on meeting analysts' expectations can lose its competitive edge. Most importantly, an effective board knows that a strong and ethical internal management team is the primary key to the success and longevity of any large organization.

Clearly, as more and more talented women join the ranks of men who historically had almost exclusive access to top leadership positions, the percentage of women corporate directors of *Fortune* 1000 companies will increase. These women may come from business, law, academia, government, engineering, or science but most will be like the amazing directors interviewed here: outstanding in their field.

Toni Rembe

Toni Rembe is a partner (retired) at the law firm of Pillsbury Winthrop Shaw Pittman, LLP, and president of a Northern California legal and social justice foundation. She has served on the board of directors of many public companies and is co-founder of the Arthur and Toni Rembe Rock Center for Corporate Governance at Stanford University Law School.

Acknowledgments

I used to read acknowledgments and wonder to myself, "How could so many people help her write that book?" Now I know—one wonderful person at a time.

Ralph Ward was the first to take a real chance on me by publishing a draft of the first chapter in the *Corporate Board* magazine. Dr. Susan Murphy (who coauthored two books on women in business with Dr. Pat Heim) provided encouragement and moral support over a period of three years. Alice Krause (who owns and operates the blog NewsOnWomen.com) is the one who kept telling me to think and write about all the progress women have made. I have never actually met these three people except over the Internet, yet I could not have done this work without their inspiration.

Frances Anderton (KCRW producer and host) was the first to interview me. She and her writer/director husband, Robin Bennett Stein, read and reread more versions of the proposal and first chapters than I ever could have imagined. I am indebted to the governance education and training provided by outstanding professionals, especially Stanford Graduate School of Business professor Maureen F. McNichols (a founder of the Stanford Graduate School of Business governance program), Susan Shultz (author of *The Board Book*), and the great team of leaders brought together by Don McCrae at the UCLA Anderson School of Management director training program.

Bonnie G. Hill sat down with me over breakfast and gave me insight into board performance and director roles that I had never seen anywhere in print. Anita K. Jones was the first woman whose biography provided the inspiration for the concept of woman who are outstanding in their field. Each of the women who agreed to be interviewed deserves special thanks for her time, her honesty, her professionalism, and her graciousness. A special thank you goes to Toni Rembe for her thoughtful Foreword. It was exciting to meet and to talk with these incredible individuals. I learned so much from researching all of their backgrounds.

Many people read and commented on earlier versions of this book, such that they may no longer recognize the final product. Anne and David Yeadon deserve special thanks for their editing and for going the extra mile for me in discussions with publishers. Frank Mittelbach, professor emeritus at UCLA Anderson School of Management, was instrumental in helping me understand business and labor economics and how to think like a businessperson. I am grateful for all the early feedback from my family (Nancy, Marilyn, Martha, and Devon) and the supportive comments from Hans, Cynthia, and David. I don't know how to tell these individuals and others how much I appreciate their tolerance of my one-way transmissions on the subject of women on corporate boards of directors.

I am grateful to Jeff Olson, Mary Cotofan, and the dedicated editors at Praeger/ ABC-CLIO and ApexCoVantage for re-crafting this work into its completed form.

Finally, I wish to thank my husband, Fereydoon, who kept encouraging me during the toughest times, who kept reading draft after draft after draft, and who kept providing ideas on a subject that he said was not really his strong suit—except that he always offered incredible insight and perspective. This book could not have been finished without his continuing patience and enthusiasm.

Abbreviations

ACT: American Conservatory Theater

ADA: Programming language named for Ada Lovelace

AECOM: architecture, engineering, consulting, operations, and maintenance

AHCPR: Agency for Health Care Policy and Research

AIG: American International Group Inc.

ARCO: Atlantic Richfield Company

AT&T: American Telephone & Telegraph Company Inc.

BBC: British Broadcasting Corporation

BHP Billiton: Broken Hill Proprietary Company merged with Billiton Company

BP: British Petroleum

C200: Committee of 200

CAD/CAM: Computer-aided design/computer-aided manufacturing

Caltech: California Institute of Technology

CBS: Columbia Broadcasting System

CCI: Cox Communications Inc.

CEO: Chief executive officer

CFO: Chief financial officer

CFR: Council on Foreign Relations

CHELA: California Higher Education Loan Authority Inc.

CIBC: Canadian Imperial Bank of Commerce

CIO: Chief information officer

CNBC: Consumer News and Business Channel

CoMAD: College of Media Arts & Design at Drexel University

COO: Chief operating officer

COSMOS: California State Summer School for Mathematics and Science

CRA: Community Redevelopment Authority

CTO: Chief technology officer

DMJM: member company of AECOM named for Daniel, Mann, Johnson, and Mendenhall

EDAW: member company of AECOM named for Eckbo, Dean, Austin, and Williams

ENSR International: member company of AECOM named for Environmental SeRvices (now AECOM Environmental)

ERA: Equal rights amendment

FDIC: Federal Deposit Insurance Corporation

FedEx: Federal Express Corporation

GE: General Electric Company

GM: General Motors

GTE: General Telephone & Electronics Corporation (now GTE Corporation)

HMO: Health maintenance organization

HP: Hewlett-Packard Company

HR: Human resources

IP: Internet protocol

IPO: Initial public offering

JPL: Jet Propulsion Laboratory

KCRW: K College Radio Workshop (public radio station owned by Santa Monica Community College District)

LACMA: Los Angeles County Museum of Art

LAN: Local area network

LLC: Limited liability company

LLP: Limited liability partnership

LP: Limited partnership

LSAT: Law School Admission Test

LSU: Louisiana State University

MIT: Massachusetts Institute of Technology

MS: Multiple sclerosis

NAFTA: North American Free Trade Agreement

NASA: National Aeronautics and Space Administration

NASMD: National Association of State Medical Directors

Nelnet: National Education Loan Network Inc.

NEPA: National Environmental Protection Act

NOW: National Organization for Women

NYNEX: New York/New England Exchange

OEM: original equipment manufacturer

OPEC: Organization of the Petroleum Exporting Countries

OS/2: Operating System/2

P&L: Profit and loss

PBX: Private business exchange

PCIP: Pacific Council on International Policy

PEIA: Public Employees Insurance Agency

PG&E: Pacific Gas & Electric Company

PIMCO: Pacific Investment Management Company

PLC: Public limited company

PLLC: Professional limited liability corporation

PSRI: Professional School Restructuring Initiative

R&D: Research and development

REIT: Real estate investment trust

RTC: Resolution Trust Corporation

SBC: Southwestern Bell Corporation

SBIC: Small business investment corporation

SCHIP: States' Children's Health Insurance Program

SEPA: State Environmental Protection Act

TIAA-CREF: Teachers Insurance and Annuity Association, College Retirement Equities Fund

UC Berkeley: University of California, Berkeley

UC Irvine: University of California, Irvine

UC San Diego: University of California, San Diego

UCD: University of California, Davis

UCLA: University of California, Los Angeles

UN: United Nations

USC: University of Southern California

USD: University of San Diego
UT Dallas: University of Texas at Dallas
WTO: World Trade Organization
WVU: West Virginia University
YMCA: Young Men's Christian Association
YWCA: Young Women's Christian Association

Overview: Women and Corporate Boards

Outstanding in Their Field is about 15 women with little in common except that they are directors at top *Fortune* 1000 public company boards. Each life story presents a unique collection of decisions made and lessons learned by the individual as she followed her chosen career into the boardroom. Most of the women acquired experience in several spheres: corporate finance and government or entrepreneurship and investment, for example. All the women are enjoying doing exactly what they love, applying their knowledge to address tough contemporary challenges, and representing the interests of shareholders to the best of their abilities and with a keen awareness of their duty of care and their duty of loyalty. These are the leaders—the women who have been nominated to public company boards of directors in today's tough, highly regulated world of contemporary governance. They are in very high demand because of their expertise and experience. If we wish to see more women directors, then we will need to ensure that there are more women like these outstanding individuals—women who are able, prepared, and willing to serve.

Every month, we see more talented, competent, and capable women being nominated to public company boards of directors, in addition to women being added to top leadership roles of leading firms nationwide and around the world. What a difference it makes when women and men collaborate to build something better— schools, houses, and businesses. This is a book about how outstanding women collaborate as corporate board members.

GOVERNANCE: WHAT IS IT?

The focus of corporate boards is building successful businesses. This book looks at how these talented women became corporate directors and how others might accomplish this goal in the future. The issue of women on boards comes down to a question of whether women are ready and willing to lead and govern in the business marketplace.

Governance, as the leadership of for-profit, publicly held stock companies is known, is a concept that has been around for centuries. It is guidance, or the strategic oversight of a public company's financial, legal, and operational performance. Governance and boards of directors came into existence in the early days of colonial America, when British companies sent emissaries overseas to check on how their invested funds were being handled by their trade partners.[1]

Governance exists because shareholders need someone to act as an agent to monitor how a business entity is using the shareholders' investments. Corporate governance is the unique responsibility of boards of directors working with executive management. Boards are the guides for contemporary businesses; they do not have operational or management responsibilities. Boards are "the bosses' boss"— they oversee and ensure that a sound strategic direction exists and is being followed properly.

Governance is a field experiencing dramatic change in the shadows of financial fiascos at companies like Enron, WorldCom, Tyco, and Arthur Anderson. Good governance is important if we want to avoid the abuses seen at those firms. Good governance is not easy to define. In part, it depends upon the enforcement of rules and regulations such as the Sarbanes-Oxley Act of 2002 (the Public Company Accounting Reform and Investor Protection Act). Passage of this bill reflected the public's pressure on Congress to restore confidence in accounting and the publicly traded securities market and ensure ethical business practices through heightened levels of disclosure and accountability of corporate executives.

Tougher new corporate compliance requirements stemming from the Sarbanes-Oxley Act and exchange regulations have increased opportunities for women to participate in corporate leadership by increasing board demand for independent directors with financial expertise and broad corporate and international experience.

BOARDS ARE CHANGING

Boards are also changing from the inside. In response to increased shareholder pressure, boards of directors are making their operations and deliberations more transparent. Boards now publish their codes of conduct and other details of their inner workings on their Web sites, under the heading of "Investor Relations," rather than merely in once-a-year proxy reports. They report details about their directors, when they were nominated, how their nomination came about, their education and experience, the other boards on which they serve, past board service, non-corporate board seats held, and whether they are considered independent or are affiliated with management, directly or indirectly through consulting or family relationships. Boards today reveal detailed information about their committee charters, who serves as a committee chair or member, the number of times the committee met during the year, and which directors are financial experts, according to the definition of the Securities and Exchange Commission. Companies may report if directors attended certified director training during the year. They detail the compensation paid to all directors and provide even more itemized information about the compensation of top executives.

Boards are making major changes to improve their internal operations. More boards elect all directors annually, eliminating staggered terms, which used to buffer members of the board from scrutiny and limit accountability to shareholders. Most boards have processes through which shareholders may nominate directors. Boards are getting smaller and more manageable. Directors are more responsible for directly contracting with auditors, compensation experts, and other consultants. Boards are more likely to have a mandatory director retirement age, term-length limits, limits on the number of concurrently held board positions, limits on the CEO's participation on outside boards, and minimum requirements as to board and committee meeting attendance. And boards are more likely than ever before to evaluate their own performance.

Boards today publish the decision-making criteria (skills and competencies matrices) that their nominating or governance committees apply in their search for new director candidates. Inexperienced directors who are not up to the challenge of the new regulatory environment are being let go. Independent nominees who meet the heightened expectations of all shareholders and stakeholders are being added. Women are benefiting from all of these changes: they are in greater demand as competent and independent-minded directors.

WOMEN ON BOARDS: TRENDS

The opportunities for qualified women to serve on corporate boards are growing with each passing year. Today, an estimated 70 percent of corporate boards are looking for "diversity" candidates—minorities and women. Yet many women-board-member advocates persist in the belief that a director role is an unmet entitlement or a right. Rather, it is recognition of the value or wisdom that an individual brings to a company in its current position of economic growth or restructuring. Today's 15 percent average occupancy—the share of seats held by women on boards listed among the top *Fortune* 500 or Standard & Poor's 200 corporations—might seem small. But it is an accurate reflection of how many women today are both capable and aspire to serve as public company directors. They are the able and the willing.

Imagine what it was like in 1971 when Patricia Roberts Harris was the only woman director on any corporate board (IBM Corporation). She also was the first African American woman director. Should we only look at her double-token status or should we look instead at the competence and experience she brought to that boardroom? Ms. Harris came to the boards at IBM, Scott Paper Company, and Chase Manhattan Bank as a lawyer, law professor, and law school dean with extensive government experience. She was the first African American woman named U.S. ambassador (Luxembourg); was dean of Howard University School of Law; and was named secretary of Housing and Urban Development, then secretary of Health, Education and Welfare, and finally secretary of Health and Human Services, all under the Carter administration.[2]

Juanita Morris Kreps is another notable female who was named the first woman board member of the New York Stock Exchange and a director at Armco, AT&T, Chrysler, Citicorp, GTE, J. C. Penney, Kodak, R. J. Reynolds, TIAA-CREF, and United Airlines. An academic economist who specialized in labor demographics, she was appointed the first woman U.S. secretary of commerce by President Carter. She was the first person honored as the director of the year by the National Association of Corporate Directors when it began bestowing the award in 1987.[3]

Shirley Mount Hufstedler is another woman who came by way of the law to directorships in the early 1980s at Hewlett-Packard, U.S. West, and Harman International Industries (where she chairs the audit committee today). She is attorney of counsel at Morrison-Foerster; was a partner in Hufstedler, Miller, Carlson & Bardsley; served 11 years as a judge of the U.S. Court of Appeals for the Ninth Circuit; and was the first female U.S. secretary of education.[4]

Other California women who led the way into the corporate boardroom include Mary E. Lanigar: one of the first women in the country to become a Certified Public Accountant (CPA), the first woman partner at a "Big Eight" accounting firm (Arthur Young & Company), and also a lawyer. She was the first woman director at Wells Fargo Co. (1973–1993), and an early director at Transamerica Corp., Lucky Stores Inc., The Pacific Lumber Co., Castle & Cooke, and the Pacific Stock Exchange.[5]

Leslie L. Luttgens was active in Bay Area civic, public service, medical, academic, and cultural activities and then became a director at five corporations: Pacific Telesis, McKesson Corp., Pacific Gas & Electric Co., Hexcel Corporation, and Crocker Bank (before it was acquired by Wells Fargo Co.).[6]

These pioneer women directors achieved their positions of leadership over 35 years ago. Today, over 1,100 women have followed in their footsteps and hold board seats at *Fortune* 1000 firms. Since Ms. Harris walked through the doors at IBM three decades ago, an average of 30 women have been added *every single year* to top U.S. corporate boards. These net numbers understate the number of women who have served at companies that were acquired and merged into others and does not include those who stepped off boards for a range of personal or professional reasons.

That bigger picture provides some perspective on today's 15 percent share of *Fortune* 500 director seats held by women. Between 1995 (when Catalyst Inc. began surveying top U.S. boards) and 2007, *Fortune* 500 firms have reduced the size of their boards from an average of 13 to 10 directors, and *Fortune* 501–1000 firms from 10 to 8 directors. In spite of that, women have increased their numbers each year (see figure 1.1).

From 1995 to 2007, the number of men on boards has declined by 884, while the number of women on boards has increased by 231 at top *Fortune* 500 firms

Figure 1.1
Total, Men and Women on *Fortune* 500 Board Seats, 1995–2007.

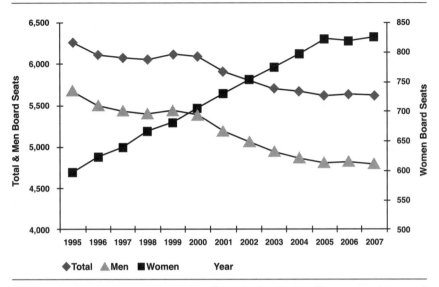

Source: Technology Place Inc. tabulations from "2001 Catalyst Census of Women Board Directors" (New York: Catalyst 2001) and "2007 Catalyst Census of Women Board Directors of the *Fortune* 500" (New York: Catalyst, 2007).

(see figure 1.2). Many companies in the bottom tier (*Fortune* 501–1000) added their first woman during this period.

Nationwide, there were 278 press releases announcing additional women named to corporate boards in 2006, and another 293 announcements in 2007, according to NewsOnWomen.com, a blog run by Alice Krause, formerly with Chase Bank (figure 1.3). This translates to an average of 24 new women named to U.S. corporate boards of directors *every month*. That's in contrast to an average of 21 women added *every year* at the top 500 firms that were surveyed by Catalyst Inc. from 1995 to 2007 or an average of 30 women added *every year* since 1971. We can see that board opportunities abound if we look at all the publicly held companies adding women to their boards across the country.

MORE WOMEN IN LEADERSHIP

There are more women added to public company corporate boards of directors because there are more talented women in top management positions from which corporations can draw directors. Women today represent our most educated professional resource.

The proof? Almost 2 million women attend graduate schools of all kinds in the United States, either full or part time (representing 59% of all enrollees). Law

Figure 1.2
Net Change in *Fortune* 500 Board Seats, 1995–2007.

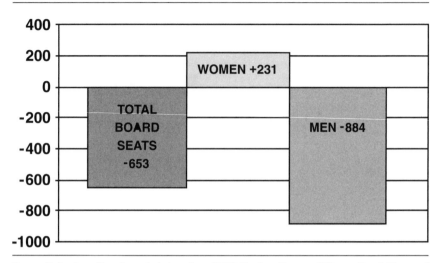

Source: Technology Place Inc. tabulations from "2001 Catalyst Census of Women Board Directors" (New York: Catalyst 2001) and "2007 Catalyst Census of Women Board Directors of the *Fortune* 500" (New York: Catalyst, 2007).

Figure 1.3
Women Directors Named to Boards in California and All States.

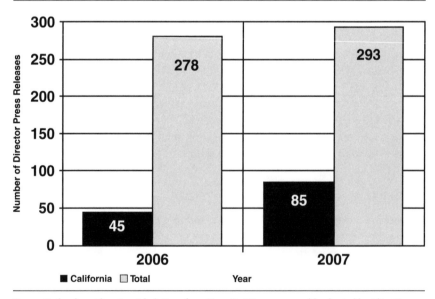

Source: Technology Place Inc. tabulations from NewsOnWomen.com, a blog hosted by Alice Krause.

schools continue to take the lead, according to the American Bar Association. Women represented only about 10 percent of first-year law students in 1970 yet now constitute 46 percent (and 48% of those receiving a JD). As a consequence, the percentage of lawyers who are women increased from 13 percent in 1985 to 30 percent in 2007.[7]

Medical schools follow close behind. Women represented 29.5 percent of applicants to U.S. medical schools in 1980–1981, and 50.4 percent in 2004–2005. Today, about 35,000 women are enrolled in medical schools. In 1970, fewer than 8 percent of U.S. physicians were women; this number rose to 12 percent in 1980, 17 percent in 1990, 24 percent in 2000, and 27.8 percent in 2006.[8]

WOMEN IN BUSINESS: THE REAL NEED

As good as this news may be, boards of directors demand an understanding of business, and this is the one area of education that needs to show greater improvement if we wish to see an increase in the number of women leaders on corporate boards of directors.

The number of women CEOs at *Fortune* 1000 firms increased 53 percent between 2006 and 2007, reaching 26 in 2007. There are an estimated 400,000 women CEOs in private (nongovernment) firms of all sizes in the United States, representing about 23 percent of the total number of CEOs in the nation. The next tier of talent consists of women in management at all levels. More than 8.5 million women are employed in management, business, and financial fields, and another 15.9 million women work in professional fields.[9]

Another potential source of women director candidates is the rapidly growing number of women-owned and -operated small businesses. The U.S. Census Bureau estimated that of the over 22.3 million businesses in the United States in 2002, 28 percent were owned by women alone (6.5 million) and another 12 percent were jointly owned by women and men. Together, these constituted about 9.2 million firms either fully or co-owned by women entrepreneurs.[10]

Thus, the issue of women on boards is partially a question of whether we are utilizing 100 percent of the educated and trained resources available to us in the business marketplace. Women are "filling the pipeline" of management, professional, and educational talent. Are we doing enough to prepare these women to move to top leadership positions, including corporate board-of-director roles? Are women doing the right things to prepare themselves for public corporate governance responsibilities?

Entrepreneurial businesses present women with the potential to build their own boards of directors and to tap other experienced women to serve on their boards. A clear opportunity for women who want to serve on more corporate boards is women-led businesses creating their own boards and naming more women directors. Barely 2 percent of all women-led businesses make it to the level of $1 million in revenue a year, and only 13.3 percent of those even have a board of directors.[11] If women do not understand how a board of directors could help their own business grow and thrive, this might indicate how much women need to learn about the benefits of governance and how good board leadership could help their companies thrive and succeed.

Executive consultants tell women and men alike that what gets you to middle management is not what will get you to the top leadership roles. For women as well as men, there are unique talents and skills required at the very top strategic levels of leadership. Women need to know what governance is, why it exists, what it accomplishes, and how it is done.

It is not enough that corporate boards, as part of their good governance practices, deliver more and better-quality information: more women have to read and understand that financial information and what it implies in terms of investment value. It is not enough that women merely represent 80-plus percent of the consuming power of our economy: more women have to understand the savings and investment side of the marketplace as well.

The reason to add diversity to a corporate board is not simply an issue of equity or justice. The real reason to add individuals with different backgrounds to a corporate board is the need to tap the intellectual and experiential perspective available from the larger candidate pool of independent-minded people (regardless of age, color, race, religion, or gender). Diversity on a corporate board is akin to diversity of an investment portfolio: too many of any one particular element tends to expose the holder to a greater average risk profile, thus diluting the potential return.

Put another way, one of the reasons the marketplace failed to catch the problems hidden in companies like Enron was that there were too many people with the same backgrounds and experiences looking at only part of the patterns of risk to which the companies were exposed. Lemming-like behavior increases the odds of running over the edge of the cliff together.

The real challenge is to increase the number of women educated in business. Today, women still represent an average of only 30 percent of the enrollment at U.S. business schools, 22 percent of the faculty, and 15 percent of the trustees. Another Catalyst Inc. survey of women in business schools found that 85 percent of the female respondents believed strongly that experience added significant value to their own careers.[12]

RAISING EXPECTATIONS

Today, women are asking, "How do I get to the top of my career and fulfill my potential?" The achievement of becoming a director on a corporate board provides a clear opportunity for competent and willing women. The question is: "Who has to do what?"

The media and advocates of women on boards have tended to expect more of corporations than they do of the women director candidates. Advocates argue that more action is required of corporations, that boards only want sitting CEOs, or that the same women are being appointed to multiple boards. They also repeat many of the old wives' tales regarding women and boards, for example, that getting on a nonprofit board or on a local government commission qualifies one to serve in the highly competitive and financially demanding world of a for-profit corporate board.

Significant progress has been made since a woman was first named director in 1971, but as recently as the early 1990s, adding women to director positions was considered unrealistic. Alice Clark Ronce, executive search professional and legal researcher, was one of the first to interview women on corporate boards. She cited one woman director in 1991 who told her that "anyone who would look for ways to increase the number of [female] board members [is] 'Don Quixote in a dress.'"[13]

Today, when women are surveyed about their business school experience, 87 percent express the belief that business school curricula need to "feature more women business leaders as role models." And 77 percent of the men surveyed reached the same conclusion.[14]

CURRENT RESEARCH: CALIFORNIA WOMEN DIRECTORS

Corporations are finding some of the best and most talented women in leadership for their boards of directors. The goal of this book is to learn from the top female business role models serving as directors in our publicly held companies. Our research focuses on the *Fortune* 1000 firms based in California as of 2006–2007. The state had 101 firms on this list of top U.S. corporations. Those firms had 114 women directors on their corporate boards. This was the "laboratory" in which we investigated different questions about how the women directors succeeded. Who are they? Where did they come from? What were their backgrounds, experience, and education? How did they do it? The women and the California companies on which they serve as directors are listed in appendixes 1 (by company) and 2 (by name).

Why focus on California? Because, in the past two years alone, the number of women directors added to corporate boards in that state was almost three times the number announced for the next-highest state (New York). What could we learn by examining the women directors on California boards? The women directors in this sample came to their board roles by way of six possible career paths (see figure 1.4 and table 1.1). In the past, women directors' experience was primarily in the nonprofit, academic, and government sectors. We found that in today's economy, significantly more women are entering the boardroom along the professional paths: investment, entrepreneurship, and—statistically, the most important route—the corporate path.

Other insights from this research include the fact that, on average, women in this sample are relatively young: 56.5 years of age, roughly nine years younger than their male director counterparts (see figure 1.5). Some women directors are in their early forties or late thirties. About 15 percent of the women in our sample are 65 years or older and may be retiring in the near future, which presents opportunities to bring new governance talent on board.

Figure 1.4
Six Paths to the Boardroom.

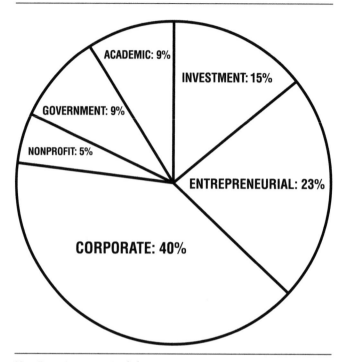

Note: Percentages are rounded.
Source: Tabulations from proxy statements and research conducted by Technology Place Inc. covering backgrounds of women on California *Fortune* 1000 boards.

Table 1.1
Combined Experience of Women on Corporate Boards of California *Fortune* 1000 Companies

Path	# Occurrences	Percent
Nonprofit	10	5.3
Government	16	8.5
Academic	16	8.5
Investment	28	14.9
Entrepreneurial	43	22.9
Corporate	75	39.9
Total	188	100.0

Figure 1.5
Age of Women on California *Fortune* 1000 Boards: 2006.

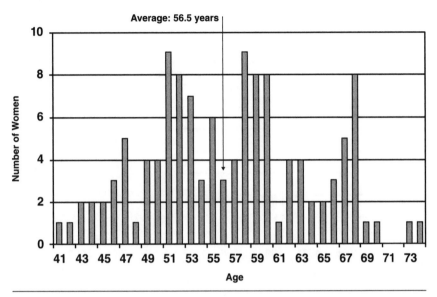

Source: Tabulations from proxy statements and research conducted by Technology Place Inc. covering backgrounds of women on California *Fortune* 1000 boards.

The women directors at top California firms actually live and work all over the country and abroad, which suggests that boards are not limiting themselves to the local marketplace. Forty-nine percent (55 of the women directors) came from outside California: three came from Finland, Hong Kong, and the United Kingdom, while the remainder came from 19 states other than California. Thus, corporate boards are looking everywhere to find the best available director talent, and women directors show a willingness to cross the country or the oceans to serve on corporate boards where they believe they can make a genuine contribution.

The number of women added to boards is increasing every year. On average, the women surveyed joined their current boards in 1999 (see figure 1.6). Thus, most of them have direct personal experience with the challenges of the dot-com bubble; the tough, highly regulated post-Sarbanes-Oxley environment; and the uncertainty of the subprime mortgage meltdown. These are not easy times to be a director, yet women are demonstrating a willingness to join boards in large numbers.

Our survey of the women directors combined information from annual proxy statements, company press release announcements about the women nominated to their boards; and general information from corporate, academic, and other research sources. Next, we interviewed two to three women from each path. We asked about their backgrounds, their career histories, and their board-of-director experiences. Unlike most surveys of women directors, the goal of this research was

Figure 1.6
Year Named to Board, California *Fortune* 1000 Women Directors.

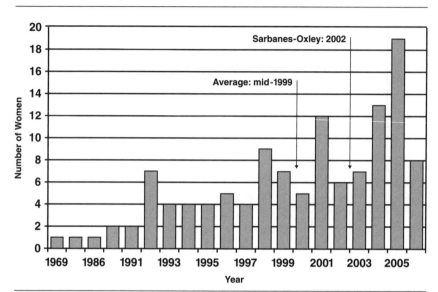

Source: Proxy statements and research conducted by Technology Place Inc. covering backgrounds of women on California *Fortune* 1000 boards.

to let the women speak for themselves. How did they see the value they brought to the boardroom and what do they advise women who are interested in following in their footsteps? We asked questions like:

- Where did you start your career?
- How did you become interested in business?
- What were your educational choices?
- What were your early experiences like?
- What career path did you follow?
- Did you acquire or develop some unique skills?
- Did you attain roles at the top level of corporate management?
- Did you partner or collaborate with others in some special way?
- What was your first board experience?
- On how many boards do you serve?

OUTLINE OF CHAPTERS

The pages that follow present the findings of research and interviews with 15 women directors on top California-based *Fortune* 1000 companies. Six chapters focus on each of the different paths into the boardroom. The introduction to each chapter describes the path, the findings that are common to all the women who pursued that path, commonly held beliefs about that path, and insights drawn from the interviews and analysis—lessons learned.

Within each chapter, we present biographies of selected women directors. Each biography is a stand-alone business case of the decisions and choices of one woman who became a corporate director. Each biography concludes with the insights extracted from her experiences.

There are no bad or wrong paths into the boardroom. All career options are viable, as demonstrated by the women we met and interviewed. Today's women directors follow jagged paths more than a straight course, although a dominant route tended to serve as a hub around which the individual women expanded their influence and contacts and enhanced their skills and expertise. Many women gathered experience along multiple paths, which suggests that part of their value as directors is the breadth of their competencies and interests.

Chapter 2 discusses the women who chose the nonprofit career path into the boardroom. It examines whether charities, symphonies, museums, and hospitals represent an important route to corporate directorship. The chapter looks at how nonprofit organizations have changed and how the women have changed their own views of the nonprofit sector of the economy.

Chapter 3 focuses on the women directors with careers in government. It asks whether they have succeeded as elected governmental candidates or whether they were appointed because of their unique expertise. Are the women local and state politicians or have they served on the national and international stage?

Chapter 4 features women who pursued the academic path, profiling teachers, professors, deans, chancellors and provosts who become directors. It describes the administrative side of academia as a key aspect of this route into the boardroom and how today's women directors have become constant learners.

Chapter 5 discusses the investment path, describing the women who are at securities firms, venture partnerships, or angel-capital organizations. These are the women who came to a board role via the money networks and took a stake in start-up firms en route to their first board seats.

Chapter 6 focuses on women who followed the entrepreneurial path into the boardroom. These are the women who pursued a dream and built business entities themselves. The evidence shows that women directors are equal-opportunity business partners, creating diversity-based growth and profit-oriented enterprises rather than simply "going it alone" as small, self-contained entities.

Chapter 7 describes the majority of directors in our sample: women who built their careers within the traditional corporate framework, climbed the ladder of success, and established strong credentials in technology, finance, law, or retail. These are the women who survived the wars with corporate competitors and achieved their own executive ambition.

THE WOMEN INTERVIEWED

It is not that women directors are out there on some remote pedestal. They are all real women who made the decisions to endure, persevere, and excel. Their stories inspire our admiration and respect. Once you meet these women and become familiar with the major steps in their careers, you might select from their experiences those lessons that are relevant to your life, your time, and your current efforts.

Gayle Edlund Wilson and Andrea L. Rich discuss their careers in the non-profit world. Linnet Frazier Deily, Linda Griego, and Sally K. Richardson came to their board roles through government service. Alice Bourke Hayes and Mary S. Metz came to their board roles by the academic career path. Leslie Myers Frécon, Donna Frame Tuttle, and Deborah Ann Coleman followed a few of the wide variety of career paths that have opened up recently in the investment/securities area. Judith L. Estrin and Lucille S. Salhany came to corporate director leadership roles by the entrepreneurial path. Janet Morrison Clarke, Judith M. Runstad, and Kathleen A. Cote came by the corporate pathway with an emphasis on retail, law, and technology.

This book shows women how to look for leadership role models among the wide variety of styles, careers, paths, and choices of businesswomen in the 21st century. If women aspire to leadership, they will raise their own expectations and not merely remain outside observers, helpers, and supporters. They will take on the mantle of leadership.

LESSONS LEARNED

These women were chosen to serve because their experience added value to their boards. Any woman *can* become competent, qualified, and capable of assuming a board role. However, not every woman *will* become a corporate director, and not every woman *should:* it is an achievement, not an entitlement.

We extract, from their experience, lessons and advice for other women who aspire to follow them into the boardroom.

- What does leadership look like today?
- What does good corporate governance look like?
- How can top companies become more diverse?
- How might a company with outstanding women directors thrive and grow?

One executive recruiter who specializes in board searches reported that "Our experience suggests that, rather than [the number of women on corporate boards] being a problem on the demand side, it seems to be more a case of a limited supply of women directors who are prepared and ready to serve."

How does a woman find a corporate board role? She doesn't. She builds a career of achievement and leadership. When a board of directors needs her skills and competencies, it will find her. And she will recognize it as an opportunity too good to refuse.

Mothers Teresa:
The Nonprofit Path

This chapter focuses on whether charities, symphonies, museums, hospitals, and other eleemosynary organizations constitute an important route to corporate directorship. The chapter looks at how nonprofit organizations have changed and how the views of the women who have worked in the nonprofit sector have changed.

Judith M. Runstad, a real estate and land-use lawyer who serves on the board of Wells Fargo Bank, provides some historical perspective on the way it was when women were first brought onto corporate boards and how much has changed since then.

> There used to be a spot on the boards for the woman community volunteer, like Mary Gates, Bill Gates's mother, truly a lady in every sense of the word.[1] She was a terrific role model for me. They were the women, almost a generation ahead of me, who were very active in the community, but who had been shut out of the professional world. Community work was a way for them to go on boards. It may have been tokenism, but the companies benefited by finding great board members. And the women benefited: when opportunity comes along, you have to grab it.

RELATIVE IMPORTANCE

Several women directors mentioned that service at nonprofit entities, community service, and work for charitable organizations once were a common route into the boardroom for women. That began to change in the early 1990s as more women who had been educated in the 1970s and 1980s began moving into the professions. It also was an era when service on a corporate board was more an honor than a position associated with the responsibilities and liabilities of contemporary boards. Governance at nonprofits today requires more knowledge of business and economics, which enhances opportunities for women who follow this path to add real value to nonprofit and for-profit boards.

Using corporate proxy statements for California *Fortune* 1000 firms in 2006–2007, we tallied the total mentions of experience and clustered common types of backgrounds for the 114 women directors in our sample and then tabulated their relative importance. From this analysis emerged six paths that described the different categories of experience that the women directors chose. Our analysis of their biographies and experience confirmed that nonprofits, charitable work, and community service are not as strong a path into the boardroom as are other careers (see figure 1.4).

Only 10 women in our sample possessed experience predominantly in the nonprofit arena (table 2.1), or 5.3 percent of all experience cited in figure 1.4. Even though today the number of women who follow a nonprofit career path is relatively small, their competencies are impressive—which is why they were chosen to serve on public company boards. Who are the women who followed this path? What types of experiences are included in this category?

Angela Glover Blackwell began a distinguished law career at Public Advocates, a nationally recognized public interest law firm, litigating class-action suits in support of employment, education, health, and consumer affairs efforts for the underrepresented. She formed the Oakland-based National Community Building

Table 2.1

Nonprofit Path: Experience of Women on Corporate Boards of California *Fortune* 1000 Companies

Paths into the Boardroom					Name	Company
N			E		Angela Glover Blackwell	Levi Strauss & Co.
N	G				Linda L. Chavez	ABM Industries
N				C	Martha R. Ingram	Ingram Micro
N					Linda K. Jacobs	Jacobs Engineering Inc.
N					Risa Juanita Lavizzo-Mourey	Beckman Coulter
N	A				Andrea L. Rich	Mattel
N		I			Anne M. Tatlock	Franklin Resources
N					Virginia Mae Ueberroth	First American Corporation
N					Mary Lee Widener	First American Corporation
N					Gayle Edlund Wilson	Gilead Sciences

Note: N = Nonprofit; G = Government; A = Academic; I = Investment; E = Entrepreneurial; C = Corporate.

Network and the Urban Strategies Council to create social and economic opportunity through comprehensive community-building strategies. She was senior vice president of the Rockefeller Foundation, a global philanthropic organization committed to the well-being of the disenfranchised. She founded and currently heads PolicyLink, a nonprofit urban strategies advocacy organization in Oakland, California.

Linda L. Chavez's began her career in local government, after which she became a syndicated columnist and a political analyst for Fox News Channel. She is founder and chair of the Center for Equal Opportunity, a public policy research nonprofit in Sterling, Virginia. The organization "supports colorblind public policies and seeks to block the expansion of racial preferences and to prevent their use in employment, education, and voting."[2]

Risa Juanita Lavizzo-Mourey is the only doctor among the women directors in this sample. She has held academic positions in the medical departments of major universities, as well as government health care positions, and her extensive public policy career has provided her with an unparalleled knowledge of health care economics. She currently heads the Robert Wood Johnson Foundation, managing a $370 million grant budget for the nation's largest health care philanthropic organization.

Anne M. Tatlock has spent four decades as a highly regarded money manager and global securities investment advisor, rising to the position of CEO of Fiduciary Trust Company International and vice-chair of Franklin Resources. She has served on more and diverse nonprofit boards than any other female director primarily because of her financial capabilities. Those capabilities and her leadership in the global financial marketplace also are why nine separate nonprofit organizations brought her onto their boards as a trustee and/or as their CFO.

Mary Lee Widener has a long history creating national and local nonprofit entities to provide education and counseling to low-income families trying to enter homeownership for the first time. It was her bank lending background and ability to build financially sound institutions, specifically Neighborhood Housing Services of America, that brought her to the attention of First American Corporation, on whose board she serves. For over 30 years, Ms. Widener has developed her unique brand of mortgage lending products and services, using a combination of nonprofit and for-profit delivery methods that attracted the attention of investors in the secondary financial marketplace and made her advice invaluable during the subprime mortgage crisis.

Two women managed the affairs of nonprofit foundations created by their families' wealth. Linda K. Jacobs was on the staff of the Near East Foundation, a private nonprofit organization dedicated to urban and rural development in the Middle East and Africa. Later, she became president of Middle East Technology Assistance, a nonprofit focused on Middle East rehabilitation development projects. Virginia Mae Ueberroth describes herself as a community volunteer, serving as chair of the Ueberroth Family Foundation, which provides charitable grants to youth, education, and cancer beneficiaries.

A typical pattern for the women in the sample is that they invested some portion of their career in not-for-profit endeavors that were tied to a subject area central and important to their own interests. They approached the nonprofit as seriously and in as business-like a manner as if it were a for-profit endeavor. They meshed the mission of their nonprofit endeavors with their professional competency. Their choice of a nonprofit was an opportunity to expand into a new market or to exercise leadership.

Many of the women chose or were chosen by nonprofits after they reached leadership positions in their professional careers and often after they achieved a board role. Thus, the nonprofit path was not so much a route into the boardroom as it was a purposeful extension of their specific skills and expertise.

Over half of the women (58%) holding board seats in our sample reported, in their proxy backgrounds, a combined total of 223 individual organizations, foundations, charities, and other service entities to which they belonged. That translates into an average of three charitable or nonprofit entities for every woman who mentioned some nonprofit membership or involvement.

Women today are members of a wide variety of nonprofit organizations. Noteworthy among them are academic foundations, college and university fund-raising and advisory groups, and business school boards of trustees, which have many similarities to mutual and trust funds in the corporate marketplace. Women directors were named to public policy nonprofits such as the Urban Land Institute and state and local public policy institutes. Other women mentioned nonprofit professional affiliations, such as the American Institute of CPAs, the Financial Executives Institute, and the American Bar Association or state counterparts.

There was very little cross-membership among the organizations mentioned by the women directors in our sample. Only a few belonged to organizations on which other women directors also served, which suggests that the women tended to find their own leadership arenas. The women appeared to choose nonprofits where they could make a unique personal contribution.

MYTH BUSTING

How do the data dispel common myths about the nonprofit path into the boardroom? Women still are told that the best way to get onto a corporate board is by way of a major charity. Prominent members of several women-in-business advocacy groups have encouraged women to volunteer for nonprofit boards and to do more public speaking in order to increase their visibility and thereby be invited to join a corporate board. Yet, the Chicago-based Committee of 200 reported that women have made progress in only 2 out of 10 categories nationally, as monitored by their index over the four years, 2002–2005: as chairs of charities and foundations and as keynote speakers at major conferences. Progress in these two areas has not translated into an increase in the number of women on for-profit boards. The Committee of 200 reported that the share of women on boards rose barely 3 percent over a year, and the number of women in venture capital, a prime feeder to board roles, declined by 24 percent.[3]

Figure 2.1
Women Directors at Top Nonprofits and Top Corporations in Chicago.

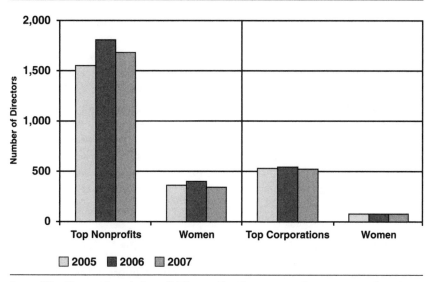

Source: "The Chicago Network Census" (Chicago: The Chicago Network: 2005, 2006, and 2007).

Another prominent women's advocacy group, the Chicago Network, surveyed women on board positions at the city's largest 30 to 35 nonprofit organizations in 2005, 2006, and 2007 (see figure 2.1). The Chicago Network has surveyed women in board-of-director positions at Chicago's top 50 public companies since 1998. They too discovered that lots of women volunteering at nonprofit organizations have not translated into more women serving as directors, CEOs, or top-tier executives at for-profit corporations.[4]

Another typical recommendation is that women should substitute visibility as a nonprofit volunteer for real corporate board experience in order to show a capacity to work in group settings or to widen their networks. This is an extension of the argument that the low percentages of women directors represents a problem on the demand side of the equation: companies do not invite enough women into their boardrooms. The real challenge seems more related to the question of how to increase the supply of women with practical business-building experience.

The data suggest that women who acquire more business experience and a better understanding of governance at coeducational public and professional public policy groups are in great demand by corporations to serve on public company boards. In order to increase the supply of women in corporate leadership, including boards of directors, women must acquire learning experiences that relate to business, market economies, governance, and the leadership skills that are transferable to the public company marketplace. Increasing the involvement of professional women in mixed-gender public and professional policy activities appears to be a more successful strategy than single-gender support networking.

The women in our sample did not pursue nonprofit director roles because of a belief that it might be a launchpad from which to catapult a personal board position search. They did not view their nonprofit exposure as either a training ground or a networking experience. Their approach to their nonprofit work was as serious and business-like as if it were a for-profit endeavor. They chose the nonprofit entity because they had a primary competency that they wanted to develop further through that organization.

The nonprofit organizations they chose included civic, cultural, medical, and educational entities involving both men and women rather than single-gender groups. Committee structures existed to delegate functions, develop research, foster debate, and refine policies to move toward solutions. The women participated in the problem analysis and policy development processes along with their male peers. The nonprofits they chose provided excellent governance training and insight into strategic decision making. The women learned how to lead, not simply how to follow or to network.

LESSONS LEARNED

What lessons did the women draw from the nonprofit path? The women who chose a nonprofit path were well aware of the tough management and financial requirements facing for-profit corporate directors in the post-Sarbanes-Oxley environment. They recognized that the heightened expectations facing corporations are beginning to trickle down to nonprofit settings. The women brought a strong understanding of financials to their nonprofit endeavors. They demonstrated a willingness to invest in their own education to prepare themselves adequately to handle contemporary for-profit board responsibilities and to apply that knowledge elsewhere in their not-for-profit work.

For-profit corporations are getting more involved in socially aware and socially responsible programs, both directly and indirectly. Corporations are adding board committees to advise them about public policy and stakeholder interests in their business areas. Many of the women directors in our sample serve on such committees because they bring an appropriate business perspective to the committee deliberations.

Donors and administrators at nonprofit entities also are pushing their organizations to improve their accounting, auditing, and financial controls and become more business-like. Nonprofits today must show they are both efficient (measured by the percentage of the entity's endowment actually spent delivering on its mission) and effective (measured by the share of fund-raising costs as a percentage of contributions). A nonprofit path into the boardroom is no longer the easy route to a director role *for a woman*. Women who say they feel more comfortable in a not-for-profit role than in a for-profit business are learning that contemporary nonprofits face the same financial challenges as for-profit businesses. As a result, the women who are willing to invest more to educate and prepare themselves to serve at top governance levels—in either domain—are finding that they are more valuable as directors on both nonprofit and for-profit boards of directors.

THE WOMEN INTERVIEWED

The women directors who were interviewed are Gayle Edlund Wilson and Andrea L. Rich. Both of their careers demonstrate how public institutions today require strong management and financial accountability in order to deliver on their missions and the promise of service to their constituencies, just as corporations are challenged today to face heightened customer and shareholder expectations.

Women directors continue to participate in community service and charitable endeavors in addition to their professional career choices. Nonprofit entities (within and outside corporations) are facing greater scrutiny of their operations and financial viability. Women are taking on greater responsibility for those challenges. Professional women still benefit from and contribute to nonprofit endeavors in their own way. What has changed is the presumption that the nonprofit route is either an easy path or a dominant path into the public company boardroom for women in leadership in the 21st century.

DIRECTOR PROFILE: GAYLE EDLUND WILSON

Gayle Edlund Wilson, age 65 at the time of our interview, took the nonprofit path into the boardroom: she describes herself as a volunteer consultant with experience from the Junior League, the Ralph M. Parsons Foundation, and a host of other charitable nonprofit organizations. She has served on two public corporate boards and three government boards. She has served as director on an alphabet soup collection of academic nonprofit entities and as a trustee at the California Institute of Technology for over a decade. When women say they believe nonprofit organizations are the easy path into the boardroom of for-profit corporations, they perhaps underestimate the caliber of the contribution that women like Gayle Edlund Wilson provide as nonprofit volunteers and corporate directors.

EARLY YEARS

Ms. Wilson was an actress from the time she was four years old, playing in amateur and professional theater in her hometown of Phoenix, Arizona. Her parents made sure she had the opportunities for music and dance lessons. "I thrived on it. I was a pom-pom girl, but I was also a serious student."

Her life took a serious turn during high school when her father died of cancer and her mother went back to work. She was redirected from an acting career by her mother, who said, "No more of this frivolous stuff. If you want to go to Stanford, you've got to focus on the academics."

Ms. Wilson's initial career interest in science came from random beginnings, but she took advantage of the opportunity. As a result of a high school chemistry teacher's encouragement, she participated in the Westinghouse Science Talent Search (now the Intel Science Talent Search). She was one of 40 finalists selected from thousands nationwide in a competition based on a research project, grades, teacher recommendations, and a major test. In those days, girls competed only against each other (10 girls that year). Finalists were invited to present their original research at a major event held in Washington, D.C., before a group of nationally recognized scientists.

Ms. Wilson was a straight-A student and valedictorian of her high school class. Family friends talked to her about Stanford University, took her to local alumni events, and wrote letters of recommendation on her behalf. She was accepted at Stanford and showed up on campus never having seen it beforehand. While a junior at Stanford, she met her first husband, a third-year law student there. He graduated and got a job in San Diego; they were married in 1963 and moved there.

Even in the mid-1960s, Ms. Wilson didn't consider taking shortcuts with her education. When they moved to San Diego, she still needed 28 more units to finish her Stanford degree and so signed up for classes at San Diego State University. Stanford required that the last 15 units be completed on campus, so she traveled back up north during the summer, graduating Phi Beta Kappa with a major in biology in 1965.

> There was never a question whether I would finish my degree. I had just a few units remaining and was interviewing for a job in San Diego. They had seen so many students who had not finished, and they treated me as if I had never gone to college at all. I tell kids today that it's not important where you go or even what your grades are in college—what *is* important is that you have the tenacity to see it all the way through. That's what really counts.

Like many married women of that time, after college she had two children and began considering what form of a career could accommodate her family life. "That was the pattern of the day," she commented. "We had few role models. My mother was the typical stay-at-home mom, and I was just like her: the carpool mom, the team mother, the room mother. I followed the path of having my children first, and then considering a career."

While in her twenties, she helped found the nonprofit San Diego Speech and Hearing Center Auxiliary. By the time she turned 30, her children were in school full time, and she was ready to get involved in her community.

> In some ways I felt like I was coming out of a cocoon, because I was ready to spread my wings and do something important. I remember reading Gail Sheehy's book, *Passages: Predictable Crises of Adult Life*,[1] where she described the path I took: have your children first and then have your career. It was the typical pattern of the day. The whole woman's movement was going on in the mid-70s and the last question you wanted to hear was "So, what *do* you do?" If you were just a stay-at-home mom, you were dismissed.

To answer the question of "What *do* you do?" she went to work part time in the paralegal program at the University of California, San Diego. Even though she had never had a real job herself, she became an employment coordinator, helping students write resumes, develop interview skills, and apply for private-sector jobs. She began performing again at age 30. "I auditioned for a charity musical review, which truly brought back all of the good feelings I had experienced growing up. I made new friends and had terrific fun. It was a catalyst that changed my life by raising my level of confidence."

EARLY BOARD EXPERIENCE

Her first formal encounter with governance was at the Junior League, an organization of "women committed to promoting voluntarism, developing the potential of women, and improving communities through the effective action and leadership of trained volunteers."[2] The wives of the men in her husband's law firm sponsored her as a member of the San Diego chapter.

> I loved the Junior League and got great training from them. I was already disciplined and reliable, but they taught you to not give volunteering a bad name. If you say you're going to do something, you better do it and do it well. I took it as seriously as a paid job.

She slowly worked her way up, serving as chair on many committees. Then, at age 35, she became president of the San Diego chapter during its 50th anniversary year. "We put on a musical show as a fund-raiser, whose monies went to landscape a 'vest-pocket' park in downtown San Diego. As president, I had a starring role in the show. I loved it."

The next year, she took on her first governmental board, serving on the San Diego Park and Recreation Board. When her husband decided to go on a sabbatical and teach law at the University of California, Davis, they relocated to Davis, where she had to start from scratch again.

> It was becoming obvious to me that I needed an MBA, but Davis did not have a business school, so I signed up to take economics and accounting as independent classes. Econ was like a foreign language to me—very theoretical. I struggled at first, but I was competitive too and wasn't about to be intimidated by it all.

When she and her husband returned from Davis, she attended the business school at the University of California, San Diego, for a year and a half. "I wish I'd started my business degree earlier, but there were other priorities at the time. I wish I had been able to finish it."

SCIENCE SERVICE/CENTER FOR EDUCATIONAL EXCELLENCE

She and her first husband divorced. In 1983, she married the politician Pete Wilson, and they moved to Washington, D.C., where she got back in touch with Science Service (today the Society for Science & the Public), the organization that hosted the Westinghouse Talent Search. They invited her to view the science projects and talk with the student finalists as they presented their research at the National Academy of Sciences. During the week's events in Washington,

Ms. Wilson met Admiral Hyman G. Rickover, who invited her to join the board of his newly created nonprofit organization, the Center for Excellence in Education. He was impressed by her science background as a Talent Search finalist, her nonprofit governance experience, and the fact that she was married to a U.S. senator. Admiral Rickover had founded the center in 1983 with Joann DiGennaro in McLean, Virginia, with the mission of nurturing "careers of excellence and leadership in science and technology for academically talented high school and college students."[3] Ms. Wilson served on that board for 20 years, retiring finally in 2005. "Every year there was a fund-raiser for the center. All nonprofit work has a fund-raising component—don't kid yourself that it doesn't."

The center holds a six-week residential program, the Research Science Institute, for high school students who are talented in math and science. The program was located initially at Xerox and then moved to George Mason, then Georgetown, and finally settled at MIT. The center selects 50 U.S. and 20 foreign students annually, so that the American scientific leaders of tomorrow know their international counterparts. Ms. Wilson served as chair of the center's board of trustees in 1993 and 1994.

CALIFORNIA INSTITUTE OF TECHNOLOGY

Her interest in science and math education caught the attention of the nominating committee at the California Institute of Technology, which invited her to join their board of trustees in March 1995, recognizing that "her knowledge of educational issues both locally and nationally will be a wonderful asset to the Institute."[4] She was well known to a number of Caltech trustees.

She serves on a number of specialized Caltech committees: the visiting committee of the Division of Biology, the executive committee, the institute and alumni relations committee, the campaign leadership committee, and the Jet Propulsion Laboratory (JPL) committee. Currently, she is chair of the nominating committee and earlier she was on the presidential search committee.

Ms. Wilson's experience and contacts in Washington, D.C., led her to become an advocate for Caltech on Capitol Hill, educating members of Congress about the importance of funding for basic scientific research and for space science and encouraging their support of the NASA budget. As a member of the JPL committee, she worked to update congressional members on JPL's unmanned space projects, the exploration of Mars, and other planetary expeditions. She said, "After eight years in Washington, I was able to talk about both the value of the science research and the value of the public investment for the state, because California was in direct competition with other states for research funding."

CALIFORNIA STATE SUMMER SCHOOL FOR
MATHEMATICS AND SCIENCE (COSMOS)

Ms. Wilson used the knowledge and insight she gained from working with the boards at Caltech and the Center for Excellence in Education to develop her idea for a residential summer math and science program to support California's most talented students. Admiral Rickover's program was very competitive: only 50 U.S. students a year take part. And states such as Illinois, Virginia, Texas, and North Carolina had already invested in high school science programs for their high-achieving students.

> Because it was so competitive, California could expect to have just two students a year accepted into the [Center for Excellence in Education] program. But I felt that every high school in the state had at least one student who could benefit from this kind of exposure and experience. I could envision three residential high school academies of science in California alone. I could hardly believe that California, home to the most Nobel laureates, didn't have such a program.

When the Wilsons returned to Sacramento in 1987, Ms. Wilson talked to then-Governor George Deukmejian's education advisor and asked, "How could we do something like this?"

Originally, she was confronted with a lack of funds to establish a high school science program. Later, at the end of Pete Wilson's term as governor, the plan for a residential science program in California was funded literally in the last hours of the last budget of 1998. The legislation (AB 2536: California State Summer School for Math & Science) allocated $1 million in planning money to the California State Board of Education to develop a program modeled on the California State Summer School for the Arts, with the same fee, age groups, and structure. Ms. Wilson observed, "It's easier to get something through the legislature if it's similar to an existing program than if it's a completely new concept. It was a model that had worked since about 1985."

Ms. Wilson had worked closely with Marion Bergeson (head of the California State Board of Education and, previously, the California secretary of education and child development) and assembly member Charles "Chuck" S. Poochigian, who took the bill through its legislative hurdles. Some women are deterred from board roles by the fact that they have not been invited to join the board. Ms. Wilson pursued board opportunities when she believed she could add real value.

> I had worked closely with Marion to implement the program, e-mailing her every once in a while, asking for a status update. Even so, nobody thought to invite me onto the board, so I had to initiate it myself: "Don't you think I should be on the board?" Finally, I was appointed in the spring of 2000 and went out to visit COSMOS that first summer, where I saw, personally, what a life-changing experience this program was for these students.

The University of California system took COSMOS under its wing in 2000, designing and implementing this educational enrichment program and beginning with two campuses—UC Santa Cruz and UC Irvine. UC Davis was added in 2002, and UC San Diego in 2005. The first two campuses started with approximately

150 students, while the later campuses started with 80 the first year and ramped up to the full 150 students by the third year. San Diego reached that full level in 2007.

Ms. Wilson's economics background provided a foundation for her work because COSMOS requires private sources to augment state funding. The fee for the summer of 2007 was $2,200 per student—covering room and board for four weeks. The total cost is closer to $6,200 per student, which includes salaries for professors, teaching assistants, and research assistants; field trips; and lab use. Full scholarships are provided for students who are accepted but cannot afford the fee. Thus, altogether, about $1.4 million in new money is needed each year.

"I never thought of myself as a fund-raiser," she said, "but I've been very successful at getting private donations for the program. I have talked to many of the major corporations and foundations in the state. This now is my primary non-profit focus."

ATLANTIC RICHFIELD BOARD

In January 1999, Ms. Wilson took on her first public corporate board role at Atlantic Richfield (ARCO). She was recommended to the board by Kent Kresa, a fellow Caltech trustee, who was chair of the ARCO nominating committee.

At ARCO, I learned a lot about the oil industry. There is no real transferability of experience between nonprofit and for-profit boards: they are dramatically different. Nonprofit organizations may provide a path in terms of the people you meet, but the competency required at for-profit companies is quite different.

CIVIC AND FOUNDATION BOARDS

While a director at ARCO, she joined a number of civic boards, including the Center Theatre Group, the Children's Hospital Los Angeles Foundation, and Phoenix House California. As First Lady of California, she was honorary chair for the California State Science Fair and the California 4-H Foundation. President George W. Bush appointed her to the board of the National Commission on Voluntary and Community Service. She chaired the advisory committee of California Court-Appointed Special Advocates and was spokesperson for both BabyCal (the California perinatal outreach campaign) and the California Mentor Initiative.

Ms. Wilson joined the board of the Ralph M. Parsons Foundation in 2000. The foundation provides grants in higher education; social impact, civic, and cultural issues; and health. She knew a number of the board members through her other nonprofit and political experiences. Today, Elizabeth Lowe (a Los Angeles community activist in children's programs) and Ms. Wilson are two female directors among nine board members.

CALIFORNIA HIGHER EDUCATION LOAN
AUTHORITY INC. (CHELA)

Ms. Wilson's understanding of competition in the marketplace from her business education helped her in 1999 when she was named to the nonprofit board of CHELA Education Financing Inc. CHELA was founded in 1979 in San Francisco to provide direct loans to higher education students. By the mid-2000s, the student loan industry had become highly regulated, with complex and sophisticated financing. Nonprofits like CHELA were having difficulty competing with well-subsidized entities. Sallie Mae, also founded in 1979 as a government-sponsored public entity, was the dominant lender. CHELA went private between 1997 and 2004 and terminated all ties to the federal government. "After awhile, it became obvious that CHELA had to sell its assets," she concluded. "As a board, we went through 22 meetings in one year to resolve the sale."

In October 2005, CHELA sold all its assets to the National Education Loan Network, based in Lincoln, Nebraska. The proceeds of that sale were used to create The Education Financial Foundation of California, renamed the College Access Foundation of California in April 2007.[5] Ms. Wilson said, "We give money to groups that give the college scholarships directly to motivated economically disadvantaged students."

Ms. Wilson is one of two female directors among nine board members of the College Access Foundation. Carlene M. Ellis also came over from CHELA, with a business background at Intel Corporation. "At every board, even nonprofits, the demand is for specific skills, such as someone who could back up the chair of the audit committee. Carlene Ellis gives our board experience from a corporate background in compensation and investments."

CALIFORNIA INSTITUTE FOR REGENERATIVE MEDICINE

Ms. Wilson was appointed by California Governor Schwarzenegger to serve briefly (December 2006–January 2007) on the Independent Citizens' Oversight Committee, overseeing the California Institute for Regenerative Medicine created by the passage of Proposition 71—the Stem Cell Research Initiative.

> I knew right from the start that I shouldn't have been on the [Oversight Committee] board. I really didn't know how time consuming it would be. I served on the facilities search committee but later decided I wasn't the best choice for a government board—too many regulations…prevent you from doing what you believe you need to do. Other people have more patience with that than I do. I decided that board just took too much time away from everything else.

CONSTANT LEARNING

Ms. Wilson has taken advantage of the director training provided by her corporate boards and also has invested in her own personal executive development.

CHELA encouraged their board members to take director training classes and paid for the board's attendance at the Stanford Law School's Directors' College to learn about the audit committee and other committee work. CHELA also brought companies in to provide training to the whole board. She attended the Stanford director training program in 1999 and again in 2000. On her own initiative, she also attended seminars and director education programs in other cities, including those sponsored by the San Diego–based Corporate Directors Forum. "Anybody who has no background with boards really should take this kind of director training. It is particularly important with all of the changes resulting from Sarbanes-Oxley. Some people will say, 'I know all this'—I'm not one of them."

GILEAD SCIENCES INC. BOARD

In October 2001, Ms. Wilson became the only female among nine directors at Gilead Sciences Inc., a biopharmaceutical company in Foster City, California. Gilead's mission is "to discover, develop and commercialize small molecule therapeutics to advance the care of patients suffering from life-threatening infectious diseases."[6]

George Schultz, former U.S. secretary of state, recommended Ms. Wilson to the Gilead board based on her science background and her work at Caltech. Even though Gilead's board has a number of prominent leaders, Ms. Wilson is not one to be easily intimidated.

There are two of us on the board with science backgrounds, but the other is a Nobel Laureate (Dr. Paul Berg of Stanford University Medical Center). That doesn't scare me. My strength is helping to figure out the information that the whole board should receive about the company's R&D. Most of the board members are not scientists: they are business people. Every year I attend Gilead's two-day International Science Advisory Board meeting, where it's like drinking from a fire hose of information. It's a lot to digest, but I realize that I'm not expected to understand all of the complex chemistry or biology presentations. What is important is to have a good grasp of where and why the company is investing its R&D.

She served on Gilead's compensation committee until July 2005 and then moved over to nominating and governance, of which she's been chair since July 2005. She was named to Gilead's scientific committee in January 2006.

LESSONS LEARNED

Ms. Wilson's perspective on the value of women on boards is influenced by her public corporate, governmental, and nonprofit board experience. She has unique insight into the challenges faced by today's corporate directors as they search for talented female candidates who are ready and willing to serve on contemporary boards. "I think every board, today, is looking for competent women," she said, "but I don't believe in bringing a woman on a board just because she's a woman. I want the skill set the person represents. If they're combined, that's great."

An example of just such a combination was the Gilead nominating committee's announcement in January 2007 that Carla Anderson Hills, another outstanding director candidate, had been selected because of her skills and extensive experience in "investment, trade and risk assessment issues abroad, particularly in emerging markets."[7]

Ms. Wilson describes her director responsibilities as a search for ways to balance, represent, or incorporate a variety of shareholder and stakeholder interests. "You can't have a women's agenda, a black agenda, or a Mexican American agenda. It's a big turnoff. It's either a company agenda or it's nothing."

Ms. Wilson says that the boards on which she has served have not used headhunters as much as they use the personal "who you know" approach. Board congeniality is a significant factor.

> At CHELA, they brought in three new board members at once, and the dynamics changed dramatically. CHELA and ARCO both used headhunters, but Gilead, Parsons, and Caltech have not and are not likely to use headhunters for board searches. We added three directors in one year at College Access Foundation, and it took a great deal of work to integrate the new people onto the board.

One director colleague told Ms. Wilson that "We didn't bring you on this board just because you're the wife of a politician." Her science experience and her ability to communicate science to the layperson are her most valuable assets. She believes you need to bring something significant to every opportunity. "I know some women in their forties who think they should be able to do what I do. They think all they need is a title."

Ms. Wilson describes herself as a "professional volunteer" and nonprofit consultant. She is not a director at some cushy consumer or soft-goods company but rather is a highly regarded science advisor and experienced board member at a top science corporation and at entities providing financial support for higher education. She is focused on early childhood health and excellence in math and science education.

Gayle Edlund Wilson is the wife of the former California state governor Pete Wilson. She served as First Lady of California from 1991 to 1999; before that, her husband was a U.S. senator from 1983 to 1991. She has two adult sons by a previous marriage.

She says: "My husband is now chairman of the World War II Museum in New Orleans, and I want to be involved in that. I have two sons, grandchildren, and a husband who is very involved. You have to make choices so you can have some balance in your life."

First, she raised a family; after that, it was "Nelly, bar the door" if anyone thought of keeping her from pursing the opportunities available to her. Her science education was the technical foundation on which she built her leadership roles, first as a finalist in the national Westinghouse Science Talent Search competition, then in her undergraduate education, and later when she renewed her involvement in the Science Talent Search program. Ms. Wilson didn't just join organizations to volunteer or network; she learned about governance by chairing committees at the Junior League and working to ensure her organizations succeeded. She continually invested in her own education in very challenging fields: economics, business, governance, and the latest board regulations. Ms. Wilson developed the attitude required to succeed. She can talk with Nobel laureates and hold her own. She can sit with PhDs and speak their language. She keeps her focus on the future—making it possible for the California economy to have the best and the brightest young scientists and mathematicians by putting a little old-fashioned shoulder to the wheels today. She took the road less traveled and made it possible for thousands of high school students to become as excited and as challenged as she was (and is) by the marvels of science and math.

Ms. Wilson sums up her success in this way: "I paid my dues. I do my homework. I'm reliable. I show up. Every once in a while I have a good question."

Director Profile: Andrea L. Rich

Andrea L. Rich's experience spans academics, public university administration, and public arts management. Dr. Rich, age 64 at the time of our interview, was instrumental in creating the communications studies major at the University of California, Los Angeles, and she combined and transformed several schools during one of the university's most treacherous budget-cutting cycles. She came to a corporate boardroom by the nonprofit path, after guiding the Los Angeles County Museum of Art to a sound fiscal and artistic foundation, demonstrating how public-benefit institutions today require strong management and financial accountability in order to deliver on their missions and on their promise of public service to their constituencies.

THE EARLY YEARS

Andrea Beck Rich was born in San Diego in 1943, the younger of two children. Her parents ran a clothing store. She enrolled at UCLA initially to study elementary education and become a teacher, "to have something to fall back on," she said. She changed her major to theater and then to speech (public and competitive speaking).[1] Although a good debater, she didn't enjoy the confrontational aspects, so switched her major to English. She graduated summa cum laude in January 1965 with a BA in English and was elected to Phi Beta Kappa. She tried student teaching but decided that wasn't for her. While she was considering whether to join the Peace Corps, a conversation with a professor opened up the possibility of graduate study. Subsequently, he helped her gain a four-year Chancellor's Teaching and Dissertation Fellowship, whereby she earned an MA in 1966. She married Los Angeles film and television director John Rich in the same year. They had two sons. She received her PhD in 1968 from the speech department, a small spin-off of the English department.

SPEECH INTO COMMUNICATIONS STUDIES

Dr. Rich and a colleague, Paul Rosenthal, proposed expanding the classical rhetorical speech curriculum into a modern major, communications studies, in which students would study the social sciences and the impact of television, radio, and other media. It became an interdisciplinary curriculum leading to a bachelor of arts in 1972 and remains a vibrant academic program today.

Dr. Rich taught communications studies and published two books on interracial communications, receiving UCLA's Distinguished Teaching Award in 1974. During the late 1960s and early 1970s, she was involved in interdisciplinary faculty programs supporting the arts and communications, and she was active on committees to improve the quality of undergraduate instruction. In spite of her academic success, neither she nor her colleagues in the speech department were awarded tenure. A member of the chancellor's office invited her to join UCLA's academic administration, where she could continue her work improving instructional support programs.

UCLA ACADEMIC ADMINISTRATION

Dr. Rich was named assistant director of the Office of Learning Resources in 1976. Over the next four years, she consolidated several disparate faculty services into a cohesive program that became the Office of Instructional Development, leveraging what already existed with a new mission and strategic vision. She became director and then assistant vice-chancellor, a position she held until 1986. The department initiated a number of innovative programs: training for teaching assistants, counseling, summer writing classes for freshmen, and special math programs to support the faculty in their pedagogy and supplement direct services to students. The Office of Instructional Development continues to be a highly valued faculty and student support service 30 years after its creation.

UP THE CHANCELLOR LADDER

As assistant vice-chancellor, Dr. Rich supervised an array of campus-wide faculty and student support services. She rose through the academic administrative ranks from assistant executive vice-chancellor to vice-chancellor for academic administration and then executive vice-chancellor and chief operating officer, reporting directly to UCLA chancellor Charles "Chuck" E. Young. During this time, she was responsible for all state funds with specific requirements and position controls over the assignment of academic employees.

Dr. Rich was the second-highest ranking officer at UCLA, overseeing a huge academic enterprise: the College of Letters and Sciences, 13 professional schools, and the medical center. The position was not for the faint hearted. During her final four years at UCLA (1991–1995), she was deeply involved in some of the most difficult organizational issues faced by the university:

1. The reorganization and consolidation of the UCLA Medical School and the UCLA Hospital
2. The acquisition of the Hammer Museum and Westwood Playhouse
3. A student demonstration and hunger strike over a proposed Chicano studies department
4. The radical restructuring of the professional schools in response to the state's fiscal crisis

UCLA'S MEDICAL QUAGMIRE

In the early 1990s, commercially managed care programs were replacing medical fee-for-service arrangements as insurance companies and hospitals tried to control escalating medical costs. UCLA's medical complex was split: the dean of the medical school reported to Dr. Rich, while the director of the hospital reported to the chancellor. A blue ribbon study committee concluded that that divided structure limited effective oversight, and Dr. Rich was asked to address the financial and organizational concerns.

She gathered together a council of doctors and medical administrators to redesign the campus's medical strategy and streamline their combined programs. The two offices (the medical school and the hospital) were consolidated, and a new leadership position with oversight and accountability for both was created. A search committee, whose work lasted three years, met with heads of medical schools all over the country until it finally selected Gerald Levey, who had a business and medical research background from the University of Pittsburgh School of Medicine, to fill the position.

In assessing that experience, she said, "I came to understand and respect the academic medical enterprise because I had that learning opportunity. We ended up trusting each other because of all the time we spent learning and listening together."

ARTS MANAGEMENT AT UCLA

UCLA had a strategic plan to develop its west campus into a focal point for the arts, which would improve public access to campus museums and serve as a site for a cinema to showcase the university's inventory of archived films. Around the same time, Occidental Petroleum Corporation was renovating four floors of its Los Angeles headquarters, just south of the UCLA campus, for a museum of art and cultural center to be named after Armand Hammer (the firm's founder, CEO, and chairman) and to house his vast personal art collection. Three shareholder lawsuits had been filed alleging that the renovation expenditures were an improper use of corporate assets. When Dr. Hammer passed away in 1990, the new CEO, Ray Irani, inherited the quagmire of disputes with shareholders and tax authorities. Dr. Rich initiated discussions between UCLA and Mr. Irani, which resulted in UCLA's takeover of the museum. She saw it as "an opportunity for everyone." The university needed a publicly accessible exhibition area, the museum was without a director or leadership, and Occidental Petroleum was being hurt by the shareholder disputes.[2] An agreement was negotiated, and UCLA assumed management of the Armand Hammer Museum and Cultural Center the following year.

Dr. Rich's key contribution was her ability to spot strategic opportunities that could be implemented, incrementally, in spite of the fact that the strategic vision, as originally planned, would not be realized due to the tight economic times.

DEMONSTRATIONS AND HUNGER STRIKE: CHICANO STUDIES PROGRAM

Centers for ethnic studies (Chicano, Afro-American, Asian American, and Native American studies) had existed on the UCLA campus from the late 1960s. In the early 1990s, there were two proposals to elevate the Chicano studies program to a departmental level. Both were denied. On April 28, 1993, Chancellor Young rejected the latest request for an independent department, but he made the announcement one day before the funeral for farmworker union leader César Chávez. Rumors circulated at the funeral that budget pressures threatened complete abandonment of the Chicano studies program. About 100 demonstrators, half of them non-students, occupied and vandalized the UCLA faculty center to protest what they believed was closure of the entire program. Dr. Rich was in charge of the campus while Chancellor Young was away on a business trip to Asia.[3]

> I was in the faculty center on that day with emeritus faculty at a special lunch. Suddenly, one of the demonstrators picked up a trash can and threw it through the plate glass window. They stormed the center. I began ushering the faculty out the back door. The students held some of them hostage and wouldn't leave. The campus police had only a handful of officers on campus, so we had to call in the city police department. The police told the demonstrators to leave; they refused. The police arrested them.

Six students and an assistant professor began a hunger strike at the administration building, ultimately reaching 10 strikers over 13 days. Dr. Rich's challenge was to manage the situation until Chancellor Young could return to renegotiate his decision. Her job was not to address the status of the Chicano Studies program. She had been an advocate of interdisciplinary programs for many years and had written extensively about interracial communications. Her responsibility that summer was to manage the campus unrest and ensure campus security. After Chancellor Young returned, a compromise was announced and the hunger strike ended in early June.

BUDGET CRISIS: PROFESSIONAL SCHOOLS
RESTRUCTURING INITIATIVE

In May 1991, Governor Pete Wilson signed legislation calling for major cuts in public support for all levels of education in California. UCLA had to deliver the equivalent of a 10 percent across-the-board budget cut within a year, necessitating a tough decision to either eliminate faculty positions or consolidate departments. Dr. Rich's challenge was to achieve the budgetary reduction requirements while ensuring that the highest-quality programs remained supported. She also had to work through UCLA's process of shared governance, whereby the administration controls the budget, while the faculty has authority to approve all academic programs. These two functions are highly interdependent: the different interests have to work together. Dr. Rich created an academic planning and budget advisory committee representing all the major campus constituencies to explore ways to solve the crisis. Even as they met, trying to determine how to phase in budget reductions, California's state finances went from bad to worse. Her job as vice-chancellor had familiarized her with the budget and strategic plan for every department; thus, she knew what the future disciplines were and where UCLA had to work to meet future growth. She came up with a very controversial solution: to merge selected schools and put weaker schools inside stronger ones where they might have a chance to prosper.

Dr. Rich proposed creating a new School of Public Policy (now Public Affairs) to concentrate research and programs with an impact on, and relevance for, public policy. The schools of social welfare and urban planning and the public policy part of public health were consolidated into the new School of Public Policy. Architecture was brought into the School of Art, and library sciences into the School of Education. The small undergraduate nursing program would be terminated while the graduate nursing program was to be strengthened and better integrated into the university's medical training program.

Over the next nine months, Dr. Rich answered questions and addressed concerns raised by the deans, department heads, and faculty in the Academic Senate. Rightfully, they demanded explanations, and she provided them with the information they needed to sign off on the proposed Professional School Restructuring Initiative (PSRI) with a two-thirds vote of approval. These were tough business decisions, but clearly the only choices under the circumstances. "That scale of change is easier to accomplish in corporate life than in academic life or the arts—they have completely different value systems."

The PSRI became well known nationwide and was written up in the *Chronicle of Higher Education*.[4] Dr. Rich traveled around the country, spoke about the PSRI at educational conferences and university research and provost conferences, and came to the attention of top universities. She was a candidate for the head of two major universities but withdrew her name from consideration.

I was not looking to leave UCLA. I was not unhappy. The PSRI was a huge job, but it was fun. I was active in all of it, very involved, and gained a lot of insight into processes, how to analyze them and figure out why they weren't always working.

At UCLA, Dr. Rich was a leader in efforts to improve undergraduate education, renovate instructional facilities, and restructure academic programs to gain greater financial efficiencies and academic quality. Her most memorable achievements at UCLA were the establishment of the communications studies major and the creation of the Office of Instructional Development. Both are strong and vital parts of the campus today.

The university honored her in two ways. Dr. Rich had proposed consolidating the events for three teaching recognition awards (for tenured faculty, non-tenured lecturers, and teaching assistants) into one large gala banquet for all award winners. When she left UCLA in 1995, they renamed the event the Academic Senate's Andrea L. Rich Night to Honor Teaching. Six years later, she was named an honorary college fellow during the annual fund-raising dinner hosted by the provost of the College of Letters and Sciences. At that dinner, Albert Carnesale, Chancellor Young's successor, awarded her UCLA's highest recognition: the UCLA Medal in Humanities.

ARTS MANAGEMENT AT LACMA

An executive recruiter contacted her about a newly created job as head of the Los Angeles County Museum of Art (LACMA), which had been without a leader for two years. Said Dr. Rich, "I had a sense of the market's timing and thought it would be better for me to take the initiative than to let things happen. I felt I had one more shot at a big job."

When she became the first president and chief executive officer of LACMA in November 1995, neither the art interests nor the trustees knew what to expect of her.[5] Dr. Rich said, "I told [the board] that there probably would be a backlash of some sort [to my appointment], but not to worry about it because once we got going, it would fall away."

The museum's mission was to acquire, preserve, and exhibit great works of art. Dr. Rich's public education background and experience had trained her to view the museum as a public service: a taxpayer-supported, nonprofit, and tax-exempt public facility of Los Angeles County. She was equally concerned about the public benefit that the arts would provide and how to effectively use public tax monies. "I get enormous pleasure when I see the public well served."

She made LACMA financially solvent and efficient by spending money strategically and with a commitment to the unique diversity of the Los Angeles community. She and her board developed a strategic plan, a physical plan, and a fund-raising plan to guide all operations. As a result, they expanded the capacity of LACMA to deliver the art experience to the community many times over.

Dr. Rich learned that money to support the arts was scarce, but that it was available in abundance to support arts education, so she launched the Arts Education

Initiative—a $3.2 million pilot project to restore arts programs and education in area schools through collaboration with the Los Angeles Unified School District, four area universities, and eight local museums. She strengthened LACMA's public programming through expanded funding from foundations such as the W. M. Keck Foundation, the James Irvine Foundation of San Francisco, and the Maxwell H. Gluck Foundation of San Pedro. In April 2003, the Annenberg Foundation made a $10 million gift to establish a director's endowment fund supporting core programs, including special exhibitions, art acquisitions, and art education activities for at-risk youth.

The museum's endowment rose from $49 million to $125 million. A major capital campaign raised $156 million, which supported the first phase of a physical expansion designed by the Italian architect Renzo Piano and increased the operating endowment. Additional fund-raising came from the newly expanded 54-person board of trustees, including a $50 million gift from Eli Broad for the 60,000 square-foot Broad Contemporary Art Museum.

Recognizing that LACMA could not compete with European or East Coast museums for classical collections, Dr. Rich focused instead on art that reflected the diversity of the Los Angeles community so that the museum could be "world class in its own unique way." Several significant acquisitions completed over the next six years added major works from Mexico, Latin America, Korea, and Islamic countries.[6] In October 2004, she finalized a five-year collaboration with the UCLA Chicano Studies Research Center for a Latino arts initiative covering exhibitions, publications, educational activities, research projects, artistic collections, and community relations.

Dr. Rich resigned from LACMA in November 2005. She learned that managing the diverse interests of the huge LACMA board was as much a challenge as guiding the artistic side of the public art environment. Curators, artists, critics, and trustees focus on the acquisition and display of great art and tend to be less concerned with the financial or administrative prerequisites. Her experience at LACMA underscored the reality that management of the arts, as a profession, needed a strong hand to establish a solid business foundation and direction.

CORPORATE BOARD ROLES

The headhunter who had called Dr. Rich about the LACMA position reconnected with her about a director position at Mattel Inc. in El Segundo, California. In November 1998, Dr. Rich's nomination was announced by Mattel chair and CEO Jill E. Barad, who said, "At both UCLA and LACMA, Andrea has established a reputation as an incredible manager and visionary. She is brilliant, and will bring a new and important perspective to our board."[7]

Dr. Rich joined Mattel's board just as it was absorbing Pleasant Company, a Wisconsin direct marketer of books, dolls, clothing, and accessories under the American Girl brand name, and initiating the acquisition of the Learning Company Inc., an educational game software company whose valuation soared along with other dot-com businesses. When the digital software game market burst, the board asked for

Ms. Barad's resignation in February 2000. Robert Eckert was selected as chair and CEO three months later. Today, Dr. Rich is a member of the governance and social responsibility committee and the compensation committee. She has been joined by two additional women directors: Kathy Brittain White and Frances D. Fergusson.

In February 2006, Dr. Rich was invited to be a founding director of a start-up bank, the Private Bank of California. In October of the same year, she was invited to be a director of Douglas Emmett Real Estate Investment Trust. She describes those nominations as coming by way of "serendipity." The boards tapped her for her financial competence and her ability to represent shareholder and stakeholder interests: experience demonstrated at both UCLA and LACMA.

Steve Broidy, chair of the Private Bank of California, knew Dr. Rich through his foundation work and support of LACMA. Regulators suggested that the bank might benefit from broader representation from the community. Up to that time, the board consisted primarily of lawyers, including Melanie K. Cook, who knew Dr. Rich as her former professor.

David Kaplan had known Dr. Rich's work when he was a member of the UCLA Academic Senate. His son, Jordan L. Kaplan, was CEO of the Douglas Emmett Company, which was putting together a board before going public. The company needed a director with experience on a public company board, somebody familiar with contemporary corporate governance issues. Dr. Rich became chair of the nominating and corporate governance committee and a member of the compensation committee.

ACADEMIC AND NONPROFIT BOARD ROLES

Dr. Rich was named a trustee of Pitzer College in Claremont, California, from 1998 to 2001. Her more recent association with the Claremont schools came by way of Stephen D. Rountree, a long-time executive vice president of the Getty Museum and now president and CEO of the Music Center of Los Angeles. Mr. Rountree, a member of the board of trustees of Claremont Graduate University, was instrumental in developing the university's MA in arts and cultural management, a joint program of the School of the Arts and Humanities and the Drucker School. When Dr. Rich retired from LACMA, he persuaded her to teach one spring semester course: Theory and Practice of Arts Management. She was named to the Claremont McKenna College board of trustees in 2007.

Dr. Rich continues to be very active in the nonprofit community as a trustee of the Jules Stein Eye Institute at UCLA. She was invited by Gloria Molina to be on the board of trustees of the La Plaza de Cultura y Artes Foundation (one of 16 California Smithsonian affiliates), where she was tapped to help them write their long-term strategic plan.

LESSONS LEARNED

Dr. Rich was a leader in academia and public university administration. Yet those institutions were late in acknowledging her accomplishments. It was not until she left UCLA to take the reins at LACMA, turning around the museum's finances and strategic direction, that the business community tapped her for corporate board positions. Once she began speaking publicly about the PSRI to the larger national audience, her financial and organizational problem-solving skills became more widely visible and valued.

The work she did at LACMA was a logical extension of her achievements on campus. She created new institutions with a stronger financial foundation, undertook mergers and acquisitions of new collections, pursued new funding sources, redefined the mission and the market, and overhauled operations and financials. These were the same technical and collaborative skills she used at UCLA in co-creating the communications studies major, consolidating the arts, reorganizing the medical enterprise, and implementing the PSRI. She stood toe-to-toe with strikers at UCLA and with the artistic community at LACMA; each constituency learned that her priority was to protect their long-term financial viability rather than simply debate short-term differences.

Dr. Rich's professional experiences are precisely the capabilities for which public company boards of directors are searching today:

- A willingness to start at the bottom and work her way up
- The ability to handle a wide variety of management challenges at large and complex organizations
- The courage to take measured risks and face confrontation
- A reputation for vision and innovation

From her own perspective, Dr. Rich sees many of the steps in her career as simply fortuitous and serendipitous. A bank, an REIT, a global toy company, medical institutions, and a prominent graduate school now call her a director or trustee. Dr. Rich is an example of an institution builder devoted to public service. She is one who can envision future opportunities and also collaborate to put into place strategies that will achieve those visions.

Politicians:
The Government Path

Women directors with careers in government chose a wide variety of political paths at the international, national, state, and local levels. The women who came by this path typically were appointed to positions because of their professional knowledge in a specific subject area, such as finance, health care, or international trade. After they were appointed to top-level administration policy committees, departments, or agencies where their expertise was highly valued, they earned the attention of corporate boards that could benefit from their competence and knowledge.

RELATIVE IMPORTANCE

The political or governmental career path was cited by 16 women directors (8.5% of all experience cited). Their competencies included telecommunications, technology, tourism, international trade, and economic development (see table 3.1). At the federal level, the women acquired experience in defense, security, environmental regulations, and health care matters. Local and community economic development groups brought them onto gubernatorial or state/regional commissions. Women directors were named to one or more agencies involved in the alphabet soup of financial institution regulations: the Federal Reserve banks, the Federal Deposit Insurance Corporation, the Federal Home Loan Bank Board, and the Securities and Exchange Commission. A few women were named to state cabinet positions, where they focused on finance, health care, or travel/tourism from a public policy perspective. Only one woman, Kathleen Brown, succeeded in attaining elected office, as California state treasurer. However, even losing elections as governor, senator, or mayor seemed to count for something: those women were considered willing to dare and to challenge the status quo. This added to

Table 3.1

Government Path: Experience of Women on Corporate Boards of California
Fortune **1000 Companies**

Paths into the Boardroom					Name	Company
	G				Charlene Barshevsky	Intel
	G	I		C	Kathleen Brown	Countrywide Financial
N	G				Linda L. Chavez	ABM Industries
	G			C	Linnet Frazier Deily	Chevron Corporation
	G	A	I		Nancy-Ann Min DeParle	DaVita
	G	A	E		Diana Lady Dougan	Qualcomm
	G		E		Linda Griego	Granite Construction
	G	A	E		Anita K. Jones	Science Applications Inc.
	G		E		Monica C. Lozano	Walt Disney
	G			C	Rebecca Ann McDonald	Granite Construction
	G	I	E		Roslyn B. Payne	First American Corporation
	G			C	Aulana L. Peters	Northrop Grummond
	G	A			Sally K. Richardson	Molina Healthcare
	G				Ronna Romney	Molina Healthcare
	G				Donna Tanoue	Longs Drug Stores
	G	I	E	C	Donna Frame Tuttle	Hilton Hotels

Note: N = Nonprofit; G = Government; A = Academic; I = Investment; E = Entrepreneurial; C = Corporate.

their aura as qualified and independent-minded candidates for public company service.

DIVERSE EXPERIENCES

Three women in our sample were named ambassadors.

- Charlene Barshevsky was U.S. trade representative under President Bill Clinton.
- Diana Lady Dougan was assistant secretary of state and the first statutory U.S. coordinator for international communications and information policy under President George H. W. Bush. Her specialty was the emerging markets involving telecommunications and information industry multilateral trade agreements.
- Linnet Frazier Deily was U.S. trade representative under President George W. Bush.

Several women were named department heads at the federal cabinet level or just below.

- Anita K. Jones was named director of defense research and engineering at the Department of Defense under President Clinton, based upon her extensive computer security background.
- Linda L. Chavez was director of the U.S. Civil Rights Commission under President Ronald Reagan, who tapped her for her experience as a minority rights advocate.
- Donna Frame Tuttle was undersecretary of commerce for travel and tourism and deputy secretary of commerce during the Reagan administration.
- Nancy-Ann Min DeParle was associate director for health and personnel in the Clinton administration's White House Office of Management and Budget and was later named administrator of the Health Care Financing Administration (now Centers for Medicare & Medicaid Services) in charge of Medicare and Medicaid programs.
- Risa Juanita Lavizzo-Mourey was deputy administrator of the federal Agency for Health Care Policy and Research (now the Agency for Health Care Quality), a member of the Clinton White House Task Force on Health Care Reform, and a consultant to the White House on health policy issues.

The Federal Reserve System and federal financial commissions have benefited from the legal and business education and the financial expertise of several women directors. Six women served as members or chairs at branch banks or advisory councils of the Federal Reserve Bank: Linnet Frazier Deily, Linda Griego, Claudine B. Malone, Cynthia H. Milligan, Judith M. Runstad, and Mary Lee Widener. Donna Tanoue was named director of the Federal Deposit Insurance Corporation by President Clinton. Aulana L. Peters was a commissioner of the Securities and Exchange Commission. Roslyn B. Payne was president of the Federal Asset Disposition Administration, an organization established by the Federal Home Loan Bank Board to manage the orderly disposal of property assets held by bankrupt savings and loans during the thrift industry crisis of the mid-1980s until the Federal Asset Disposition Administration was replaced by the congressionally authorized Resolution Trust Corporation.

Other women have been very successful at the state levels of government.

- Kathleen Brown was elected state treasurer of California.
- Monica C. Lozano was elected to the California State Board of Education.
- Donna Tanoue served as the first commissioner of financial institutions in the Division of Financial Institutions, Hawaii Department of Commerce and Consumer Affairs. The commissioner is appointed by the director of commerce and consumer affairs, subject to approval by the governor.

- Nancy-Ann Min DeParle was the commissioner of the Tennessee Department of Human Services.

The women directors surveyed have served in political and governmental roles primarily because of the unique expertise that they could bring to the deliberations. They did not seek political power so much as political powers sought their wisdom and advice.

- Susan Westerberg Prager was asked to provide testimony before the U.S. House Judiciary Committee regarding the Civil Rights Act of 1997 and to serve on the bipartisan and nonprofit California Commission on Campaign Finance, a private organization.
- Risa Juanita Lavizzo-Mourey is a highly regarded authority and advisor in the field of public health care, nationally and internationally.
- Rebecca Ann McDonald was on the advisory committee of the Export-Import Bank of the United States as an oil industry production representative under both Presidents Clinton and Bush.

Women directors showed strong interest in public policy and international affairs organizations where they could listen to global political leaders speak in their area of expertise and access innovative research in their field of interest. A prominent organization with several women directors is the Council on Foreign Relations (CFR), the powerful private organization of 4,200 of the nation's political elite, and publisher of the prestigious journal *Foreign Affairs*. Patricia E. Mitchell, Anne M. Tatlock, and Miriam L. Haas mentioned they are members of the CFR. Other members include Monica C. Lozano, Linda L. Chavez, Linda Griego, Diana Lady Dougan, Aulana L. Peters, and Kathleen Brown.

The Pacific Council on International Policy is the public policy group (founded by Linda Griego with John Branson, president of Edison International, and Warren Christopher, President Clinton's secretary of state) as a West Coast spin-off of the CFR. All the members of the CFR listed above, except Linda L. Chavez, are also members of the Pacific Council on International Policy.

Women directors come from both sides of the political aisle. Democrats include Clinton appointees Charlene Barshevsky, Kathleen Brown, Linda Griego, Anita K. Jones, Nancy-Ann Min DeParle, Sally K. Richardson, and Donna Tanoue. Anne B. Gust was a campaign coordinator for Democrat Jerry Brown's campaign for attorney general and is now his special advisor in that office. Monica C. Lozano was appointed a University of California regent by Governor Gray Davis, a Democrat. Mary Lee Widener was active in the California State Democratic Party and received federal appointments from Presidents Reagan and Carter.

Republicans appointments under both Presidents Bush went to Linda L. Chavez, Linnet Frazier Deily, Diana Lady Dougan, and Ronna Romney. Roslyn B. Payne served in a federal agency during the Reagan years. Ms. Deily was named a University of Texas regent by then-Governor George W. Bush. President Reagan named

Aulana L. Peters a representative of the Democratic Party to the Securities and Exchange Commission, the membership of which is divided between parties.

Opportunities for women to find their appropriate place on top governmental committees and commissions are on the rise. Women in leadership bring their unique brand of independent thinking, experience, and wisdom to public policy roles, increasingly at the international level.

MYTH BUSTING

The most common myth about the political path is that volunteering on local or municipal commissions is one way into the corporate boardroom. In our sample, the women on boards were selected by government boards, bureaus, and departments that believed they could add value to the problem-solving process based on the expertise they had developed up to that point in their careers in finance, banking, real estate, health care, or technology. Most of the women on boards who came from the government experience pathway were named to top political positions with top compensation, not volunteer posts.

LESSONS LEARNED

The share of women elected to national office is only slightly larger than the share of women on corporate boards. In the 111th Congress, women will hold 90 (16.8%) of the 535 seats overall: 17 of the 100 seats in the Senate and 73 of the 435 seats in the House of Representatives. In 2009, 73 women held statewide elective executive offices across the country, representing 23.2 percent of the 315 available positions.[1] Elected office has yet to be shown to be a viable career path into a boardroom for women. Kathleen Brown is the only director in our sample who was elected to statewide office. As state treasurer in 1991–1995, she was the fourth woman of six who ever served in elected office in California state history.

Ronna Romney wrote a book on the unique challenges that women need to address in the political field.[2] Ms. Romney's interviewees noted that women have difficulty raising funds, especially the crucially important "early money," and face especially harsh criticism for negative campaigning.

Linnet Frazier Deily and Donna Frame Tuttle both mentioned that their government experience was built on the foundation of the business skills they acquired in negotiating deals and finding common ground among different interests. They both contrasted this ability with the adversarial nature of legal training.

Roslyn B. Payne, Mary Lee Widener, and Aulana L. Peters developed creative new business or regulatory models in the fields of real estate, finance, and accounting, and their proposals have been adopted as legislation or public policy by the agencies where they served.

Anita K. Jones, Risa Juanita Lavizzo-Mourey, Sally K. Richardson, and Nancy-Ann Min DeParle demonstrate that women in government are not simply shy, retiring tokens—they have taken daring leadership positions and challenged the status quo without hesitation.

THE WOMEN INTERVIEWED

The three women who were selected as representative of this pathway into the boardroom are Linnet Frazier Deily, Linda Griego, and Sally K. Richardson. They have tremendous breadth of experience, spanning local, state, national, and international political or governmental competencies, which is exactly why the corporate directors invited them on board.

More women pursue government and political positions in response to the increased number of opportunities for women to work in regulatory agencies and politics at the local, regional, and national levels. The proliferation of new regulatory entities in the financial field, especially, opens up many new opportunities for women directors to acquire governing and governance experience uniquely suited to corporate board-of-director responsibilities.

Director Profile: Linnet Frazier Deily

Linnet Frazier Deily was born in 1945 and raised on a 250-acre farm in McKinney, Texas, in rural Collin County. "My parents were always talking about world events, politics, and international affairs around the dinner table," she said "That piqued my interest long before college."

She came to her corporate board roles primarily as a result of her international negotiating experience as U.S. trade representative to the World Trade Organization, a position to which she was appointed by President George W. Bush. In preparation for that role, she acquired almost three decades of financial experience at banks and financial service firms in Texas and California.

EARLY YEARS

Said Ms. Deily, "I had been to the UN [and] seen the General Assembly during the summer after I graduated from high school. Those were the days when people still held very high hopes that the UN could provide international guidance to solve future problems." In 1967, she earned a BA in government from the University of Texas at Austin, where she was involved with the Model United Nations. She received her MA in international management from the University of Texas at Dallas in 1976. While at UT Dallas, she took a course in international banking taught by Dick Backus, senior vice president in the international area of Dallas's Republic National Bank. He offered her a summer job writing country studies. At the summer's end, she moved into the bank's management training program. By 1980, she had become senior vice president of international management with administrative responsibilities for the bank's branch operations in London and Singapore and representative offices in São Paulo, Brazil; Caracas, Venezuela; Mexico; Hong Kong; and Tokyo. "I traveled to Brazil a number of times and spent quite a bit of time in London working on computer projects there."

She married Myron "Mike" Bonham Deily in 1981 and relocated to the West Coast when he was named head of strategic planning at Bank of America's North American division.

FIRST INTERSTATE: CALIFORNIA

Ms. Deily's expertise in corporate and global finance was refined and enhanced at First Interstate Bank in California. "A friend from Dallas sent my resume to some people at First Interstate Bank, where it was handed around to the head of human resources. Bruce Willison invited me to join him at corporate banking at First Interstate Bancorp, the holding company. It was just the two of us."

First Interstate, via their franchisee First Interstate Bank of Denver, bought IntraWest Bank of Denver and asked Ms. Deily to take charge of the merger. When it was finalized in October 1983, it was one of the largest bank acquisitions in the United States—with a combined asset value of $2.4 billion.

Next, Ms. Deily was invited by Mr. Willison to become senior vice president in charge of finance, administration, and strategic planning at the world banking unit of First Interstate of California. In July 1984, she participated in her second major bank acquisition: the London merchant banking operations of Continental Illinois Ltd. Shortly afterwards, the world banking group was formally spun off to form a new bank, First Interstate Bank Limited, to serve large corporate customers. Ms. Deily became its chief financial officer.

In 1986, she was asked to head up the Los Angeles division on the retail side of First Interstate Bank of California. A year later, she was named executive vice president.

FIRST INTERSTATE: TEXAS

The savings and loan industry went through accelerated growth throughout the 1970s, followed by deregulation in the early 1980s. Some major thrifts overextended themselves. First Interstate saw them as acquisition opportunities by which it could expand its cross-state presence. The combination of deregulation, managerial problems, and poor lending practices in both energy-related industries and commercial real estate hit Texas banks especially hard. In the summer of 1986 the state passed emergency legislation authorizing out-of-state acquisitions of Texas banks. Two of the state's largest commercial entities were sold without government assistance: Texas Commerce Bancshares was taken over by Chemical New York Corporation, and Allied Bancshares was taken over by First Interstate Bancorp.

She recalled, "After we bought the bank in Texas, it was said that our senior management looked around to see who could 'speak the language.' I was chosen." Ms. Deily and her husband moved back to Houston in 1988 when she took over as president and chief operating officer of First Interstate Bank of Texas, a 123 branch bank network in the state. She and her team turned the bank around the hard way, taking it from a loss of over $100 million to a high-performing institution entirely through private capital. In January 1991, she was named chief executive officer of First Interstate Bank of Texas and, a year later, she became chair.

While still in Houston, she also served on the First Interstate Bancorp managing committee, based in Los Angeles, which oversaw corporate, retail, and trust operations across the company. She chaired the retail council, with responsibility for the firm's overall retail presence.

HOUSTON INDUSTRIES BOARD

In 1993, she became director of Houston Industries (later CenterPoint Energy), her first public corporate board. Other board members knew her through a number of shared community organizations in Houston and recommended her for consideration by the chair, Don Jordan.

> Houston has a closely linked business community. The value that I brought to that board was my public company experience. Most of the other board members came from the private industry environment. Today, Sarbanes-Oxley has formalized many public company standards. Private companies might not be as familiar with those requirements.

CIVIC LIFE

Ms. Deily and her husband became more involved in local business and community activities. In 1992, she became a board member of the Houston Museum of Fine Arts and a member of the Greater Houston Partnership, one of the city's major business organizations. She was named chair of the World Trade Supervisory Committee of the Partnership; chair of Central Houston, the downtown business association; and a member of the board of the Texas Medical Center. The following year, she also chaired the Houston United Way campaign.

In 1994, she was asked by First Interstate to take on corporate-wide responsibility for government affairs in recognition of the fact that the banking industry was facing a host of new legislation and regulations. As one of the top four executives at First Interstate, she was also asked to represent the firm as a member of the Bankers Roundtable in Washington, D.C., a national association promoting the business of banking and encouraging the development of sound banking and financial policies and practices. Membership in the Roundtable is reserved for senior executives of the 125 largest banking companies in the United States. She became First Interstate's representative to the American Bankers' Association political committee in Washington, D.C., which was established to strengthen the legislative presence of the banking community in Washington. And she served as a director on the board of the Consumer Bankers Association. Together, these commitments meant a minimum of another two days a month on Capitol Hill.

In February 1995, Texas governor George W. Bush appointed her to a six-year term as a regent for the University of Texas. She had not been involved in Texas

Republican politics, but First Interstate of Texas was the lead bank for the Texas Rangers, of which Mr. Bush was one of the managing partners.

She was the national president of the Chicago-based Committee of 200 during its 10th anniversary year, 1992–1993. In 1997, she was honored as an outstanding business leader by Northwood University in Dallas, Texas. Previously, she was a director of the American Conservatory Theater in San Francisco, and a member of Catalyst Inc. and the Women's Museum in Dallas in 2000–2001. She was named one of *Fortune* magazine's Top 50 most powerful women in business in October 2000. About that honor, she said, "It was special because Dawn Lepore, chief technology officer of Schwab, was also recognized."

According to Ms. Deily, "I've always enjoyed being involved in local community activities. I've always believed in giving back. I was able to change the banks' officer appraisal system at First Interstate of Texas to include consideration of community services and to allow people time off to perform those tasks."

In June 2001, the University of Texas at Dallas named her a distinguished alumna. In November 2002, McCombs School of Business at the University of Texas at Austin inducted her into their hall of fame.

In 2005, President George W. Bush named Ms. Deily to a three-year assignment on the J. William Fulbright Foreign Scholarship board, the organization that approves every scholarship granted worldwide. "We review about 6,000 applications a year," she said. "It's particularly heartwarming to read the profiles of these very talented scholarship candidates."

CHARLES SCHWAB & CO.

Her last day at First Interstate was April 1, 1996, when the bank was acquired in a hostile takeover by Wells Fargo. Recalled Ms. Deily: "A fellow that I knew in the search industry just called me one day, asking if he could be of help. He offered to introduce me to people he knew in San Francisco. There's a lot of serendipity in life."

The following October, she was named enterprise president of Charles Schwab institutional group where she was responsible for providing support services to 5,700 independent investment managers and overseeing more than $100 billion in assets nationwide. Charles Schwab & Co. Inc., one of the nation's largest financial services firms, was growing rapidly by bringing in talent from outside.

In 1998, she became president of Schwab's retail group, responsible for all general investment services: 370 branches, 6 major investor call centers, specialized retail and electronic brokerage services, Internet retail activity, and a staff of 10,000 employees. During her tenure, Schwab added a million new retail accounts a year (reaching 5.7 million) and increased investment assets by over $250 billion. After two years in that position, Ms. Deily joined Schwab president and CEO David Pottruck in a newly created office of the president, where she was responsible for services to wealthy customers, Schwab's expansion into banking, and other client investment services. As vice-chair of Charles Schwab Corporation, she supervised the company's strategic direction and integration of the company's client-focused enterprises and was a member of the executive committee.

In December 2000, she was selected by the directors of the Federal Reserve Bank of San Francisco to represent the 12th district to the advisory council of the Federal Reserve Bank's board of governors. The advisory council has representatives from each of the 12 Federal Reserve Bank districts.

> My sense was that the Fed recognized that the lines were blurring between banking and brokerage services. They needed more input from the retail brokerage side, and Schwab was the obvious premier provider in that category. [I] might have been [an] attractive [candidate] as a representative with experience from both these perspectives: banking and brokerage.

U.S. TRADE REPRESENTATIVE

When asked about how she came to be named U.S. trade representative, she recalled,

> I was talking with several people in the administration in D.C. about coming to work there. Robert B. Zoellick, U.S. trade representative, wanted a businessperson as U.S. representative to the World Trade Organization, the negotiation forum of 140 international trading nations. He knew the WTO decisions were made unanimously. If the U.S. had a representative with a legal background, there might be the tendency to look at the discussions litigiously, contentiously. A businessperson would be familiar with "doing deals"; a businessperson would have the view that deals had to be mutually agreeable, that everyone has to pay something, and that everyone has to work together.

In March 2001, President George W. Bush appointed Ms. Deily ambassador and deputy U.S. trade representative to the WTO. From 2001 until June 2005, she was chief of mission of the U.S. trade representative's office in Geneva, Switzerland. She led the U.S. delegation to the WTO, supervising the team during the Doha round of trade negotiations.

> I spent my time on agricultural issues, industrial products, service businesses, and trade facilitation—all of those issues. I was very active in a number of different cases where the U.S. either was pursing trade settlement or defending itself against disputes in Geneva. Just getting the Doha negotiations to launch was a major task unto itself. Keeping the negotiations organized and moving forward [was] the priority during 2002 and 2005.

The importance of the Doha round of multilateral trade negotiations was summarized by Carla Anderson Hills in a special World Trade Organization edition issue of *Foreign Affairs:* "These negotiations hold the promise of raising standards of living worldwide, alleviating global poverty, removing inequities in the trade regime, and enhancing international stability."[1]

LUCENT TECHNOLOGIES INC. BOARD

In November 2005, Ms. Deily was named a director on the board of Lucent Technologies Inc. (now Alcatel-Lucent). "Lucent liked my international experience. They needed someone familiar with the consumer marketplace who understood how to make technology decisions based on good knowledge of the consumer base."

Ms. Deily is a member of Alcatel-Lucent's governance and nomination committee and the compensation committee. She is one of three female directors, including Lucent president Pat Russo, who welcomed her on board with the following compliment:

> Linnet's extensive experience in executive management and international trade makes her a valuable addition to the board as we focus on accelerating Lucent's pace for profitable revenue growth. We look forward to working with Linnet and utilizing her expertise to move our company forward in a dynamic global marketplace for communications technology.[2]

CHEVRON CORPORATION BOARD

In January 2006, Ms. Deily was added to the Chevron board of directors, where she is a member of the audit committee. She said, "For Chevron, the international experience was also important, to help them understand the larger marketplace."

She was the sole female on Chevron's 13-member (now 15) board. She was first identified by one of the non-management directors and was named to the audit committee largely because of her extensive financial expertise.

HONEYWELL BOARD

In March 2006, she was named a director of Honeywell and a member of their audit committee and their retirement plans committee. "Linnet's expertise in international trade coupled with her strong leadership experience will make her a valuable addition to Honeywell's board of directors," said Dave Cote, chairman and chief executive officer of Honeywell. "We look forward to her contribution to our efforts to expand globally and build a growth-focused company."[3]

Added Ms. Deily, "The committee roles are just part of the board assignment: you go where there's a need and where your experience fits. Usually there's a rotation of assignments."

LESSONS LEARNED

Linnet Deily brought business-based corporate financial expertise into governmental positions at the Federal Reserve advisory council and the U.S. trade representative's office, where she was instrumental in keeping the Doha round negotiations on track. She's also been tapped by civic and nonprofit boards, where her financial expertise is valued. In February 2007, she was named to the board of Houston Endowment Inc. "It's a pure pleasure. They do great work as a philanthropic endowment, giving about $70–80 million a year to the arts, education, health, and the environment. I knew several people on the board and was asked to join when other directors retired."

Like her peers, she's a constant student of governance, attending Stanford Law School's Directors' College (June 2006) and UCLA's director training program (October 2007). "It's a good idea to keep up to date on the major issues. Most directors are quite savvy about their responsibilities. I'm likely to do director training once a year or every other year just to pick up nuggets of ideas."

The knowledge she brings to her corporate board roles include finance, technology, deal making, and a strong global perspective. Linnet Deily is a builder of financial institutions and highly valued for her international experience.

DIRECTOR PROFILE: LINDA GRIEGO

Linda Griego, age 60 at the time of our interview, came to her board roles by many paths, but in her key leadership roles she followed the political/governmental path as deputy mayor, community economic development expert, and candidate for mayor of Los Angeles. Her years as head of Rebuild/LA after the Los Angeles riots provided the fulcrum around which many other corporate and nonprofit director opportunities developed. She calls herself a "public policy wonk." She is a small business entrepreneur who didn't think she could get a bank loan, yet she ended up being a community development banker and bank builder herself.

EARLY YEARS

Born in Tucumcari, New Mexico, "about 200 miles from nowhere," she was raised by a grandmother whose dream was that she graduate from high school. "I grew up in poverty. My family worked in a small-town bakery. At age 13, I used to do the payroll taxes and checks on Saturdays."

Ms. Griego came to Los Angeles by way of Washington, D.C. "Right after high school, I went to work for my hometown congressman, Tom Morris, whose wife Connie was my first-grade teacher. I was on my way out of poverty." Later, she became a legislative aide to California U.S. senator Alan Cranston, first in Washington, D.C., and then in California. "He was one of my best mentors."

She met her husband, Ron Peterson, while he was in law school and they both worked in Senator Cranston's office. They were married in 1970 and moved to Los Angeles, where he started his career as a litigator.

Ms. Griego surpassed her grandmother's expectations, graduating from college while working full time. Ms. Griego took part-time classes in D.C., then one year at Pomona College. "Pomona was the right-size school. I was very interested in their economics program. But I missed working for Senator Cranston, so I switched to UCLA and went back to work in his Westwood office." She earned a bachelor of arts in history from UCLA in 1975.

PACIFIC BELL

Ms. Griego's private-sector employment began with a challenge from a telephone company executive, a pattern that would reoccur. While representing Senator Cranston at a labor conference, she sat on a panel with a telephone company executive "who was making a lot of noise about women in nontraditional jobs." At that time, AT&T was operating under a Justice Department consent decree to open up more jobs to women in areas that had not been available to them before, such as installation, repair, and construction.

He made this remark about women not wanting to break their nails or muss their hair. I told him, "You missed the whole point. It has nothing to do with broken nails. It has everything to do with how much those jobs pay, which, at that time, was at least $14 an hour. That income could send your kids to college or buy a home. The jobs currently available to women are entry-level telephone operator positions at minimum wage. You won't know how well women will do on those jobs until you give them a chance."

A few weeks later, Pacific Bell (then owned by AT&T) invited her for a job interview. It took all day, but their interest seemed genuine. "It was one of the longest, toughest interviews I'd been through. Very physical. They did a terrific job." At the end of the interview, she was offered a job in charge of installation and repair crews. Over the next three years, she rose to management positions at Pacific Bell, in spite of supervisors who told her that she was a threat to their annual bonuses because she was a woman with no field experience. She said, "My view is that when you work hard, it all works out. Ultimately, one particularly skeptical supervisor ended up working for me."

SMALL BUSINESS ENTREPRENEUR

Ms. Griego's introduction to the small business world was like that of most women: doing what she knew best. She decided to start her own business after leaving Pacific Bell when the Baby Bell breakup relocated her job and team to San Francisco. In 1980, she opened Chili Stop, a 16-seat New Mexican café and market specializing in red and green chili.

It was the only food I knew how to cook. That was long before anyone knew anything about Southwestern food and also before the takeout craze, so I was somewhat successful. I learned so much from the experience, starting a small business, making all the mistakes without going broke. There was no way I could qualify for a business loan, so I relied heavily on credit cards.

The most important lesson she learned was "pulling the plug"—one of the hardest challenges for an entrepreneur. "I had to come to terms with the simple fact that I was making less money than when I was working for the telephone company. Those early days prepared me to struggle through many challenges. But I enjoyed learning new things and taking quantum leaps."

ENGINE CO. NO. 28

Closing the doors on Chili Stop led to her next major opportunity: renovating a historical landmark. Some customers suggested that she open a restaurant downtown, referring her to Engine Co. No. 28, an abandoned fire station built in 1912. The city wanted to sell the three-story building, which had about 20,000 square feet. She was intrigued and loved the challenge of downtown, but she got the "royal bureaucratic runaround" at city hall.

Drawing on her Washington experience, she set out to overcome the obstacles thrown her way. She partnered with attorney Hugh Biele and formed a development firm to acquire the property and renovate the building as a restaurant. Ultimately, she became the president and CEO of Griego Enterprises Inc., the firm that oversaw her investment in Engine Co. No. 28.

> I had always been an entrepreneur but had yet to learn how to become a business partner. If I made a mistake, I took full responsibility and thought losses should come out of my share of the investment. My partners made it clear that we were in the project as a team. I'll never forget that important lesson. We don't make it alone.

The redevelopment project put her in direct contact with a skeptical adversary, the Community Redevelopment Authority (CRA) of Los Angeles, which was not very receptive to women developers. "I was warned by a CRA employee that 'If you really want this building, you've got to bring a man to represent you. Otherwise you will get turned down.'" After a consultation with her partner, they found a man with extensive construction management experience to strengthen the team.

She found other people in the city who were rooting for her and who helped her to succeed. Said Ms. Griego, "Maureen Kindel was president of the board of public works. Even though she didn't know me, she backed me and helped turn around resistance from city hall."

THE POLITICAL PATH

Ms. Griego began taking on leadership positions on local commissions and elsewhere in the public sector. Those leadership engagements would make her a strong candidate for corporate board positions.

In the late 1980s, the CRA was rocked by major scandals. Its administrator resigned amid controversy involving a board member and its legal counsel.

Ms. Griego had been very outspoken about the CRA based on her experience with Engine Co. No. 28. In 1991, she was appointed deputy mayor in charge of economic development, with oversight responsibilities for the departments of public works, building and safety, and planning, and the CRA, a position she held until 1993. "My job was to streamline the permitting process and attract new business. However, after just a few months into the job, riots rocked Los Angeles in April 1992 and at least 10,000 jobs were lost. Hundreds of buildings were destroyed. Damages were estimated at over a $1 billion."

She also was designated the city's liaison to the federal government after the riots. In 1993, after a brief candidacy for mayor on a platform highlighting the challenges facing small businesses during the economic recession, Ms. Griego took on an assignment as special advisor for economic development in Southern California to U.S. secretary of commerce Ron Brown.

THE REBUILD/LA YEARS

According to Ms. Griego, "Los Angeles was reeling in the recession. Corporations were shedding jobs, not creating them. We'd lost about 250,000 aerospace and related jobs in Los Angeles County. One of my assignments was to analyze the impact military base closures would have on the Southern California economy."

Her work at commerce led to her involvement with Rebuild/LA Inc., a nonprofit corporation formed immediately after the Los Angeles riots by Mayor Tom Bradley and California governor Pete Wilson. Peter Ueberroth, who had led the financially successful 1984 Los Angeles Olympics, was asked to head a community-wide effort to restore the health and vitality of Los Angeles. Rebuild/LA had only a five-year window in which to accomplish its goals. During the first two years, Mr. Ueberroth took a top-down approach, going to major corporate officers and telling them that the inner city had been abandoned, and that now corporate America had to do its share. He put into place a structure and process for the private sector to contribute to the solutions in South Central Los Angeles.

Ms. Griego took over as president and CEO of Rebuild/LA in 1994, initiating a bottom-up approach. This role became one of the more important leadership positions of her career.

> I used the Marshall Plan as my model. After World War II, small manufacturing businesses in Europe were rebuilt using that concept. We looked for cooperative opportunities where we could help small manufacturers link to other more successful firms, joint venturing, and taking on bigger orders, relying on each other to divvy up the work to get the job done.

During her three years at Rebuild/LA, 17 new stores were brought into the city's economically disadvantaged neighborhoods, 35 supermarkets and 149 gas stations were repaired or rebuilt in the riot-affected areas, and countless small to midsize manufacturing firms were given help to create jobs and rekindle growth in South Central Los Angeles. She used resources such as Dun & Bradstreet, the

Urban Land Institute, volunteer students from UCLA and the University of Southern California, and CORO, the nonprofit leadership training entity, to conduct research and develop databases describing the inner city. She built a consortium of community colleges, private employers, and public agencies to develop vocational and job-training curricula to meet the needs of manufacturing firms in the neglected areas. Rebuild/LA encouraged companies such as supermarket chains, Payless, Blockbuster, Taco Bell, Pizza Hut, and Chief Auto Parts to build anew and/or relocate stores in disadvantaged neighborhoods, persuading them with Rebuild/LA's economic data.

She encouraged the pension funds to invest in area small businesses. Her work with commerce secretary Ron Brown helped open doors to pension funds such as the California Public Employees' Retirement System. Secretary Brown also was the point person for NAFTA. In April 1995, Ms. Griego was appointed by President Clinton to serve on the NAFTA North American Development Bank community adjustment committee (under the U.S. Treasury), where she stayed until 2000. With these public positions, she began broadening her understanding of bank operations and their relationships to local economic development.

> It was recognized that passage of NAFTA would hurt some communities all over the country depending on whether they were directly competitive (like North Carolina textile and Southern California food-processing firms). It was not just border towns that would be hit. The adjustment committee advisory board was to provide loans to those communities that needed help transitioning into new types of business.
>
> The board reviewed loan applications almost as if it were a bank. We used the U.S. Department of Agriculture's rural loans program as a model because they did a great job handling the credit reviews with very few defaults.

FIRST INTERSTATE BANK BOARD

The combination of her business, public-sector, and banking backgrounds began to catch the attention of the for-profit corporate world. During her mayoral campaign, Ms. Griego gave many presentations to chambers of commerce and to other possible source of business support. During one such event, she met executives of First Interstate Bank, with whom she discussed the business environment in Los Angeles. They liked what she had to say.

Ms. Griego was invited to join the board of directors of First Interstate Bank. "The value I brought to First Interstate was my background working with small businesses of many kinds, my knowledge of the local economy, and a wealth of contacts drawn from years of research inside the communities."

It was her first corporate board. "I was thinking back to the days when I couldn't get a business loan, and now here I was on a bank board." She served on that board until the bank was acquired by Wells Fargo in 1996. She served on the audit, credit, and community reinvestment committees.

LOS ANGELES COMMUNITY DEVELOPMENT BANK

Another challenging public-sector bank assignment that she accepted was as director, then head, of the nonprofit Los Angeles Community Development Bank, which was established in 1995 by the U.S. Department of Housing and Urban Development together with the city and county of Los Angeles as a public-private partnership to respond to the Los Angeles riots. The Community Development Bank was to make loans to businesses located in the high-poverty areas most in need of jobs to either increase their existing job count or bring new jobs into the area.

Ms. Griego was a director of the bank and later was interim CEO and president, replacing C. Robert Kemp, who had served as its president since May 1996. He was stepping down for health reasons. She held that position while a committee searched for a permanent replacement (July 1999–January 2000).

TOKAI BANK BOARD

The banking community continued to be impressed by her willingness to serve in the face of large challenges. After First Interstate Bank was acquired by Wells Fargo, Ms. Griego was invited to join the board of directors of Tokai Bank, a Japanese-owned bank, again because of her knowledge of the small business marketplace in Los Angeles.

In the case of Tokai, we had a program to finance restoration of historical buildings on Spring and Main streets in Los Angeles. My background as a developer of a historical landmark and proponent of adaptive reuse of historical buildings was very helpful to Tokai. I brought extensive knowledge of community-based organizations. I was the first woman on their board. The chairman of the parent company in Tokyo was the one who highlighted my experience to the board and "sanctioned" me.

She served on the board of Tokai Bank from 1997 through 2000 and was on their audit and community reinvestment committees. Additional bank assignments included the board of United California Bank, where she was on the trust committee from 2000 to 2002, and the bank advisory board of U.S. Bank from 2003 to 2006.

FEDERAL RESERVE BANK SAN FRANCISCO BOARD

Ms. Griego's work at Rebuild/LA and at First Interstate brought her to the attention of the local Federal Reserve Bank board. She was a director of the Los Angeles branch of the Federal Reserve Bank of San Francisco from 1998 to 2003.

When I was at Rebuild/LA, my staff arranged a bus tour of small manufacturers in East and South Central Los Angeles to show the directors of the Federal Reserve the business environment of these communities. They spent a day touring the companies we were trying to help. Later, during the takeover of First Interstate by Wells Fargo, I testified before the Federal Reserve about the closure of bank branches. I wanted the Federal Reserve to be aware of the negative impacts of closing First Interstate branches in neglected neighborhoods. After that, I was asked by the Federal Reserve to join their Los Angeles branch board.

She was selected as a representative of the banking community and chaired the audit committee.

I've spent a lot of time in the last two decades on audit committees, getting a great deal of practical financial experience. Some people say they won't go on the audit committee because they think it's boring. I seek audit committee assignments because of the knowledge obtained through the organization's financial channels.

PUBLIC POLICY AND NONPROFIT BOARD EXPERIENCE

Ms. Griego has had highly visible nonprofit board roles, including leadership engagements where she helped to create institutions of public policy and research focused on the California economy and the national and international communities.

In 1995, she joined John Bryson, president and CEO of Edison International, and Warren Christopher, former U.S. secretary of state under President Clinton, as a founding board member of the Pacific Council on International Policy (PCIP). It is a Los Angeles–based organization established in partnership with the Council on Foreign Relations, designed to give more effective voice to West Coast perspectives on critical global policy issues. PCIP does this by building a nonpartisan network of globally oriented business, civic, and government leaders (over 3,500 members); convening exchanges with policy makers and opinion leaders from the United States and around the world; generating fresh ideas, timely research, and innovative proposals on issues shaping the global agenda; partnering with organizations around the world to promote mutual understanding and coordinated action; and informing policy elites and the public about global challenges and opportunities.

Seven other prominent leading female directors are members of PCIP. Said Ms. Griego, "I wonder how many of us women would be on the Council on Foreign Relations if it had not been for the PCIP. Having a broad-based national network such as the Council on Foreign Relations has allowed me to meet executives from all over the nation."

Ms. Griego was named to the nonprofit board of the Robert Wood Johnson Foundation (headed by Risa Lavizzo-Mourey, president/CEO, with Nancy-Ann Min DeParle, another director). Her first term was 1995 to 2003; then she was invited back in 2005.

Around the same time, she was a director at the Tomás Rivera Policy Institute, housed at the University of Southern California's School of Policy, Planning, and Development, a widely respected national Latino think tank.

I was on the Tomás Rivera board for 10 years beginning in 1995. Originally located at Pitzer College at Claremont, the institute relocated to the University of Southern California School of Policy, Planning, and Development. While I was chair of the institute board, we chose USC to have greater access to more resources and more collaborative opportunities with other departments in support of the institute's research on education, voting rights, immigration, and other public policy issues.

My interest in public policy issues has always been a top priority. I've always had very close ties to UCLA. I was on the foundation board. I owe a lot to UCLA. Being a senior fellow that first year of their public policy school was quite an honor. I really enjoyed meeting people like Michael Dukakis and sharing ideas about rebuilding South Central Los Angeles.

In September 2005, she was named a director of the Public Policy Institute of California, a San Francisco–based private, nonprofit organization dedicated to improving public policy in California through independent, objective, nonpartisan research.

In August 2006, she was named a trustee of the David and Lucile Packard Foundation, which provides about $250 million a year in grants to nonprofit organizations in three areas: conservation and science; population; and children, families, and communities.

BLOCKBUSTER INC. BOARD

Ms. Griego was a director of Blockbuster Inc. from July 1999 though May 2005, again through an association built up during her leadership of Rebuild/LA. "Blockbuster was interested in locating stores in inner-city neighborhoods, and I knew those communities well through my Rebuild/LA experience. The value I brought to that board included my knowledge of the local economies, the permitting process, and the community support groups. My banking and financial background also helped."

GRANITE CONSTRUCTION BOARD

From August 1999 until March 2007, she served on the board of Granite Construction, a diversified civil contractor and construction material producer. She was the second female on the board (Rebecca Ann McDonald was the first); she chaired the nominating and corporate governance committee and was a member of the audit compliance committee. "Again, my background at Rebuild/LA brought me to Granite's attention. I worked to get construction companies to donate construction management software to high schools."

SOUTHWEST WATER COMPANY AND AECOM BOARDS

Ms. Griego was a director at SouthWest Water Company, a small water provider and waste-water management company from October 2001 through April 2006. She joined Maureen Kindel, who had been the sole woman on the eight-member board since 1997. Ms. Griego returned to the board in December 2006. She now chairs the nominating and governance committee and serves on the financial planning and investment committee.

Another SouthWest Water board member recommended her to the board of AECOM, a global engineering design and management company that consolidated the former firms of DMJM Harris, EDAW Inc., ENSR International, and Korve Engineering. She was named a director in June 2005, serving on the audit, compensation, and governance committees.

CITY NATIONAL BANK BOARD

She was named a director of the City National Bank Board in October 2006, the sole woman director on the 12-member board, where she was named to the wealth management and fiduciary committee. City National Corporation president and chief executive officer Russell Goldsmith welcomed her with these words: "Linda Griego is a successful entrepreneur and civic leader with significant experience in banking and as a director. She understands the clients and communities we serve and will make a strong contribution to our organization."[1]

Ms. Griego, who had met Mr. Goldsmith when they both were on the Federal Reserve Bank board, said, "A lot of the recruitment for boards comes from people who know you on other boards. They know your style, whether you come prepared, whether you're a knowledgeable person. I do the same thing myself."

CBS CORPORATION BOARD

In March 2007 Ms. Griego was elected to the board of CBS Corporation, where she is the sole independent female director among 14 directors.[2] She has been named as a member of the audit committee.

LESSONS LEARNED

Concluded Ms. Griego, "There's no such thing as an easy path to the boardroom. It's board experience that counts: business experience, knowledge of the community, government and governance expertise. It all helps you get there."

She achieved her board positions by using the skills she developed through extensive exposure to business challenges within political frameworks. She continues to learn and gives credit to the director training programs she has attended for "rounding out my board skills, particularly in updating my knowledge of audit and compensation committee work."

Ms. Griego is the managing director of the Oso Ranch and Lodge in Chama, New Mexico.

My family has very long ties to northern New Mexico. This ranch is 20 miles north of my great-great-grandmother's ranch. I never left my roots—you're from New Mexico forever. I grew up in communities where there were no jobs, where you just had to leave. In the future, I plan to do some economic development in northern New Mexico—call it giving back to my community.

Director Profile: Sally K. Richardson

Sally K. Richardson, age 75 at the time of our interview, came to her board role through her work in public programs and her expertise in Medicaid and other public health insurance programs. She started at the state level and rose to federal office, serving at the very top levels among politically notable leaders addressing key national health care challenges. In May 2003, she became the second of two women and one of five independent directors on the board of Molina Healthcare Inc., where she is a member of the compensation committee and the governance and nominating committee.

EARLY YEARS

Ms. Richardson grew up in Huntington, West Virginia, in the rural western part of the state.

> I was a slow starter both academically and in life in general. Mother persuaded our father to give my older sister and me the best educational opportunities and chose an all-girls' college preparatory boarding school, the Baldwin School in Bryn Mawr, Pennsylvania. I followed in my sister's footsteps, went to Baldwin for my last two years in high school, and graduated from Vassar in 1954 with a bachelor of arts and a double major in music and drama.

Regarding her first job, she said:

> My mother let me visit a college roommate in Washington, D.C., for Thanksgiving. When I got there, I answered a newspaper ad, had an interview, [and] accepted a secretarial job with an economic research firm. I called Mother

and told her I was employed [and] had a roommate and a place to live. It was the only way I could get out on my own.

Her father, a respected attorney, heard that West Virginia's Senator Revercomb was looking for a secretary, and Ms. Richardson was hired. Then her father was diagnosed with a brain tumor and became a total invalid after surgery. Ms. Richardson came home to help her mother care for her father at night, while working during the day as a secretary for her brother-in-law, who took over responsibility for the law office. After her father died in the spring of 1956, she found work as one of three young women "information representatives" hired by the Columbia Gas System to cover each of the company's major eastern divisions. Her district was the Charleston district, which included Kentucky, Virginia, West Virginia, and a small part of western Maryland. The women were responsible for presentations at businessmen's local civic organizations like Rotary and Lions' clubs, at which they explained how the gas industry worked, from discovery and drilling through its end uses in industry and local households. Their goal was to show that Columbia Gas was a solid citizen and to create good community relations to stand the company in good stead, especially when it came time to request rate increases.

I met my husband in Charleston. We were married in 1961. The work was interesting, but very sexist. When I became pregnant, I lost my job because in those days there was no such thing as maternity leave. We had our first child in 1962, and two years later her sister was born. They are both terrific women.

Ms. Richardson and her husband, Don "Rich" R. Richardson, a professional engineer, were friends with John "Jay" D. Rockefeller IV, who in 1968 was elected secretary of state of West Virginia.

When I was first married, I stopped working to stay home and raise my two children. When Jay Rockefeller ran for governor in 1972, both girls were in grade school, so I decided I could work during the day and take care of them after school. I mentioned to a mutual friend that I'd love to work on Jay's campaign, and the campaign director asked me to become the volunteer coordinator.

WEST VIRGINIA WESLEYAN COLLEGE

Mr. Rockefeller lost the governor's race to Republican Arch A. Moore Jr. but was named president of West Virginia Wesleyan College. He invited Rich Richardson to join him at Wesleyan as vice president of administration and finance. "We picked up our family and moved to Buckhannon, right in the center of the state."

She was asked to work in the admissions office to try to reverse declining enrollment at the college. With the backing of the president, Ms. Richardson and her husband put together a strategy. When they left the college two years later, the changes the Richardsons had made to the system had increased admissions by almost 60 percent, and incoming academic scores were at their highest levels in 20 years.

Jay Rockefeller decided to run again for governor in 1976. They returned to Charleston, where Rich Richardson became campaign manager. Ms. Richardson worked with the local field operations, making campaign contacts with county-level people and coordinating communications, programs, and strategy. Mr. Rockefeller won, and he asked if they would manage his transition team. When the office was running smoothly, Mr. Richardson left government to establish his own consulting business. For the next six months, Ms. Richardson continued as the governor's special assistant for human services. The welfare commissioner asked the governor to allow Ms. Richardson to be his assistant commissioner. She continued in that role for the next year, dealing with planning, communications, research, and the Medicaid program, and serving as liaison between the department and the legislature.

WEST VIRGINIA DEPARTMENT OF WELFARE/DEPARTMENT OF HEALTH

Governor Rockefeller invited a native West Virginian, George Pickett, to return from California as a public health director and reorganize, consolidate, and streamline all the pieces of health care located throughout West Virginia's various departments. Mr. Rockefeller recruited Dr. Pickett to build a truly broad-based health department.

He asked Ms. Richardson to be Dr. Pickett's deputy director to help him learn the ropes. Ms. Richardson describes Dr. Pickett as

a brilliant physician, pretty forthright and not suffering fools easily. Ours was a tentative relationship at first. George had only one deputy position, and he probably wasn't happy about not having his own choice in selecting that person. I gave him all the space I could, while also trying to earn my way and learn what the job was all about.

When Dr. Pickett moved on to the University of Alabama's medical school at Birmingham, Ms. Richardson served briefly as acting director and led the search for a new physician director. The state recruited L. Clark Hansbarger, another native West Virginian, and a pediatrician who was running a community health center in southern West Virginia.

Clark knew how to deal with the community in the whole array of health services delivery. He taught me so much about how to bring stakeholders into the decision-making process, making the effort to reach consensus so that people felt their views had been heard and well considered.

WEST VIRGINIA HEALTH CARE COST REVIEW AUTHORITY

In 1981, at Governor Rockefeller's request, West Virginia established a program that brought key components of the National Health Planning and Development Act of 1975 under one umbrella organization—the Health Care Cost Review

Authority. Ms. Richardson accepted Governor Rockefeller's invitation to chair the Authority. Over the next two years she developed and guided the Authority's operations while becoming actively involved in a number of programs dealing with state health policy. She was invited onto key advisory committees and boards that were dealing with programs and strategies at the national level. She tapped into federal technical support and user liaison programs that gave annual workshops for state officials and legislators on health planning.

She said, "I was really beginning to get a better handle on, and a better understanding of, health policy. They demonstrated how public policy could be more productive when it was based on information, knowledge, and hard data."

HEALTH MANAGEMENT STRATEGIES

Governor Rockefeller successfully ran for senator after two terms as governor. His successor, Arch Moore, did not want a Democrat to continue as chair of the Health Care Cost Review Authority, and so he replaced Ms. Richardson when her term ended.

I left state government and went to work as a private consultant, forming an organization called Health Management Strategies, to advise hospitals and other health care institutions in the state about certificates of need and health care planning. I ran it for four years [1985–1989] before returning to state government.

She also became an adjunct faculty member to the Department of Community Medicine at West Virginia University School of Medicine. In 2004, the University of Charleston in West Virginia gave her an honorary degree in law in recognition of her contributions to health care public policy.

PUBLIC EMPLOYEES INSURANCE AGENCY

Gaston Caperton, a prominent Democrat who had developed a major national insurance company, became governor of West Virginia. After he took office in 1988, he called her "out of nowhere" and asked if she would run the Public Employees Insurance Agency (PEIA) for him. The PEIA was in trouble; its new third-party administrator did not have the ability to handle the large volume of claims.

It was a huge mess. Once the system began missing payments, it all started to pile up. People couldn't see their doctors because the doctors didn't think they would get paid. Public entities in West Virginia employed about 250,000 people. We worked with the third-party administrator to fix its system, and—when it continued to fail its processing standards—we rebid the contract and awarded it to another administrator with large government experience. By 1991, the new administrator had the situation under control.

More importantly, we changed the governance structure of the agency. It had been run by the five statewide officials elected to constitute the board of public works. Their decisions were based more on their concern for the public employee members than on the financial stability of the health insurance program. As a result, the rates set for the current and retired employees were not increased sufficiently to keep up with the increasing costs of their health care. It was a difficult lesson for both the insured members and the board to learn.

Ms. Richardson and her team proposed legislation, with the governor's support, for a PEIA finance board to replace the board of public works with wider stakeholder representation and the charter to establish an annual plan incorporating both benefits and costs to the insured and to the public employer agencies. "The system is still in place because it makes so much sense, all the way from public input through modifications to implementation."

By 1993, the PEIA system was fixed and working well. Claims payments were under control. Physicians were satisfied. Regular meetings were held with the providers.

CLINTON HEALTH CARE TASK FORCE

By now, Ms. Richardson was very involved in policy work through her memberships in several national associations. In February 1993, she was pulled out of a community meeting in Charleston and told to call the White House. Totally astonished, she immediately found a phone.

A very young woman asked me if I could come to work on the Clintons' White House health care reform task force. They needed some folks with expertise in rural health care. I called the governor's office and asked for a leave of absence. He agreed and said, "Godspeed!" I packed over the weekend and moved to Washington the next Monday morning.

The Clinton task force operated outside of the mainstream of government, which allowed it to be a high-pressure total-emersion operation. Its Achilles' heel was the organizers' commitment to immediate implementation upon passage. They realized that the existing federal rule and regulation processes could stall implementation for a year or more. So their goal was to write a piece of legislation that would be self-implementing. Even though it was one of the most remarkable documents ever written, ultimately it fell under its own weight in terms of the processes within the congressional legislative system.

The task force work required a three-month leave of absence. She returned home to Charleston in May.

HEALTH CARE FINANCING ADMINISTRATION,
U.S. DEPARTMENT OF HEALTH AND HUMAN SERVICES

From 1989 to 1991, Ms. Richardson had served as chair of the steering committee on managed care for older persons and persons with disabilities for the National Academy for State Health Policies. The National Academy had been started by the states as a policy-level organization for health care. There she had met and worked with Bruce C. Vladeck—whom she described as "probably the brightest person I ever met in my entire life." Dr. Vladeck was appointed head of the Health Care Financing Administration (now the Centers for Medicare & Medicaid Services) under the Department of Health and Human Services in May 1993, just as Ms. Richardson returned to West Virginia from the Clinton task force. "Bruce Vladeck was a phenomenal leader. He wanted to reorganize the agency into an entity focused on its constituencies."

Medicaid was significantly different from Medicare; it was a joint federal-state program. The federal government developed the policy framework for eligibility benefits and financing, as well as the rules and regulations under which the program would be governed, but it left a wide range of design and administration issues to the states. Medicaid primarily covers low-income families, children, and pregnant women as well as the elderly and individuals with disabilities through insurance, long-term care, and supplemental coverage for critical health protection.

When Dr. Vladeck asked her to become Medicaid director, there was a great deal of distance between the states and the federal government. Neither one trusted the other. One of her first jobs was to get the two to sit down and talk to each other. She used her relationships with the National Association of State Medical Directors (NASMD) to find ways to address the different ways the two levels interpreted Medicaid law and regulations.

One of the greatest pieces of good fortune I had was my deputy director, Rozann Abato. At her suggestion, we wrote a set of ethical principles about how the federal agency would relate to state Medicaid directors and vice versa. They described the commitments that we made as federal and state parties in search of common ground. Some principles were written from the federal point of view, while others were written from the state perspective. We presented our charter of ethical principles and won the approval of the executive committee of the NASMD. Dr. Vladeck gave his support, and he and the chair of NASMD held a public signing ceremony with the state directors. It was hokey, but it worked. We began meetings on a regular basis and lived by that charter in all of our relations with the states.

Dr. Vladeck asked Ms. Richardson to become acting deputy director for the Health Care Financing Administration in 1996. His own term ended the following year, and he returned to New York as a vice president of research at Mount Sinai Medical Center. When Nancy-Ann Min DeParle succeeded him as administrator of the Health Care Financing Administration, Ms. Richardson was named director of the Center for Medicaid and State Operations, where she stayed until 1999.

THE STATE CHILDREN'S HEALTH INSURANCE PROGRAM

In 1997 Congress passed the Balanced Budget Act, which created the State's Children's Health Insurance Program (SCHIP), a major $24 billion program with much higher matching levels than Medicaid for states to encourage them to provide health insurance for America's needy children who are not eligible under states' Medicaid programs.

Ms. Richardson's contribution to the streamlined effort was the creation of a department-wide team that kept all of the department's other agencies fully informed with access to, and input into, the SCHIP implementation process, providing a fast track for the normally time-consuming intradepartmental approval processes. Her coordination of responsibility among members of that group provided her with a direct and close understanding of implementing programs at the federal level.

INSTITUTE FOR HEALTH POLICY RESEARCH
AT WEST VIRGINIA UNIVERSITY

As the Clinton years were coming to an end, Ms. Richardson had to decide to stay in Washington or return home to West Virginia.

Rich and I have been married 45 years. We had talked about leaving West Virginia, but we both decided that we wanted to come home rather than live the life of a Washington consultant. Hilda Heady, a bright, wonderful woman I had met through the Health Care Cost Review Authority, had left as head of Preston Memorial Hospital to start the Rural Health Education Partnership program at West Virginia University, originally funded jointly by the Benedum Foundation and the Kellogg Foundation.

Ms. Heady called Ms. Richardson to see if she might be interested in returning to work for West Virginia University. Ms. Heady already had prepared the way. She had approached the head of the Health Sciences Center to encourage him to hire Ms. Richardson to run a health services policy center and guarantee start-up funding for three years. She had asked Beverly Walter, the Claude Worthington Benedum Foundation's vice president for health grants, to fund the start-up of an institute for health policy research at West Virginia University.

Hilda invited me to come to West Virginia University to meet Bob D'Alessandri, the vice president for health sciences there. We quickly came to terms. It was so wonderful for me to have a great job to come home to. We decided the institute should be located in the Charleston division of the Health Sciences Center because Charleston is the hub of government in the state.

In 1999, Ms. Richardson was named executive director of the Institute for Health Policy Research and an associate vice president for the Robert C. Byrd Health Services Center of West Virginia University. The institute operates on a $1-million-a-year budget "focused on research that can both inform and support policies that improve services and health for communities and populations."[1]

Ms. Richardson continues in an advisory capacity and as a member of the National Rural Health Association, which currently is preparing an in-depth issues paper on Medicaid. In May 2007, she received the association's Gorin Award for Outstanding Achievement in Rural Health.

MOLINA HEALTHCARE INC. BOARD

Ms. Richardson became a director at Molina Healthcare in May 2003, joining Ronna Romney as the second female director. Molina is a managed health care company that was founded in 1980 by C. David Molina, an emergency room physician who took over three health clinics from bankrupt Maxicare in 1989 then expanded to 30 Los Angeles–area health clinics focused primarily on the poor Hispanic population. As the company prepared to go public in 2003, they were advised by George Goldstein, their chief operating officer, who had helped them expand into other states (Michigan, Washington, Utah) and acquire an insurance organization in New Mexico. Molina needed more independent directors on their board as a requirement of going public. Mr. Goldstein had worked with Ms. Richardson and Dr. Pickett when they were developing a system of community health centers in West Virginia under the National Service Corps and later at the Health Care Financing Administration, where he was a consultant.

> George recommended me for consideration as an independent director. He called and invited me to visit in Long Beach. The first person I met with was a man who had worked with the original Dr. Molina and was a hospital administrator at Dr. Molina's hospital. He was absolutely dedicated to the Molina family. He showed me everything. His sincerity and commitment were a tremendous example of the ethics of the organization.
>
> Next, I met with George and learned the nuts and bolts of how Molina operated. I had dinner with Mario, the president, and his younger sister, Bernadette. We had a good evening and got to know each other a bit. I went back to Charleston without knowing what would happen. Mario called me a week later to ask if I would consider coming on the board. He wanted me to have conversations individually with each of the other directors. I met with some and had phone conversations with the rest of them. They voted to put me on the board, and I was convinced it was worth doing.

Ms. Richardson is an appointed member of the compensation committee and the governance and nominating committee. It is a small board, now with six outside directors, so that all the directors can attend all the committee meetings, including the meetings of the audit committee. "It's efficient as long as we're able to have the time to do it," she said. "Even though we don't get paid to sit in on the other committee meetings, it's a real assist in understanding all the issues without any extra cost."

It was a major transition for Molina to go from a family-owned and -operated health care provider to a public company regulated by Sarbanes-Oxley. Ms. Richardson brought to the board a working knowledge of how the Medicaid program operated, how state variances worked, and effective methods of implementing

Medicaid in different states. Having worked at the federal level, she knew its views of state Medicaid programs. Having worked at the state level, she knew how states approached their Medicaid challenges and opportunities.

> I've worked with Molina on board education. I know many state and federal experts who are willing to provide the board with the latest and most current best practices, and to advise on strategic planning from their federal and individual states' perspectives. Since Molina went public, strategic planning has become an annual process to assess where the company is in achieving its strategic goals and what changes need to be made going forward. It is a single corporation with divisions operating in different states, all owned by Molina. The company has branched out to become a Medicare HMO—a much more difficult population to serve than Medicaid moms and kids. That makes it more important to concentrate on where we want to be strategically and then set benchmarks to measure our progress and success. Molina has brought in skilled leadership to facilitate that process. We want to come away with something we can move toward over the next three years.

LESSONS LEARNED

Ms. Richardson's chosen career offers many lessons for those who might follow in her footsteps along either the health care or political pathway. A key takeaway is the many mentor relationships that she has encountered along the way. Rather than search for mentors to help her, Ms. Richardson found talented people along the way who realized that her strengths were the factors that could benefit them.

A primary example is her collaboration with her husband, Rich. They are an incredible team: they have created the admissions strategy at Wesleyan College, collaborated on Governor Rockefeller's campaigns, and evaluated together their many geographic relocations.

> You need to know the kind of husband that I have. When I was in Washington, I'd travel back to West Virginia on some of the weekends, but for 70–80 percent of the time, Rich would make sure, far more than I could, to come to Washington, D.C., for the weekends so we didn't spend any appreciable time apart. If I went somewhere to speak, he'd come there to be with me.

Another example was her professional association with Jay Rockefeller. "It was certainly one of the fortuitous things in my life to have Jay Rockefeller as a boss, a friend, and sometimes a collaborator."

Her work with George Pickett began without promise but endures today.

> It was a wonderful relationship by the time our work together finished. George was my mentor as much as Jay. He taught me about budgets, health care services, how you really manage the health care system by what you do

with the financing, with the dollars that you have. He gave me a couple of really strong years learning about health care. And we became really good friends.

L. Clark Hansbarger was also one of her mentors.

Clark could handle any and all comers. From him, I learned how important it is interact with people—even in negative circumstances—in a way that makes them feel better about themselves. George and Clark gave me my schooling in public health. Those two men really helped me understand the health concepts and also the perspective of why and how important working for the public's health is.

Governor Caperton began by asking her to step down as the state party chair, then they both benefited immensely when she led the cleanup of the PEIA financial mess that he inherited. In addition to these men, there were many women whom she considers mentors or collaborators.

Despite the fact that I knew nothing about the Medicaid program at the start, Rozann Abato was the kind of deputy director who knew that it was important to the agency that I succeed. She taught me faster and harder than anybody ever had a right to expect. She backed me up on everything I did and made sure that I understood the consequences of all the choices that I made. If it hadn't been for Rozann, I'm sure I would have fallen flat on my face. I really owe my federal success to her.

Ms. Richardson gives equal credit to all the women (Debbie Chang, Hilda Heady, and Beverly Walter, among others) who individually and collectively both enriched Ms. Richardson's life and career and benefited from their association with her. That truly is the meaning of mentorship.

This is where I want to be. I'm still working full time. I'm 75 years old. I'm not interested in any additional boards. I hope to begin to pare down my responsibilities at WVU maybe next year. Rich and I have just bought an old farmhouse in the county where Mother, my sister, and I used to spend summers with my grandmother. Who knows, I might even begin polishing up my gardening skills and cleaning up our canoe.

4

Les Belles Lettres:
The Academic Path

The women who followed the academic path into the boardroom did so primarily as deans, chancellors, and provosts, rather than as teachers or professors. The administrative side of academia, more than the classroom, is a key route into the boardroom because the financial challenges of leading academic institutions share similarities with those facing public company boards of directors. It has been observed that today's women directors have become constant learners, a capability that corporate board directors are finding valuable in their highly regulated environments.

RELATIVE IMPORTANCE

Sixteen women directors (8.5% of the experience cited, see table 4.1) came to their board roles by the academic path. Higher education and academics play a very important role in preparing women directors for their board roles. The women directors interviewed in all career fields often mentioned educational excellence as a primary personal interest.

Academically oriented women on boards do much more than simply get tenure and teach. Many were top administrators of universities, professional, or graduate schools. As academic administrators, they learned that their ability to manage budgets meant they could accomplish the academic improvements they sought for their schools, faculty, and students.

DIVERSE EXPERIENCE

Three women are current or former presidents or deans at university institutions. One is a former executive vice-chancellor.

Table 4.1
Academic Path: Experience of Women on Corporate Boards of California
Fortune **1000 Companies**

Paths into the Boardroom						Name	Company
		A			C	Sara L. Beckman	Building Materials Holding
		A				France A. Córdova	Edison International
	G	A	I			Nancy-Ann Min DeParle	DaVita
	G	A		E		Diana Lady Dougan	Qualcomm
		A				Alice Bourke Hayes	Jack in the Box
	G	A		E		Anita K. Jones	Science Applications Inc.
		A		E		Janet E. Kerr	CKE Restaurants
		A		E		Claudine B. Malone	Science Applications Inc.
		A				Mary S. Metz	Longs Drug Stores, PG&E
		A				Patricia E. Mitchell	Sun Microsystems
		A				Susan Westerberg Prager	Pacific Life
N		A				Andrea L. Rich	Mattel
	G	A				Sally K. Richardson	Molina Healthcare
		A				Shirley M. Tilghman	Google
		A		E		Kathy Brittain White	Mattel

Note: N = Nonprofit; G = Government; A = Academic; I = Investment; E = Entrepreneurial; C = Corporate.

- Shirley M. Tilghman is the current president of Princeton University and Howard A. Prior Professor of the Life Sciences there. She is a founding director of the Lewis-Sigler Institute for Integrative Genomics at Princeton University and chaired Princeton's Council of Science and Technology.
- France A. Córdova is the newest president of Purdue University, having just completed five years as chancellor of the University of California, Riverside, and six years as vice-chancellor for research at University of California, Santa Barbara.
- Susan Westerberg Prager is the former president of Occidental College in Eagle Rock, California, and previously was provost at Dartmouth College, dean of the UCLA School of Law, and the Arjay and Frances Fearing Miller Professor of Law at UCLA. Currently she is executive director and CEO of the Association of American Law Schools.

Two women currently head up a department or center at their universities.

- Anita K. Jones is the Lawrence R. Quarles Professor of Engineering and Applied Science in the Department of Computer Science, School of Engineering and Applied Science, at the University of Virginia.
- Janet E. Kerr is a professor at the Pepperdine University School of Law and executive director at a venture-supporting collaborative that she co-founded, the Palmer Center for Entrepreneurship and Technology Law, located at Pepperdine in Malibu, California.

Other female directors had noteworthy academic experience as a complement to careers that primarily followed a corporate, investment, entrepreneurial, political, or nonprofit path.

- Cynthia H. Milligan is the dean of the College of Business Administration at the University of Nebraska–Lincoln. Claudine B. Malone was a professor or lecturer at Harvard University, Georgetown University, and Colgate-Darden Business School of the University of Virginia. Both of these directors have primary careers as entrepreneurs.
- Sara L. Beckman is a senior lecturer in the Operations and Information Technology Management group at the Haas School of Business at the University of California, Berkeley. Her primary path was corporate, with an emphasis on technology.
- Nancy-Ann Min DeParle is an adjunct professor at the Wharton School of the University of Pennsylvania. Her primary career has been as a lawyer, then Tennessee commissioner of human services, administrator of the federal Health Care Financing Administration (now Centers for Medicare & Medicaid Services), and now managing director of a medical investment advisory firm.

A number of the women started out as teachers at various levels then changed career paths either for financial reasons or because they found other more challenging professional interests that they wanted to pursue elsewhere.

MYTH BUSTING

The most common myth about the academic path into the boardroom is that women need to be tenured professors at Harvard University or another Ivy League university in order to be considered for a corporate board role.[1] The women who followed the academic path suggested that they are valued by boards more for their administrative leadership in academia than as tenured professors. Two women in our sample (Andrea L. Rich and Claudine B. Malone) mentioned they did not achieve tenure, but that appeared not to be a barrier. Ms. Malone did not receive tenure at Harvard yet served on more boards than many men because she is a recognized expert in finance and accounting. Even the women who chose a primary career path other than academia still invested heavily in their undergraduate education, advanced degree programs, and continuing education with a special emphasis on business, economics, and finance.

DEGREES EARNED

Women directors in our sample are some of the most highly educated people in the marketplace. Ninety-three percent of the women in our sample reported earning at least a bachelor's degree in a wide range of serious subject fields, including economics, finance and accounting, engineering, the sciences, technology, and management. Twelve women received bachelor's degrees from Stanford University, seven from Vassar College, and four from the University of California, Berkeley.

The women earned 66 master's degrees and 35 doctoral degrees, or an average of 1.74 advanced degrees each. Eight women earned double master's degrees, and five of them an MBA. Harvard and Stanford each granted 22 degrees from their business schools, law schools, medical schools, or the university itself. International institutions conferred a total of 13 degrees.

Of the 35 doctoral degrees earned, 23 (66%) were in law and 10 (29%) were PhDs in fields of study including industrial engineering, engineering management, computer science, physics, public health, medicine, physiology, biochemistry, and business education. One woman earned an MD, and one woman earned a doctorate in business education.

A WEALTH OF HONORARY DEGREES

Eighteen women in our sample earned special recognition, with a total of 40 honorary degrees. Not all the women touted their honorary degrees. Shirley M. Tilghman, president of Princeton University, has received 10 honorary doctorates in science from Duke, Yale, Oxford, Dickinson, Rider, Western Ontario, Toronto, Harvard, New York, and Rockefeller universities. Yet not one of these was mentioned in her proxy statement biography.

Alice Bourke Hayes received six honorary degrees. Four were given to Patricia E. Mitchell, three each to Carol A. Bartz and Mary S. Metz, and two each to Barbara Bell Coleman and Monica C. Lozano.

Eleven other women received one honorary degree each from such distinguished institutions as Carnegie Mellon University (Anita K. Jones), Purdue University (Marjorie Magner), Loyola-Marymount University (France A. Córdova), and the University of Sheffield in the United Kingdom (Penelope L. Hughes).

ACADEMIC TRUSTEESHIPS

A major component of the academic experiences of these women directors was their service on school or university boards. Three-fourths of the educational experience cited by the women directors involved service on a board of trustees at their university, college, or school. The remaining one-fourth cited educational involvement as one of their outside interests in proxy statement biographies. And 12 percent of the experience cited was service on foundations or endowment boards, and often those were education oriented.

A common pattern was that as a successful student, a woman was invited to be a representative to the board of trustees or governors of her undergraduate or graduate program. That exposure provided invaluable lessons about governing an institution, how the institution is structured, what strategic planning and financial challenges must be faced, how effective committees operate, and how mixed-group collaboration can succeed. The woman might have stayed on and become a full trustee or she may have left and returned to a full trusteeship position later in her career. Regardless of the timing, this experience provided some of the earliest and best director training, according to the women interviewed. It also created long-lasting personal relationships with female and male leaders in the community.

MANAGING THEIR OWN EXECUTIVE EDUCATIONS

The American Association of University Professors suggests that, even today, female faculty are more likely than their male counterparts to stay in adjunct teaching positions (academia's low to middle management levels). The association found "a significantly higher proportion of women among non-tenure-track faculty than among tenured factulty."[2]

In our sample, the women who became directors went far beyond the middle ranks of adjunct teachers and rose to top administrative leadership roles. Many of them pursued business education at the undergraduate or graduate level or in postgraduate extension or certificate programs. The women also described their enthusiasm for top-quality executive education that helped them understand the boardroom and how to manage their governance challenges. Linda Griego said, "I'm not the type of director who feels she has nothing else to learn. You have to be exposed to best practices. You hear the good and the bad: all of it is invaluable. Director training has made me a better board member. You have to stay on top of the issues. You just have to do it."

While some directors might feel intimidated by the classroom setting, the women directors in general and the women from academia in particular were enthusiastic about opportunities to learn the latest information about directors and governance through their investment in continuing education.

The women who came by way of the academic route also involved themselves in a wide array of entrepreneurial, political, and corporate ventures that gave them experience, perspective, and contacts in the many complementary fields that affected their primarily academic careers. Academic women are perpetual students in the most positive sense in that they are constantly challenging themselves to gain new knowledge and insight.

INVESTING IN THE NEXT GENERATION

Women directors invested in educational opportunities for the next generation. Claudine B. Malone established three awards at Wellesley College in honor of her mother "to recognize outstanding academic achievement combined with accomplishment as a citizen of the college."[3] Mary "Nina" R. Henderson established an endowment for the Nina Henderson CoMAD Business Plan Competition at the College of Media Arts & Design at Drexel University "to encourage students to take an idea through a feasibility study/market analysis to a full business plan, and consequently build a new venture."[4] Kathy Brittain White donated $2 million to Arkansas State University College of Business to establish a fellowship in management information systems for tenured and tenure-track faculty with strengths in database management, information systems, and network administration. Margaret "Meg" C. Whitman, former president and chief executive officer of eBay Inc., and her family committed $30 million to Princeton to construct a sixth residential college: Whitman College.

Three women and their family charitable trusts have made significant donations over many years to support their alma maters: Doris Fisher has been a major fund-raiser at Stanford University and, with her husband, a major investor in the Knowledge Is Power Program public charter school program. Miriam L. Haas and her family have been major donors to the University of California, Berkeley. Martha R. Ingram and her family have been primarily contributors to Vanderbilt University in Nashville, Tennessee.

THE WOMEN INTERVIEWED

The two women selected as representative of the academic path both received doctorates: Alice Bourke Hayes and Mary S. Metz. Their academic and professional backgrounds are in biology and French, but in both cases their administrative experience is what qualified them for public company board roles.

More women than ever before are rising to the top positions of president, dean, and provost of U.S. colleges, universities, and graduate schools. According to the American Council on Education, the percentage of presidents of colleges and universities who are women more than doubled from 9.5 percent in 1986 to 23 percent in 2006.[5] Corporate boards will increasingly tap individuals at the presidential level (and the chancellor, provost, and administrative tier just below it) as academic administration becomes a stronger training ground for women in business leadership.

DIRECTOR PROFILE: ALICE BOURKE HAYES

Alice Bourke Hayes, age 70 at the time of our interview, came to the boardroom by way of the academic path. She has been a biology scientist, educator, and academic administrator who led three universities (Loyola, Saint Louis, and San Diego) at Jesuit campuses where women, historically, were expected to be "quiet supporters" rather than leaders. In a career that spans almost five decades, she has served on civic, nonprofit, academic, and accreditation boards and commissions and has a resume so long that "not even my mother will read it." She was one of three female corporate directors at Jack in the Box (through February 2008) and the sole female on the board of ConAgra (through September 2008).

> In the '50s, we were not career oriented. In the back of our minds, we just assumed that some nice man would take care of us—a husband, a father, or a brother. I first took a biology class because I had to, not because I was thinking of a career at all. I stayed with biology because I loved it.

THE EARLY YEARS

Raised in Chicago, she won a scholarship to attend Mundelein College, a private, independent all-women's college in northwest Chicago. To augment that financial aid, she worked as a researcher for the *Encyclopaedia Britannica* at the John Crerar Library in Chicago, specializing in biology,

> I was an "answer lady." If someone had a question that was not answered in the *Encyclopaedia,* they'd send it in, and a team of us would research it. I was responsible for the science questions. They trained us well, gave us all the research techniques that you could ever want. That job prepared me, to this day, to find anything I need and to be open to questions.

She earned her bachelor's degree in biology from Mundelein in 1959, magna cum laude, with the honors of the college key and as an academic scholar. She was studying for her master's in biology as a university fellow and a teaching assistant at the University of Illinois at Urbana-Champaign and was planning on getting her doctorate there.

She said, "I met my husband, John Hayes, while we were in college. He was an accountant. He had a beautiful, orderly mind." They were married in 1961 when he came out of the army. Since they were living in Chicago, she accepted a job offer from Loyola University Chicago, where she became a biology instructor in the Department of Natural Science, putting on hold for the next five years her plans for a doctorate while she focused on space biology research funded by NASA.

LOYOLA UNIVERSITY CHICAGO

Loyola provided her with her first exposure to the administrative side of academic life. Dr. Hayes was elected by her colleagues to be chair of the Department of Natural Science in 1967, the same year she became an assistant professor.

> When I first accepted the department chairmanship, I didn't think I was embarking on an administrative career. I felt it was just my turn to be chair. It was awkward for the university to have a department chair who didn't have a doctorate, so the academic vice president suggested I take a sabbatical and go back to get my doctorate.

Dr. Hayes went to Northwestern University in Evanston on a National Science Foundation fellowship, was a visiting lecturer in biological sciences, and finished her PhD in 1972. Her thesis was on the factors that regulate and influence the growth of bean plants, a continuation of the work she'd done for NASA. From the mid-1970s through the early 1990s, she researched and wrote extensively on the factors that influence leaf form and shape, which in turn determine the effectiveness of leaves in photosynthesis.

Her academic career soon became two pronged: an administrative path emerged in parallel to her teaching path within the science community. She was reappointed as department chair at Loyola in 1971 and then became assistant dean at Loyola in 1977, working half time as an administrator and half time teaching for the next three years. She said, "I made a conscious decision to become an assistant dean because there were things that I wanted to see happen at the university administrative level that I couldn't see happening from my position within the faculty."

The Department of Natural Science had successfully introduced biology and environmental science programs into the curriculum of non-science majors. As assistant dean, Dr. Hayes was able to broaden that strategy to a university-wide perspective: "It was important for the university to have science classes for non-science students because, ultimately, as citizens they would be voting on science issues, living in a science environment, and using the results of science." She stayed on that administrative track and became a full-time associate academic vice president in 1980 and then vice president of academic affairs in 1987.

The women on boards of directors are a living embodiment of the expression "If you want something done, give it to a busy person." No one is more accurately defined by it than Dr. Hayes. While she was rising in the academic, research, and administrative ranks, John Hayes came down with multiple sclerosis. As a scientist, she knew the inevitable prognosis for the disease. They faced the challenge of that reality for the next 10 years. With his encouragement, she stayed the course with her dual academic-administrative role, in addition to taking care of him. When he passed away in 1981, she wanted to continue their battle against his disease. "I wanted to fight MS! That's why I wanted to be on the MS board."

The National Multiple Sclerosis Society's Chicago–Northern Illinois chapter was one of her earliest experiences with a nonprofit board. She was vice-chair from 1984 to 1987 and chair of two major projects, Word Encounter and Readathon, which raised over $2 million a year. The national MS board was a chance for her to apply her knowledge of how to manage and leverage financial resources. She built a personal network of support that helped her through that difficult time and established friendships that she cherishes today.

SAINT LOUIS UNIVERSITY

Dr. Hayes's second major university opportunity happened when Father Lawrence J. Biondi took over the presidency of Saint Louis University in Missouri in 1987 and invited her to join him there. He had been dean of the College of Arts and Sciences at Loyola University, reporting to Dr. Hayes in her role as academic vice president. For his first two years at Saint Louis, he kept trying to interest her by offering her better positions there—all of which she declined. "He finally came up with the position of provost, which was head of all of the academic vice presidents, and executive vice president, which was in charge of everybody else. That was like the chief operating officer—just a wonderful opportunity that I couldn't pass up."

Within just a few years, Saint Louis University was reclassified as a research institution by the Carnegie Foundation and today it ranks among the top research institutions in the nation. She became a different kind of "answer lady," learning how to use the budget to achieve certain goals and make things happen. "There was nobody to guide you," she said. "You had to learn these things yourself. To find something, you had to just go look for it."

While still at Saint Louis, Dr. Hayes was nominated for several university presidency posts; even though she was not looking to change. The experience of being one of several finalists interviewed by a selection committee made her ask herself new questions. "I realized that I didn't have a good vision of my own future; [I was not yet] able to answer their questions about how I would handle the future of their campus."

She began developing a mental list of her own personal criteria: "When I have my own little shop, what do I want it to be?" She decided she would like to lead a campus with undergraduate, graduate, and professional levels and enrollment of at least 5,000 students. She recognized that limits existed: she would never become a president at a Jesuit school because, in those days, only a Jesuit would be considered.

UNIVERSITY OF SAN DIEGO

In July 1995, Dr. Hayes began her third major leadership transition, leaving the Midwest to become president of the University of San Diego and professor of biology. She recalled, "When I got there, saw the place, and met the people, I could see that it was ready for things to happen. They had everything that I had decided that I really wanted. It was irresistible. And I was ready."

While at USD, she increased the endowment from $40 million to $135 million in eight years and built new facilities, including the Jenny Craig Sports Arena, the Joan Kroc Institute for Peace and Justice (providing mandatory theology, philosophy, and ethics courses), the Donald P. Shiley Center for Science and Technology, new residence halls, and parking garages. She describes the most personally satisfying part of her work at USD as improving academic quality in terms of the number and caliber of faculty while holding enrollment steady. "When a university becomes a little more exclusive, you become more attractive; you can select, every year, better and better students; shape the student body for all the qualities you want; and create a really outstanding student body."

At the start of her presidency, USD received about 3,000 applications a year for 1,000 places in the freshman class. When she retired in 2003, it was receiving over 10,000 applicants for the same 1,000 places. Evidence of the higher quality of both the students and the faculty includes the additions of a Mortar Board chapter (the national honor society) and a Phi Beta Kappa chapter. She retired from USD in June 2003 and returned to Chicago with the honorable distinction of being named president emerita.

EARLY BOARD EXPERIENCE

Her board-of-director experience followed the three major academic/administrative windows defined by her tenure at Loyola (1962–1989), Saint Louis (1989–1995), and San Diego (1995–2003). While at Loyola, she was on charitable and high school boards. She also was on her first publication board, the Civitas Dei Foundation at Mundelein College (1986–1992), which published *Chicago Studies,* a tri-yearly periodical on liturgical training.

At Saint Louis University, she added civic boards to her experience, including the Urban League of Metropolitan St. Louis, the St. Louis Science Center, and the St. Louis County Historical Society. She also was on the board of St. Louis Catholic Charities.

While president of USD, Dr. Hayes increased her involvement in local civic and community groups, academic boards, and governmental boards interested in local economic development. It was her academic administrative leadership that provided the pathway into corporate boardrooms. Her advice: "Women should look for opportunities to put themselves into positions where they will be considered for boards."

> One thing leads to another. My opportunity at Pulitzer came through my work at Saint Louis. My opportunity at Jack in the Box came through my work at USD. My opportunity for ConAgra came to through my work at Loyola as well as my work on other boards.

PULITZER PUBLISHING COMPANY BOARD

Her first for-profit corporate board was at the Pulitzer Publishing Company in St. Louis. Her nomination came through Michael Pulitzer, chair of the company, who had been on the board of directors at Saint Louis University. Said Dr. Hayes, "The Pulitzer board decided it wanted a woman on the board, that it was time to make this innovation. It was a conscious decision on their part."

Although the board wanted diversity, the real reason for her selection was that she was an outstanding candidate. Pulitzer had tapped other women, including Emily Rauth Pulitzer (widow of Joseph Pulitzer), who served on several national charitable, civic, and arts organizations, but they needed a director with financial and strategic planning experience and an independent perspective.

Dr. Hayes was also valuable to Pulitzer Publishing because she knew something about the publishing business. As an academician, she had written over 20 book reviews and had been published in *Science Books: A Quarterly Review* and *American Biology Teacher.* From 1990 to 1993 she served on the editorial board of *Initiatives,* the journal of the National Association of Women Deans and Counselors. She was a columnist for *Trusteeship,* the journal of the Association of Governing Boards, from 1996 to 1997 and had published numerous books, chapters, papers, and articles on the natural sciences and on Catholic higher education.

Dr. Hayes served on the Pulitzer board from 1993 through 2005, during two major corporate transitions, as a member of the audit and planning committees.

JACK IN THE BOX BOARD

Dr. Hayes joined the corporate board of Jack in the Box in San Diego in September 1999. Her appointment to the Jack in the Box board came through Jack W. Goodall, chair of the board, who knew her through the USD trustees. Robert J. Nugent succeeded Mr. Goodall as CEO and president of Jack in the Box in 1996 and invited her onto his board three years later. The value that she brought to that board was, first, a good understanding of the youth marketplace: the university and the company shared the same target market. Second, she had a wealth of experience with the global marketplace, an area in which the company wanted to expand.

Dr. Hayes saw that Jack in the Box was a model of good governance practices. One example was Jack in the Box's practice of rotating the committee chairs every three years. When first appointed, she immediately joined the compensation committee and the nominating and governance committee and then chaired the compensation committee beginning in February 2005. Dr. Hayes also had high regard for the company's approach to developing new managerial talent from within the corporation.

> Linda Lang became president and chief operating officer of the company in 2003 as part of Bob Nugent's succession planning: he brought several senior executive officers onto the board so we could get to know them. She has worked for Jack in the Box for about 16 to 17 years. She is just an outstanding person and brings all those skills [from] having been the COO, the president of the company, [and] she's a woman, a Hispanic, and presents a lot of assets for the board.

Mr. Nugent also encouraged board members to take director education training once every two years, as their schedules would permit. Even after a decade of corporate board experience, Dr. Hayes knew the value of continuing director training and attended programs at Stanford University (2002) and UCLA (2006). While the two programs differed significantly, she learned from both. In selecting Dr. Hayes, Jack in the Box gained a director who had invested extensively in her own executive business-oriented education. "I attended Harvard's program for presidents and the American Management Association's courses on strategic planning because I felt I needed that knowledge. That's probably the academic in me; we're always going to school. When I stop learning, that's when I stop growing."

CONAGRA BOARD

Dr. Hayes's third corporate directorship was at ConAgra in Omaha, Nebraska, in August 2001. A member of the Loyola University board of trustees was consulting with ConAgra to help them find a new director. He had known Dr. Hayes for a long time as an officer and faculty member at Loyola and recommended her to the ConAgra board. She was a member of the corporate governance and the corporate affairs committees. "In all three boards, I met with the CEO and 'ate my way' through the interviews."

Dr. Hayes speaks lightly about the informal conversations involving the CEO and the top senior board members that are the prerequisites to an invitation to become a director. "It is essential for them to get to know you and to feel comfortable with you before they nominate you as a director," she said. What is equally important is the candidate's ability to present herself well and to conduct herself in a manner that gives other directors confidence that she has the ability to perform—with them—on that particular board.

> I was the only woman on the ConAgra board at that time, but they have had talented women directors before [Jane J. Thompson and Marjorie Scardino]; for them it was not as much an innovation. But when I realized I was taking

the place of the woman ranked as #1 on the *Fortune* international list of top 50 women executives, I thought to myself, "Wow!"

Dr. Hayes's immediate predecessor on the ConAgra board was Marjorie Scardino, who became CEO of Pearson PLC, the parent company of the Financial Times Group and Penguin Publishing. Ms. Scardino also was invested as Dame Commander of the British Empire in February 2002. Tall heels to fill, indeed, but Dr. Hayes's scientific research in agricultural-related fields clearly qualified her to take on the ConAgra board assignment. Dr. Hayes also has received six honorary doctorates: one each in science and law and two each in humane letters and education.[1] She retired from the ConAgra board in September 2008.

EDUCATION SYSTEMS EXCHANGE BOARD

In 2002, Dr. Hayes became a member of the board of Education Systems Exchange, a nonprofit foundation established by American College Testing, to oversee Education Systems Inc., a corporation in San Diego that sells software for student financial aid, admissions, and alumni relations. Now vice-chair of the foundation, Dr. Hayes views her nonprofits as working boards (as opposed to governing boards) and delivers the same kind of perspective there as she does for her public companies.

When [Education Systems Inc.] develops financial aid software, they need to hear from directors like me, an academic administrator, who understands the organization's overall interests. Their products are more than just software; it's part of an enterprise resource system that must be integrated into all parts of the university.

ACCREDITATION COMMISSIONS

Dr. Hayes's experience with working boards covers a wide range of academic, civic, charitable, and community interests. She has been a global traveler to South Africa, China, the former USSR, and Mexico, often in a professional academic capacity. Through these experiences, she has become well aware of the importance of an international perspective for directors and for students in today's economy. "Everything is international now. It's not fair to your students to give them simply a local view. The world in which they will be working is going to be global. So we have to start it, get out there, and understand and relate to people in other countries."

One of several annual trips that she made on behalf of the North Central Association, a regional accreditation commission, was for the Japan Initiative (June 1992), for which she visited American universities in Japan to ensure that they met the standards of accreditation for the American students who went there so that the courses they took there would get academic credit that would be recognized in the United States. She continues to be active in the Commission on Institutes of Higher Education (since 1995) and the Illinois Board of Higher Education (since 2004).

BISHOPS' CONFERENCE

One of her toughest working board assignments was as a member of the U.S. Conference of Catholic Bishops' National Review Board for the Office of Child and Youth Protection (from 2002 to November 2004). The bishops' conference coordinates Catholic activities in the United States and established the board after instances of sexual abuse by priests became widely known. "It was a terrible phenomenon of priests abusing children—that simply could not be allowed to continue without some action."

The bishops' conference recruited lay Catholics to investigate the scope, causes, and costs of the abuse scandal. The value that Dr. Hayes provided was her scientific background, her community involvement, and her governance knowledge of both legal and financial risks within organizations. Her background and experience as administrator and educator at Catholic campuses simply enhanced that credibility.

Volunteer not-for-profit board roles typically provide a laid-back opportunity to work with political and social icons. "But this board was one of the most demanding things that I've been involved in," she said.

> We had about a dozen people on that board, each with a different skill, because we had to deal with so many different interests. Several members had really good political experience dealing with challenges in the public sector—people such as Governor Keating of Oklahoma; Leon Panetta, who had been Clinton's chief of staff; and Bob Bennett, who had been counsel to the congressional ethics committee. They were extremely helpful in establishing the project parameters.

The board conducted detailed research, and the members traveled extensively and spent many dedicated hours in meetings just as if it were a public corporate board assignment.

> We had to set up national guidelines for behavior [and] audit procedures to monitor fulfillment of the guidelines by the diocese. Then we did research to get a handle on the scope of the problem.
>
> I helped set up the scientific research. We had to do a massive, elaborate scientific survey to find out how many cases of abuse were there, where were they, and how to get a handle on the issue of priests moving from one diocese to another. At first, nobody wanted to participate because of their fear of legal liability. We held many meetings with legal counsel and the various bishops. After the initial anxiety, their cooperation was way beyond expectations. We ended up with a 98 percent response rate on our survey. In the end, they recognized they had to do it, and we were able to focus on a very dramatic pattern of abuse.

> These were the same governance challenges as in any corporation: oversight, strategy, and putting remedies into place based on the best answers that research

could provide. First, they had to set up structures to deal with the problem, then establish guidelines for implementation, then go back and check to see that they were really doing what was expected.

The skills that Dr. Hayes developed in university accreditation work are very similar to those required within large public corporations or those that she used as an "answer lady" for the *Encyclopaedia Britannica:* posing and answering good questions: "It's all the same sort of thing: does the organization have the people who are qualified, do they have the right resources, how are they operating the program, what are the outcomes, is it doing what it says it's going to do?"

WOMEN IN LEADERSHIP

Dr. Hayes has been a low-key sympathetic source of support for women in leadership. Throughout her career, she has spoken to women in management and education about preparing themselves for those roles. "In San Diego and Saint Louis, I would give lectures in classes for women in management. For fun, I have a lecture on the evolution of women, describing some of the characteristics of women that make us different from men and that are part of our understanding of women."[2]

While acknowledging that women might bring unique traits to management roles, "I don't know that there is something that is distinctively performing as a woman on a board. You are who you are," she says.

> I think there was only once in all of my work with corporate boards where I felt I might have acted like a woman. One company sent us new food products to sample and review. I realized they hadn't told us what the price would be, probably a more important part of the buyer decision than packaging. Because I was the only one on that board who did any grocery shopping, I realized they needed to know that. Later, I thought to myself, "Boy, they *do* need a woman on this board."

Her brief biographies in proxy statements understate her many memberships in women's organizations.[3] At the same time, companies like Jack in the Box, Con-Agra, and Pulitzer demonstrate that innovative corporate directors are enthusiastically ready to give competent women opportunities to serve on their boards. They see diversity in the boardroom as an indicator of independent thinking—a factor that helps ensure the board's effectiveness as a team.

LESSONS LEARNED

According to research by Margaret Neale, the John G. McCoy-Banc One Professor of Organizations and Dispute Resolution at Stanford Graduate School of Business, more homogeneous teams tend not to expect conflict, so they may not be prepared to handle conflict well. Group conflict, in the sense of intellectual conflict, debate, or controversy, actually makes a team function better and be more willing to innovate.

"One of the most interesting recent findings in the area of work-team performance," says Professor Neale, "is that the mere presence of diversity you can see, such as a person's race or gender, actually cues a team in that there's likely to be differences of opinion. That cuing turns out to enhance the team's ability to handle conflict, because members expect it and are not surprised when it surfaces."[4]

Dr. Hayes is an academic administrative leader with experience from multiple campuses in widely different locations where the challenge was to work with faculty, students, administrators, and stakeholders who represented many different perspectives. Through deliberation, debate, and negotiation, reaching toward shared goals, she developed the competencies needed to make decisions and implement change. The diversity of perspective that Dr. Hayes has brought to her corporate boards consists of experience and knowledge spanning scientific, academic, governance, and financial spheres and international exposure.

It is natural for her to look for, and to find, other women of equal competence and independence of thought who might join her as a director.

> Any woman that I know who has been on a board has taken advantage of that position to try and give other women opportunities. It happens. The women with whom I have worked on boards certainly are outstanding. As a member of the nominating committee at Jack in the Box, I feel very good about being able to encourage the board to include other women like Anne B. Gust, who came onto the board in 2003—a senior executive with Gap Inc. who successfully managed her husband's [Jerry Brown's] campaign for California attorney general. She is one sharp cookie with a wonderful sense of humor and a great business sense and focus.

Dr. Hayes's capacity for work has always seemed boundless. She continues to find answers to the challenges that come her way. Although formally retired from academic and administrative work for over three years now, she continues her many corporate and board commitments. She's not the type to just stop. Said Dr. Hayes a decade ago:

> We are learning that leadership involves understanding human behavior and performance; articulation and communication of values; shaping culture; building consensus and support; initiating and managing change. These are qualities that are as natural to a woman as to a man. Now that women have the political, economic, educational and influential abilities to be leaders, the fact that we are shorter, and soft voiced, and less violent in our assertiveness, will become unimportant, and our ability to lead others in our own way will be expressed.[5]

DIRECTOR PROFILE: MARY S. METZ

Mary S. Metz, age 71 at the time of our interview, is in high demand by multiple boards primarily because of her business and financial expertise, acquired during her time as a top academic leader at Mills College and the UC Berkeley Extension. She is a director at four corporations: Longs Drug Stores, PG&E, Union BanCal Corporation, and AT&T Inc.

EARLY YEARS

Dr. Metz was born in Rockhill, South Carolina, in 1937. She married F. Eugene Metz, an architect, in 1957; they have one daughter. In 1958 she received her BA in French and English, summa cum laude, from Furman University, a small private liberal arts college in Greenville, South Carolina. Furman was an all-men's theological academy founded in 1826, but it went coed when Greenville Women's College began sending female students there in 1933. Dr. Metz graduated with the highest academic average, earning the Scholarship Cup and the General Excellence Award as the outstanding graduate.[1] She received a National Defense Education Act fellowship in the early 1960s and did postgraduate studies as a Fulbright fellow at the Institut Phonetique and the Sorbonne in Paris. In 1966, she received her PhD in French from Louisiana State University in Baton Rouge, magna cum laude, writing her thesis on the French theater of the absurd.

At LSU, she was an advocate for students' and women's rights, first as a graduate student and later as a faculty member there. She was the first woman elected to the Faculty Senate.

> There were very few women at LSU. I was an activist there; we had a very active chapter of the National Organization for Women. In 1972, the equal

rights amendment finally got out of Congress and went to the states for ratifi-
cation. I was the president of the Baton Rouge chapter of NOW (1971–1974)
[and] headed up a huge statewide coalition of about 100 organizations, including churches, labor groups, and the American Association of University
Women, to lobby on behalf of [ratification of] the ERA.

We were concerned with many other campus issues. For example, there
was still a 10:00 PM curfew for women in dorms. Female architecture students
were barred from working very late on *charettes,* the all-night group design
session. Student housing was not available for female married students. The
law school limited admission of women to just 10 percent. I led a protest at
the graduate dean's office because they were hiring a new dean, but they had
no women candidates. Women at LSU were losing out on a lot of learning
and collaborative experiences.

I saw so much discrimination against women at LSU—both the tangible
things and the diffused stuff that you can't get your hands on, but you know
it's just holding women back. All these things ran so counter to the ways
that I had been brought up and educated with men and women together at
Furman. Even so, I guess I always protested in a manner perceived as responsible and professional.

UP THE ACADEMIC LADDER

Dr. Metz progressed quickly up the tenure ladder as a French instructor (1965),
assistant professor (1966), and then associate professor (1972), publishing three
books along the way.[2]

I always wanted to be in a position where I could make a difference. If you're
too low down in any organization, you can't make a difference. I wanted my
ideas to be taken seriously. It was very hard to be taken seriously, as you can
imagine, for a young woman in the South, in the '60s and '70s. You needed
credentials. I wanted the freedom to make good things happen. Until you
get to the top, you don't have freedom to enact things, to make decisions.

From 1966 through 1974, she was director of elementary and intermediate
French programs at LSU. When her husband was studying for his master's degree
in architecture at the University of California, Berkeley, in the late 1960s, she was
a visiting assistant professor there.

The new chancellor of LSU, Paul W. Murrill, nominated her for an American
Council on Education fellowship, part of a broad-based program to select and
advance faculty members with the potential for higher education administration. The American Council on Education wanted to identify talented female
and minority candidates. As part of that fellowship, she was required to serve
as a special assistant to the chancellor during 1974. He asked her to stay on
the following year as assistant to the chancellor. In that role, she became part of
a network of college and university administrators from all around the country.

Inquiries began to come her way from other campuses interested in recruiting academic leaders.

She recalled, "I was invited to join Hood College [a small, private liberal arts college for women in Frederick, Maryland] as the provost, dean of faculty, and professor of French. I accepted it because I wanted to see what women's colleges were like."

Founded in the 1890s, Hood originally was an all-women's college (admitting only a few men as commuter students beginning in 1971 and going residentially coed in 2003). Her position at Hood College (1976–1981) was her first significant administrative position. As provost, she made whatever decisions had to be made when the president was not available. As dean of academic affairs, she was the leader of the faculty, working with all the department heads on all aspects of academic life, curriculum, and admission standards.

> I discovered that I really loved that hybrid role. I very much identified with the faculty roles, their views, their values, and what mattered to them. I learned I have this strong organizational bent. I wasn't afraid to tackle budgets or administrative tasks, even when I'd not done it before. I learned and did the administrative work pretty well.

MILL COLLEGE PRESIDENCY

Dr. Metz remained active in higher education circles, regional meetings, and the American Council on Education, becoming known among leaders at colleges and universities across the country. A partner in a search company called, telling her a national search for the new president of Mills College in Oakland, California, was underway and that she was a top candidate for the position. She never knew who nominated her. While she felt she could have stayed on at Hood for a few years, she realized that opportunities like that don't come around every day. She and her family arrived at Mills in 1981.

Mills had an outstanding faculty; the school's standing was right next to that of the top women's colleges. Early on, Dr. Metz worked with the faculty, encouraging them to rethink and reorganize the freshman and sophomore academic experience. Mills freshmen had a great deal of freedom to select their own courses, but she saw that their first-year curriculum was not fully integrated into the overall educational experience. She brought in a new provost and dean of faculty to help develop the program. "It was clear that Mills needed to grow. I wanted the faculty to refocus the curriculum because I thought that would be key to attracting top-quality students to the freshman class. They began to change, but faculty change slowly and with great resistance. It's just natural."

Mills also had not done a fund-raising campaign for 10 years. When she was first recruited, the endowment campaign goal was $35 million; by the time she arrived on campus, the goal had been doubled. She became very involved in fund-raising for the college, ultimately raising $73 million.

The faculty, alumnae, and trustees, together, worked very successfully in many areas: we built a new library, greatly expanded and renovated the art complex, and renovated the biological sciences complex. My family and I were very involved in everything happening on the Mills campus: basketball, dance concerts, lectures, everything.

In a survey of her peer academic administrators while she was at Mills, the Council for the Support and Advancement of Education named Dr. Metz one of the 100 most effective college presidents. She was a member of the American Council on Education's committee on leadership development and also became involved in Bay Area research centers. Dr. Metz received three honorary degrees during her tenure as president of Mills College.[3]

In the mid-1980s, the Mills board grew to 35 members through the addition of trustees from the corporate world, including Sam Ginn, CEO of Pacific Bell; Eugene E. Trefethen Jr., retired CEO of Kaiser Industries; and F. Warren Hellman, co-founder of Hellman & Friedman, a top San Francisco private equity firm. Mr. Hellman became chair of the Mills College board of trustees.

During the 1970s and 1980s, liberal arts colleges in general, and single-gender schools in particular, faced greater pressure about their long-term financial viability. All but four of the nation's all-men's colleges had gone coed. The number of all-women's colleges had declined from 298 in the 1960s to 93 in 1990. Once women began to be admitted to the nation's top colleges for men, fewer female high school students chose to attend all-women's colleges. Mills's board of trustees began studying the issue and holding public meetings about the college's future financial stability starting in 1988.[4]

The trustees hired outside consultants to advise them. Their research confirmed other studies pointing to a declining share of high school graduates attending all-women's colleges: enrollment at all-women's colleges had fallen from 250,000 in 1970 to 125,000 students, roughly only 3–4 percent of the high school graduate population. The consultant presentations warned that if Mills did not go coed, "in five or six years, [Mills] would be heading into a death spiral."[5]

The primary issue facing the board was how to increase enrollment sufficiently to support Mills's annual $23 million operating budget. The graduate program, which had been coeducational from the beginning in the 1930s, was doing well with an enrollment of about 300. The undergraduate women-only program was facing increased competition for female students from other area campuses. Undergraduate enrollment had dropped to 777 in 1990. Two opposing views emerged on campus. The trustees approved a proposal for the undergraduate program to become coed. Students and alumni, on the other hand, opposed admitting male undergraduates. They demonstrated their opposition and closed the campus.

Initially, Dr. Metz had voted, along with the majority of trustees, for the campus to go coed.

I was trying to be as objective as I could. I greatly admired women's colleges. I had experienced that kind of affirming environment at Furman. For me, the crucial question was academic quality. I didn't want to be part of anything that did not have very high academic standards. I did not want Mills to go into further decline. We believed we would not lose anything for the women as we added men, attracting a high caliber of student.

Facing the reality of the strike, Dr. Metz formed a collaboration of alumnae association members, students, faculty, and college administrators to undertake several initiatives that might preserve Mills's 138-year status as an all-female college. The students and alumnae association agreed to raise an additional $10 million in endowment pledges over the next five years on the condition that trustees reverse their decision. Two weeks later, the trustees held a special meeting and voted to reverse their decision. Dr. Metz voted in support of the final decision for Mills to remain an all-female undergraduate college.

After the strike, conversations with the faculty about changes to the curriculum and with the alumnae about aggressive recruitment and fund-raising became much more productive. Together, they created a new strategic five-year plan for the school, which included the goal of enrolling 1,000 undergraduate students by 1995.

Dr. Metz decided it would be best for someone else to take ownership of the plan and its implementation. "It was time to turn the leadership over to a new team to start from this new beginning," she said.

Undergraduate enrollment at Mills in 2008–2009 reached 973 women, with a graduate head count of 508 women and men, partially due to the implementation of dual-degree programs in six fields, where a four-year bachelor's program was topped by a one-year master's degree. The annual budget at Mills now totals $77.6 million.

When Dr. Metz retired from Mills, her relations with the school, faculty, alumnae, and trustees continued to be cordial. The alumnae association gave her accolades, citations, and receptions, as did the faculty and the board of trustees. Gene Trefethen started a movement among the trustees, which was joined by the alumnae association, to fund a $1 million endowed faculty chair in her name. When they asked her what she wanted to do with the money, she said she wanted it to go "to talented and innovative younger faculty. I wanted to help attract faculty members who would be thinking forward [about] where their college and their field of study would be going in the future."

After her retirement from Mills in 1990, the college established the Mary S. Metz Honorary Chair for Excellence and Creativity in Teaching, and she was named president emerita.

PACIFIC GAS & ELECTRIC BOARD

Many of Dr. Metz's board assignments came during the mid-1980s while she was at Mills. She was very active on the Oakland mayor's advisory council, a board of top business leaders trying to revitalize the downtown area. Members included the CEO of Clorox, the head of Bank of America's East Bay regional office, and other major corporate and civic leaders.

I wasn't even thinking about boards at the time. I was just very active in San Francisco and the East Bay communities, in part for fund-raising for Mills College, but also doing the kinds of things that I thought the president of Mills College should be doing for the college and for the community.

Pacific Gas & Electric was the first corporate board Dr. Metz was invited to join (1986). She was its second female director. The first woman, named in 1980, was Leslie L. Luttgens, a civic and community leader active in various civic, public service, and cultural activities. "The context of 1986 was very different from today," she said. "In those days, boards had to look among community leaders to find women candidates. Leslie Luttgens came out of the civic leadership pathway that dominated the 1980s, and I came out of the academic pathway."

A math professor at Mills had been a childhood friend of Frederick W. Mielke Jr., the chair and CEO of PG&E. The professor mentioned Dr. Metz to Mr. Mielke, who interviewed her and invited her to join his board. Today, there are 3 females among 10 directors on the board of the firm that became PG&E Corporation in 1996. Other current directors include Maryellen Herringer and Barbara L. Rambo, both added in 2005.

PG&E was severely affected by the energy crisis that began in California in 2000. Blackouts and a declared state of emergency followed, and in April 2001 PG&E declared bankruptcy, from which the company emerged three years later.

PACIFIC BELL/AT&T BOARDS

Recalled Dr. Metz, "Just a few months after the PG&E board nomination, Sam Ginn, CEO of Pacific Bell, introduced me to Don Guinn, the chairman of Pacific Bell, who invited me to join the Pacific Bell board."

Dr. Metz served on boards where the companies kept changing beneath her. In 1986, she was the sole female director of Pacific Bell (and Pacific Telesis Group, the holding company created after the AT&T breakup in 1984). Pacific Telesis was acquired by SBC Corporation Inc. in 1997; then SBC Corporation acquired AT&T Inc. and renamed itself in 2005.

There are now 5 other women on the AT&T board among 17 directors: Lynn M. Martin and Laura D'Andrea Tyson, both of whom were added in 1999; Joyce M. Roche (1998); Patricia P. Upton (1993); and Toni Rembe (1991).

UNION BANK BOARD

An alumna from the Mills College board of trustees mentioned Dr. Metz to John Harrison, CEO of Union Bank in Los Angeles, at that time owned by Standard Charter, a British Bank. He contacted her, interviewed her, and invited her onto the board in 1988.

Union Bank became Union BanCal Corporation in 1997. Dr. Metz was joined by Aida M. Alvarez in 2004 on the 15-director board. In August 2008, Union

BanCal was bought out by Mitsubishi UFJ Financial Group. According to the *Los Angeles Times,*

> Corporate directors often are accused of being pushovers. But in the case of Union Bank, the directors pushed back at a lowball takeover offer from the Japanese corporate parent—and won a hefty premium for sharehold-ers…$73.50-a-share.…That was 27% more than the $58-a-share offer Mitsubishi made in April, and nearly 17% above the revised bid of $63 a share that the Japanese firm made last Tuesday.[6]

LONGS DRUG STORES BOARD

Dr. Metz became the sole woman on the board of Longs Drug Stores in 1991. "My nomination to the Longs board followed the same pattern. Vera Long was an alumna of Mills and the wife of one of the founders, Joe Long. I had become very friendly with her. Her son Bob Long was the chairman and CEO of Longs at the time. He invited me to join the Longs board." Donna A. Tanoue (2005) and Lisa M. Harper (2006) joined her there, now among 10 directors. In February 2007, Longs added its fourth female director, Evelyn S. Dilsaver.

SODEXHO MARRIOTT SERVICES BOARD

Dr. Metz was named to the board of Sodexho Marriott Services in October 2000.

> Deloitte Touche was the independent auditor of PG&E. One of the partners of Deloitte knew me as a member on the audit committee at a number of the companies. She also knew the head of the French firm Sodexho Alliance. As a U.S. publicly traded company, Sodexho Marriott Services needed an independent board member. I was recommended both as an independent director and also because I spoke French. Out of the blue, I got a call from France asking if I would consider being on their board. I served a year or so before the French company completed the acquisition. I served on the special committee that helped evaluate the fair value of the stock of the American firm for the shareholders.

UC BERKELEY EXTENSION

Dr. Metz became dean of the university extension (1991–1998), the continuing education arm of the University of California, Berkeley, and one of the largest outreach education providers in the country.

> Berkeley Extension received no financial support from the university or the state: it had no endowment. Every year it started with zero dollars. It was exactly like running a higher education business. It was fascinating. What

we had to sell was the excellence and the cutting-edge nature of the courses. Having the right courses and a really great faculty was not enough; you also had to market them effectively. We also had all of the logistics issues of physical facility—where to teach all over the Bay Area.

She became dean just as the California economy entered a deep recession and the Extension's enrollment started declining. She increased enrollment from 50,000 to 72,000 primarily by expanding regional training facilities. She increased the number of courses from 600 to 3,000 in the Bay Area, nationally, internationally, and online.[7] "The staff was academics who were more entrepreneurial and business minded than traditional faculty. They understood that their curriculum had to change continuously because they were educating the educated. I felt this was right up my alley."

Dr. Metz was instrumental in the Extension's winning of a $2 million grant from the Alfred P. Sloan Foundation of New York, which facilitated the school's entrée into the world of distance learning in the mid-1990s, at a time when the Internet was just beginning its commercial growth. According to a University of California press release,

> University of California, Berkeley…will launch one of the largest educational online projects in the history of the Internet. Within three years, Berkeley Extension Online will offer 175 college courses focusing primarily on continuing adult education. Berkeley Extension Online will be developed in collaboration with UC Berkeley Extension's Center for Media and Independent Learning.[8]

Upon her retirement, Berkeley chancellor Robert M. Berdahl said, "Under [Dr. Metz's] leadership, the goal of Extension has been to reinvent lifelong learning for the 21st century."[9] She was honored in 1998 with the Berkeley Citation, which "celebrat[es] extraordinary achievement in the recipient's field coupled with outstanding service to the Berkeley campus." Upon her retirement, she again was named dean emerita.

S. H. COWELL FOUNDATION

From January 1999 to March 2005, Dr. Metz was the president of the S. H. Cowell Foundation in San Francisco, an organization that seeks "to improve the quality of life of children living in poverty in Northern and Central California by providing support that strengthens families and communities."[10] She said, "I was the first woman on the Cowell board in 1991. As president, I greatly increased the number of women and diversity on the board. Every one of those women has impeccable credentials, such as Mary Lee Widener."

THE AMERICAN CONSERVATORY THEATER BOARD

The American Conservatory Theater (ACT), San Francisco's Tony Award–winning theater and training institution, had been hard hit by the 1989 earthquake. ACT reached out to Dr. Metz after she retired from Mills, asking her to join their board and help in their fund-raising to restore the theater. From 2004 to 2007, Dr. Metz was chair of the board of trustees at ACT, which offers both contemporary and classical productions and a wide range of classes. She continues today to serve as a trustee.

PERSPECTIVES ON COMMITTEES

Dr. Metz's competency as both a financial administrator and a corporate audit committee member is well demonstrated in the interview she gave to the magazine *Internal Auditor* in October 1993, which still stands today as a primer on what it takes to serve effectively as an audit committee member. In that interview, she demonstrates an incredible grasp of the history of audit regulations and in-depth knowledge of the enabling legislation and the operating guidelines of corporate accounting regulators as well as major public accounting firms.[11] Because of her breadth of experience, she is a member of six committees at these corporations and chair of three: she is on the audit committees of Longs, PG&E, and Union BanCal; the executive committee at PG&E; and the corporate governance and nominating committee and the public policy committee at AT&T. She is chair of the Longs' corporate governance and nominating committee and the public policy committees at PG&E and Union BanCal.

> Before the passage of the Sarbanes-Oxley Act, audit committees often were chaired by people like me who were financially literate, but who would not have been classified as financial experts in the sense of an auditor or a CFO. After the passage of Sarbanes-Oxley, it became clear that the board would be better served by someone with the credentials that would classify them as a financial expert.

Dr. Metz agrees that financial experts are best as the chairs of audit committees. She suggests it is equally important to populate the audit committee with members who are not financial experts, to include people who are willing to ask good questions, such as a simple "Now tell me: why is it this way?" She elaborated:

> Board members cannot assume that it would be improper for them to really question a CFO. Audit committee members might think the CFO is so smart, that that is why a director didn't quite understand what was going on. Perhaps a director didn't want to reveal any ignorance about what was going on. I don't have those inhibitions. I'm not afraid to ask those questions.

Dr. Metz describes an observation made by several board members, both male and female:

> On one board where I serve, at most board meetings the majority of questions come from the women. All the women do it, not just one woman dominating the questions. The questions don't come out all at once; they come out genuinely, over the length of the board meeting. The women are

all very different. We all come from different backgrounds. It just seems that the women are relaxed about asking questions or making comments in the board meetings. I think it's a great tribute to how corporate boards have changed.

Her experience with a variety of committees is both interesting to her and beneficial to the boards on which she serves.

All of the committees are interesting for different reasons. The audit committee is a terrific place to be if you want to understand the real workings of the corporation, because sooner or later almost everything has to come to the audit committee: all the financial aspects, the business ethics, and the corporate strategy. In terms of really understanding the company, the audit committee is the hub.

I love serving as chair of the governance and nominating committee because—with the support of the CEO—I've been able to bring three women on the board. You don't do this alone. The CEO has been a partner in that.

Being on a nominating and corporate governance committee requires a director to be much more than simply a single-issue director.

The governance issues are quite broad; they concern the independence of directors, the composition of the board, and the number of former executives. I've been fortunate to be involved in all of those discussions. Everything that you do as a board needs to be as transparent, ethical, straightforward, and as shareholder focused as you can possibly make it.

Dr. Metz sees public policy committees as an important asset to the for-profit corporate board. "I agree that the pipelines to the corporate boards are changing. I hope that they don't change so much that all of the women who come onto boards only come out of the business sector, as has been the case with most men."

LESSONS LEARNED

Dr. Metz's experience on boards spans a period of over two decades of change and changed attitudes about women on boards:

Throughout the 1980s, corporations got their first or second woman on the board. They became very content with that through the 1990s, when some of the women who had been there for awhile began retiring due to the board regulations about age or years served. So, there I was, the only woman on the board of PG&E. And I've always been the only woman on the Longs board. I found I didn't like it. For several years, I talked about it to the other board members, and they all agreed with me, but for one reason or another nothing happened. Finally, I had to be forceful and direct. In one case, I said, "I will not stand for reelection if there aren't more women on the board."

I think my greatest area of contribution to these corporate boards is that I was educated and operated in a variety of arenas: civic affairs, academic affairs, and philanthropic matters. When an issue of policy arose about how the corporation interfaced with the public, I could always look at it from multiple points of view in a way that sometimes the businessmen and women didn't quite see at first blush. Their first thought would not be to ask, "How would this issue impact the person standing next to me in an elevator?" Businesspeople on the board certainly understand the impact once we began talking about it, but their first consideration usually is the business impact.

Dr. Metz provides a grounding in reality for the corporate boards on which she serves.

When some publicity about the company comes out, I listen to how people are reacting in the elevator and what they are saying on the street or in social circles. I think I've been able to provide different perspectives on a lot of issues that shape public policy, such as when companies try to make decisions about charitable giving, about urging employees to be volunteers, or around the environment.

Dr. Metz came to her four corporate board roles because of her academic leadership and her financial expertise. She is a teacher and an educational innovator, a trusted corporate advisor, and a social and philanthropic leader. She does not easily fit into any one category but rather demonstrates how women of talent have the capacity to endure and prevail in the face of challenges. Dr. Metz is a "serial" director because the corporations on which she serves have gone through tremendous flux and change and she has endured and grown with them. Throughout her career, she has shown a unique ability to focus on her expertise and the simple task of getting the tough jobs done.

5

Angels and Venturers: The Investment Path

This chapter focuses on the women with careers in securities firms, major investment houses, venture partnerships, and angel organizations. These women came to their board roles via the money networks, taking a stake in entrepreneurial firms and acquiring shareholder interests at their first board seats. The three dominant paths to the boardroom (investment, entrepreneurship, and corporate business) tend to cluster together and could be described as the performance-based paths to a board role.

RELATIVE IMPORTANCE

Twenty-eight women (15% of the experience cited, as shown in table 5.1) came to their board roles by way of the investment path, a career route that is of increasing importance as more women pursue graduate business degrees and enter the finance and investment business sectors.

DIVERSE EXPERIENCES

The women directors surveyed pursued a number of options along the investment or securities path, some of them acquiring experience in more than one of the following endeavors:

1. *The Big Investment Houses:* Eight women came up through the ranks of major national or international securities and investment advisory firms or banks.
   - Kathleen Brown is senior private wealth management advisor and head of West Coast municipal finance at Goldman Sachs. Previously,

Table 5.1
Investment Path: Experience of Women on Corporate Boards of California *Fortune* 1000 Companies

N	G	A	I	E	C	Name	Company
	G		I		C	Kathleen Brown	Countrywide Financial
			I	E	C	Mariann Byerwalter	Pacific Life
			I		C	Safra Catz	Oracle Corporation
			I	E	C	Deborah Ann Coleman	Applied Materials
			I	E	C	Kathleen A. Cote	Western Digital
			I	E		Patrice Marie Daniels	CB Richard Ellis
	G	A	I			Nancy-Ann Min DeParle	DaVita
			I			Patricia C. Dunn	Hewlett-Packard
			I	E	C	Leslie Myers Frécon	Ryland Group
			I		C	Maureen E. Grzelakowski	Broadcom
			I		C	Michelle Guthrie	VeriSign
			I		C	Jeanne P. Jackson	William-Sonoma
			I	E		Catherine M. Klema	Watson Pharmaceuticals
			I		C	Marie L. Knowles	McKesson
			I	E		Catherine P. Lego	Lam Research, SanDisk
			I	E	C	Linda Fayne Levinson	Ingram Micro, Jacobs Engineering Inc.
			I		C	Marjorie Magner	Charles Schwab
			I			Jacqueline C. Morby	Pacific Life
	G		I	E		Roslyn B. Payne	First American Corporation
			I	E		Naomi O. Seligman	Oracle Corporation, Sun Microsystems
N			I			Anne M. Tatlock	Franklin Resources
			I		C	Carolyn M. Ticknor	Clorox
	G		I	E	C	Donna Frame Tuttle	Hilton Hotels
			I			Lida Náprstek Urbánek	KLA-Tencor
			I		C	Elizabeth Vanderslice	Xilinx

Note: N = Nonprofit; G = Government; A = Academic; I = Investment; E = Entrepreneurial; C = Corporate.

she was president of the private bank in the investment management group at Bank of America.

- Safra Catz was managing director for Donaldson, Lufkin & Jenrette, a global investment bank, and before that held several investment banking positions.

- Patrice Marie Daniels was managing director of corporate and leveraged finance for CIBC World Markets, an investment banking firm.
- Nancy-Ann Min DeParle is an investment advisor at J. P. Morgan Partners LLC.
- Catherine M. Klema was managing director of health care investment banking at Lehman Brothers, then at Furman Selz LLC, and finally at SG Cowen Securities.
- Elizabeth Vanderslice was a principal at the investment banking firm Sterling Payot Company, and then vice president of H. W. Jesse & Co., a San Francisco investment banking and business strategy consulting firm that was spun off from Sterling Payot Co.

2. *Venture Partners/Principals:* Eight women are principals or partners of financial advisory or venture capital firms that invest in emerging companies of all sizes.
   - Maureen "Moe" E. Grzelakowski is a senior advisor at Investor Growth Capital, a venture capital and private equity firm that focuses on opportunities in the information technology and health care industries.
   - Mary "Nina" R. Henderson worked with Angelo, Gordon & Co., LP, a privately held registered investment advisor focused on alternative investing.
   - Linda Fayne Levinson was a senior advisor at the venture capital firm GRP Partners, which manages investments in innovative entrepreneurs primarily in the consumer marketplace.
   - Jacqueline C. Morby is a senior director and head of the Pittsburgh offices of TA Associates, a private equity firm that manages local investments in medical device and laboratory equipment firms.
   - Carolyn M. Ticknor is a venture partner at Inflexion Partners, which looks for emerging technology investment opportunities in the Central Florida Tech Triangle.
   - Catherine P. Lego is a general partner of the Photonics Fund, an early-stage venture fund that invests in the fiber-optics telecommunications markets. Previously, she was a general partner of Oak Investment Partners, a multistage venture capital firm.
   - Michelle Guthrie is managing director of Providence Equity Partners, a private equity firm that invests in the media, entertainment, communications, and information industry sectors.

3. *Entrepreneurial Angel Investors:* Ten entrepreneurial women created their own investment entities as vehicles to foster angel or venture capital in areas of interest to them.
   - Jeanne P. Jackson formed MSP Capital LLC as a vehicle for her investment consulting business after retiring as president and CEO at Gap Inc. and Walmart.com.
   - Catherine P. Lego created her own firm, Lego Ventures LLC, to consult with early-stage technology firms.

- Roslyn B. Payne established Jackson Street Partners Ltd. as a real estate venture capital company. She also owns Dover Corporation, which provides equity capital for residential developers.
- Linda Fayne Levinson is president of Fayne Levinson Associates, an independent consulting firm that advises major corporations and start-up entrepreneurial ventures in strategy, market, and corporate development.
- Catherine M. Klema is president of Nettleton Advisors LLC, a real estate investment management firm in New York.
- Marjorie Magner is managing director and co-founder of Brysam Global Partners, funded in part by J. P. Morgan, which invests in consumer finance opportunities in emerging economies.
- Naomi O. Seligman co-chairs the CIO Strategy Exchange, which partners with Kleiner Perkins Caufield and Byers, one of Silicon Valley's preeminent venture capitalists. She is co-founder and senior partner of Cassius Advisors Inc., which provides e-commerce partnering and consulting services to technology firms worldwide.
- Lida Náprstek Urbánek describes herself as a private investor managing family wealth as the widow of Karel Urbánek, founder and former president of Tencor Instruments, a semiconductor manufacturing firm.

4. *The Major Fund Families:* Four women have found their experience is valued in their capacities as advisors to mutual funds, where they monitor securities trends and growth opportunities for families of fund.
   - Marie L. Knowles is on the board of trustees of Fidelity Funds.
   - Mariann Byerwalter is a trustee of the Schwab Capital Trust, a group of funds of Charles Schwab Corp. in San Francisco.
   - Marilyn Alexander recently retired from the boards of three registered investment companies managed by PIMCO, one of the world's leading fixed-income managers.

Women in investment are very likely to have entrepreneurial and/or corporate experience. They also are very likely to invest heavily in their own business educations, earning an average of more than two academic degrees each. Twenty-one women from the investment path earned one master's degree, and five earned a second master's degree. Seven earned an MBA as a first advanced degree, and all the second master's degrees were MBAs. Four women who took the investment path also earned JDs.

Two women, Deborah Ann Coleman (1997) and Elizabeth Vanderslice (2000), were recognized by the Aspen Institute as Henry Crown fellows. The Henry Crown Fellowship Program was begun in 1997 to develop the next generation of community-spirited leaders and to provide them with the tools necessary to meet the challenges of corporate and civic leadership in the 21st century. Each year, 20 fellows are chosen from among young executives and professionals between the ages of 25 and 45 who are nominated for their considerable achievements in the private or public sector and for their potential to provide leadership at the highest levels of corporate and civic responsibility.

MYTH BUSTING

Historically, researchers and journalists have focused primarily on the small percentage of women venture capitalists, understating the substantial progress women have made entering into the investment field.

A report of the Diana Project by the Kaufman Foundation demonstrates how much information can be hidden beneath a fascination with percentages. The Diana Project compared the presence of women in venture capital in 1995 and 2000, reporting that women represented only 10 percent of management-track venture capitalists and only 9 percent by 2000.[1] In fact, the actual number of women kept pace with the dramatic growth in venture capital activity during those years. Annual dollar value of venture capital investment skyrocketed from $8 billion to over $105 billion. The number of deals a year rose from 1,800 to almost 8,000.[2] The number of women venture capital managers increased 40 percent (from 364 to 510), and the number of women venture capital partners increased 20 percent (from 261 to 339). These were the ranks from which boards selected women investors to become directors at top venture firms.

Other trends confirm the growing presence of women in investment and venture/angel capital. According to *Forbes* magazine, when it began publishing its Midas List of the top 100 deal makers in high-tech and life sciences in 2001, there were no women on the list; in 2007 there were five women.[3] Research into the leadership of the largest university endowments and heads of top national foundations shows the appointment of more women chief investment officers, including the addition of Jane Menillo as head of Harvard Management Company, Inc. where she is responsible for the nation's top endowment.[4]

Significant progress is being observed in the representation of women within the traditionally all-male investment world. In a study of 100 angel investing organizations, the University of New Hampshire's Center for Venture Research determined that women represented 13.8 percent of angel investors, 12.9 percent of entrepreneurs who sought angel capital, and 21.5 percent of those who received angel investment funding in 2006.[5]

The center searched for possible explanations for why women historically have been underrepresented in both the angel and venture capital markets. They concluded that the choices and actions of women themselves were significant. Women seek angel financing at rates substantially lower than men: only 8.9 percent of all proposals were brought forward by women-owned businesses. However, there appears to be no significant difference between the rates at which women-owned businesses (13.3% yield rate) and male-owned businesses (14.8%) were funded. Thus, when women pursued angel financing, they had an equal probability of receiving investment.

The Center for Venture Research theorized that as more women investors acquire the appropriate expertise and experience in providing angel capital, we can expect "greater participation of women entrepreneurs in the high-growth, high-return industries typically financed by private equity."[6]

LESSONS LEARNED

A fundamental concept in business formation is that boards of directors are selected by those who own some financial interest in the entity. Control over the designation of directors comes from the underlying valuation of the company. At the start-up phase of a business entity, the investment deal allocates seats on the board of directors in proportion to angel or venture capital invested in the entity. When women participate as angel or venture capital investors or advisors, then women are included among the shareholders of start-up entities.

Greater presence of women in investment or security advisory firms will parallel increases in the number of women on boards of directors. Companies create boards when there is a need for representation of outside financial interests as part of the company's leadership. Companies add financially savvy independent-minded directors as the firms grow. Skills in demand at these growth stages of firms are not only operational and managerial skills but, more importantly, competency in governance—the guidance level of the company: the helmsmen providing strategic direction.

As more women seek advanced business education and degrees, they will add their own expertise and experience to these higher levels in the investment community. As more women are employed in the investment/securities business sectors, they will enhance their understanding of what it takes to select and fund successful businesses. As more women build viable businesses that match the interests of angel and venture capital investors, they will win funding and earn seats in the boardrooms of growth-oriented entrepreneurial firms.

THE WOMEN INTERVIEWED

The three women interviewed were Leslie Myers Frécon, Donna Frame Tuttle, and Deborah Ann Coleman. These women demonstrate exactly the capabilities required to succeed in private equity, investment funds, and angel ventures. They represent different paths into the investment field, and they share an ability to look for profits and rewards where risks can be measured and managed by shareholders and their representatives, corporate board directors.

DIRECTOR PROFILE: LESLIE MYERS FRÉCON

Leslie Myers Frécon, age 54 at the time of our interview, came to her board role as a top corporate executive with over 16 years' financial experience at General Mills, with a strong suit in acquisitions and spin-offs—competencies that she developed further through her own private equity firm, LFE Capital LLC, where today she invests in smaller Midwest-based companies with great growth prospects, often with a female focus or ownership.

THE EARLY YEARS

Leslie Myers was born in 1953 in Minneapolis, Minnesota, the oldest of four children. Her father and grandfather were entrepreneurs, so she grew up being around business. She spent two years at Smith College in Massachusetts and then transferred to Stanford University, from which she graduated with a bachelor's degree in English in 1975. "I wanted a different experience—a larger West Coast university." She worked for a year in San Francisco at *womenSports,* the magazine launched by Billie Jean King in May 1974, and then she decided to get a business degree.

> I started in arts management at UCLA, which, at the time, was one of the few MBA degree programs in that field. I had a summer internship at the Mark Taper Forum in Los Angeles. About halfway through the program, I decided that, while I love the arts, I didn't want a full-time career in that arena. I began taking finance and accounting classes and soon switched my major to finance.

Ms. Frécon graduated with an MBA in finance from UCLA in 1978. She was hired by Bank of America in their Los Angeles corporate lending department, which made commercial loans to agriculture and general manufacturing businesses located primarily in the western United States. She stayed at Bank of American from 1978 to 1981, becoming an assistant vice president.

GENERAL MILLS

In 1978, she married Alain Frécon, whom she had met while he was at Stanford Law School. Today, his firm, Frécon & Associates, specializes in commercial mediation, arbitration, and international business law. In 1981, when Mr. Frécon was offered a position at Dorsey & Whitney LLP in Minneapolis, the couple chose to move back home to a city they knew to be family friendly. Ms. Frécon recalled, "I wanted to work in a company rather than in the financial services industry—I liked the idea of being involved directly in the general management of a business."

She joined General Mills in Minneapolis as manager of acquisitions in 1981 and was named director of acquisitions two years later.

For the next seven years, I was involved in restructuring the company, which had acquired many non-food businesses during the 1970s, including Talbots, Monet jewelry, Pennsylvania House furniture, and FootJoy shoes. General Mills realized they would be a more profitable enterprise by focusing on consumer foods rather than building a portfolio of unrelated consumer-branded businesses. I was responsible for divesting the company of the non-food entities.

She had two boys in the mid-1980s while she was climbing the corporate ladder at General Mills and traveling to Latin America, Asia, and Europe. "There were no women's groups back then and few women in leadership at General Mills. Companies didn't offer child care facilities on-site or even paternal leave. In fact, there were only two or three of us who had children and then returned to work in management-level positions."

She became controller and CFO of the food service division in 1989, and of the Sperry division in 1991, acquiring in-depth understanding of the profit-and-loss operating experience and management of business entities within the larger General Mills organization.

Ms. Frécon became vice president of General Mills in 1991, one of only a handful of women at that level. In April 1993, she was named the first female and the youngest senior vice president at General Mills in charge of corporate finance. The company was anxious to promote women to senior executive positions where they would be exposed to greater responsibilities. She was actively involved in setting the strategic direction of General Mills as it transitioned from a diversified consumer products firm to a packaged consumer foods company. She managed over $5 billion in pension fund assets and financial liabilities, including $200 million in private equity investments, and led a $3 billion spin-off of the company's restaurant operations, including Red Lobster and Olive Garden. She worked with division management in expanding their businesses, which included the acquisition of Chex cereal.

EARLY GOVERNANCE ROLES

Because of her international experience, she became a board member of International Dessert Partners, the 1996 Latin American joint venture of General Mills and CPC International Inc. (which became Bestfoods in 1998). As one of the top corporate executives, she was named a trustee of the General Mills Foundation, which at that time was responsible for about $15 million in community and educational grants and scholarships. She became more actively involved in the community and a trustee of the Breck School, a private college-preparatory school in Minneapolis that her two boys attended. On the board of the Minnesota Opera Company, she helped develop a long-range strategic plan. She served briefly on the board of the Resource Companies, a wealth management firm that was acquired by U.S. Trust in 1999.

ENTREPRENEUR

Ms. Frécon said:

For some time, I had this desire to do something entrepreneurial. I was in my mid-forties and felt I'd better make the move sooner rather than later. I looked inside General Mills for opportunities but didn't find anything that really excited me. When I left the company in 1998, I didn't have another job or even a specific plan in my mind. I just had this general idea of owning my own business.

She tested the entrepreneurial waters in several directions. She started her own firm, L. Frécon Enterprises, which provided strategic planning and consulting to small businesses and helped them develop long-term growth strategies. As president of her own firm, she realized she enjoyed working with small businesses. "I found it very rewarding to be able to apply my experience and skills to help them to grow their businesses and position themselves effectively in their market."

THE RYLAND GROUP INC. BOARD

She was tapped by an executive recruiter for the director position at The Ryland Group, Inc. at about the same time she left General Mills. In 1998, Ryland was just finishing a major corporate turnaround that was started in 1993 under the leadership of R. Chad Dreier, then president and CEO.

I knew one of Ryland's outgoing directors. I thought the opportunity sounded interesting, so I called him and asked about his experience with the company—the pros and cons. The company was coming out of a shaky period, and the board itself was going through a transition. I knew the company was not without its challenges. I interviewed with the directors and liked them. I thought the industry (production home building) was very interesting. Ryland was a national company with 20 divisions across the country. For me, it was an opportunity to learn about a whole new industry and to get exposure to regional economies across the country. Intellectually, that was exciting to me. Ryland was looking for someone with strong financial experience from a *Fortune* 500 company, so I could help them in that regard. For my part, I thought it would be a great chance to learn. Plus, I was embarking on creating a whole new career. It was good timing for both of us.

When she was named to the Ryland board, she was welcomed by Mr. Dreier, who was now chair, president, and chief executive officer, with these words:

Ms. Frécon brings extensive management, financial and business development experience to the Ryland board. The election of Leslie Frécon continues Ryland's efforts to bring the diversity of both work and life experiences to the table. In this industry, more and more of the purchasing decisions are being made by women and minorities. In addition to having strong business acumen, Ryland's board of directors should be able to relate to the lifestyle and needs of the modern consumer.[1]

She was the second woman on the Ryland board: Charlotte St. Martin of the Loews Corporation had been named a director in 1996. Ms. Frécon also met Leonard M. Harlan, a Ryland board member since 1984. He was president of Castle Harlan Inc., a private equity firm in New York that he co-founded with John K. Castle in 1986.

LFE CAPITAL LLC

Mr. Harlan's encouragement was partially responsible for her decision to enter the private equity investment management business. Ms. Frécon said, "As he became familiar with my background, he became convinced that my combination of corporate finance skills—buying and selling businesses, structuring deals—and my operating experience was a great skill set for private equity. He put that bug in my ear."

Not long after that, I attended a New York event honoring the top 50 women-owned businesses. It was very inspiring to see gathered in one room so many successful female entrepreneurs. That, together with Mr. Harlan's advice, helped [me] formulate my business strategy for LFE Capital. At around the same time, I developed a relationship with the Center for Women's Business Research, where I've continued as a member of their advisory council.

The combination of these events and relationships ultimately led her to establish her own private equity capital firm, LFE Capital LLC, which she formed in 1999 and for which she started raising funds in 2001. Ms. Frécon assimilated information and research on private equity and women-owned businesses from several sources, finding opportunities that others had missed.

The Center for Women's Business Research had conducted research on the rapid growth of the women's entrepreneurial marketplace since the early 1990s.[2] Ms. Frécon learned from the center that

> Between 1997 and 2006, the percentage growth in the number of firms owned 51 percent or more by women was nearly twice that of all U.S. firms (42.3% versus 23.3%). Close to 40 percent of all nonfarm businesses in the U.S. are owned by women or by women partnering 50-50 with men. One out of every 11 women is an entrepreneur. Every minute, 5 women start a business in this country.

Ms. Frécon saw an opportunity to target the women-owned and -led business market that was not being served by traditional private equity. At the same time, she could leverage her own network of women in business to find more investment opportunities. The focus on women-owned and -led businesses was a strategy to expand deal flow by positioning LFE Capital as a preferred supplier to that market. "Raising capital is a relationship business requiring an extensive network of support. Raising capital also is key to growing your business."

She structured LFE Capital to target high-growth-potential companies that the private equity market had overlooked. LFE focused on finding women-owned and -run businesses in growth-oriented industry sectors that could benefit from access to private capital and from the fund's unique style of hands-on management.

Ms. Frécon became a member of the advisory council of the Center for Women's Business Research.

> The center looks to us to help guide their research areas. Because of my interest in funding and investing in women-owned businesses, I probably was a strong voice in favor of their research on women-owned businesses earning $1 million or more in revenues, to understand how they succeed compared to other firms, as well as a number of studies about women's access to capital.

She saw the combination of disadvantages, outlined by the research on women in business and women's access to capital, as opportunities that could be mined. The research helped her develop the strategy expressed on her company's Web site that "superior investment opportunities can be found in smaller companies."

She created LFE Capital Fund I in order to broaden the firm's potential deal selection by expanding its access to the top-tier women-owned business marketplace. LFE Capital's investments focused on two targets: (1) smaller established businesses with revenues between $5 million and $75 million and at least $1 million of annual cash flow and (2) emerging businesses with at least $5 million of revenue and break-even cash flow projected within a year. LFE Capital's typical investment is between $1 million and $5 million, with the target market of women-owned businesses. LFE Capital currently has two funds under management. Wells Fargo, an investor in Fund I, made a $20 million cornerstone investment in Fund II. The remainder of LFE's capital has been sourced from other institutions, family offices, and high-net-worth individuals.

> I'm very well networked, in particular among women in leadership. There are more women in our fund than in the typical male fund. It's not what it could be, but it's a start. Most venture capital comes from institutional investors whose money is managed in midtown Manhattan. LFE Capital is in a very small segment of the market, with $60 million in committed capital.

LFE Capital has a business advisory council consisting of over 20 business and community leaders with diverse functional and industry expertise that supports the investment activities of the fund on an as-needed basis.

> Most of the members of LFE's business advisory council are also investors of the fund. The purpose of the council is to be a resource to help us evaluate investment opportunities and to address and resolve specific issues we encounter at our portfolio firms. They believe in what we are doing; they share our goals and objectives.

Ms. Frécon is closely involved in identifying and qualifying the businesses in which her company invests. She sits on their boards as part of her job of supervising the portfolio of funds. LFE Capital Fund I invested in two medical treatment/technology firms, a regional online grocery, and four firms representing a diverse selection of business services and consumer and health sectors—industries in which LFE believes strong growth opportunities exist. Ms. Frécon believes that "small, rapidly growing businesses need top-quality management as their first, second, and third priority." Members of the management team and the investment team have to be comfortable with each other. The soundness of this approach is echoed by the Diana Project report, a study of women in private equity during 1995 and 2000:

> Most venture capital investors take an active role in the entrepreneurial companies they fund. Particularly in the early days of a company's growth, they may serve as an advisor, board member, or even part of the top management team.... The overwhelming majority of entrants come into the [venture capital] industry as experienced business leaders whose reputations and networks bring substantial benefits to the partnerships.[3]

In 2006, LFE Capital began a second fund, LFE Growth Fund II, with a target of $60 million. When companies get equity capital, essentially they are bringing in a new owner who will take a significant stake in the business, so there has to be a high level of trust in the relationship. Avant Healthcare Professionals was that fund's first investment and provides an example of how the CEO of a woman-owned business sought out LFE based on the firm's reputation as a desirable business partner. Avant was founded in 2003 by Shari Sandifer, a registered nurse with an MBA and a long track record with health care staffing firms.

> Avant Healthcare was pursued by other major private equity firms. The company wasn't quite comfortable with the offers and the relationships proposed, so they reached out to their network, which included the CEO at one of our portfolio companies. That CEO recommended that Ms. Sandifer consider LFE Capital because of their experience with our management style and our female focus. Our reputation gave us a preferred position and the proprietary deal flow. Most of our portfolio companies have come to us through our personal networks of business and professional colleagues.

LFE Capital's experience is a reflection of the findings of the Diana Project research: "investors chose to review plans based on prior knowledge of an entrepreneur's capabilities—knowledge based on a direct relationship, a strong recommendation from a trusted colleague, or a referral from another venture capital partnership looking for a co-investor."[4]

Ms. Frécon is a director of Associated Packaging Company, a Castle Harlan portfolio company. That relationship represents another example of collaboration among firms: sometimes a deal is too small for Castle Harlan; other times it may be too big for LFE Capital. By working together, Ms. Frécon and Mr. Harlan increase the deal flow available to both firms. Mr. Harlan also serves on the review board of LFE Capital Fund I. Justin Wender, president and chief investment officer of Castle Harlan, serves on the investment committee of LFE Capital Fund II. The two firms draw upon their respective networks and expertise to source and manage investment opportunities.

> There are a lot of fundable companies in the Midwest, but not as many investment funds as there are on the East or the West Coast. Here, we have broad deal selection, but less competition from other private equity firms. We'll occasionally venture out of the area, such as we did with the Florida-based Avant Healthcare, but we tend to stay regional.

ADVICE TO WOMEN DIRECTOR CANDIDATES

In addition to her association with the Center for Women's Business Research, Ms. Frécon and her firm have been supporters and sponsors of WomenVenture, a St. Paul women's career and entrepreneurial education group, and Springboard Enterprises, a D.C.-based nonprofit that "educates, showcases and supports entrepreneurs as they seek equity capital and grow their companies."[5] She's a member of the Minnesota Women's Economic Roundtable and the Women Presidents' Organization.

> We need to educate women as to investment alternatives. Often I give talks to women on that subject. Women express interest in a board role and ask, "How do I get on a board?" One of the most important pre-qualifications

for a woman to get on a public company board is public company management experience. If I had not been a senior executive in a *Fortune* 500 firm, I would not have been considered as a director candidate for Ryland. Candidates with financial expertise are highly desirable, post-Sarbanes-Oxley.

Many women seeking public company board positions are not in the executive ranks and do not have the necessary experience of working in a large public company. Some women are in their forties or fifties when they first start considering a board role, and that's almost too late to start establishing the kind of competence necessary for a public company directorship.

Serving on a nonprofit, as I do at the Greater Twin Cities United Way, might qualify a person for a private company board, but it is less relevant for a public company role. Experience as an executive, at least at the *Fortune* 1000 level, is important because a director has to know what it's like to face the issues that public company CEOs experience. Executives on top corporate boards want directors who understand the world in which they live.

Ms. Frécon has been a member of the Ryland audit and finance committees since 1998 and the audit chair since 2000.

Some directors will hesitate to accept an audit committee assignment because of a perceived greater risk. I feel that my obligation is to serve on the committees where the board needs me. If I'm asked to chair the audit committee, then it is my responsibility to perform. You have to take the assignments that come to you. I consider it all part of what is involved in being on a board. I don't believe I'm naive about it. It's part of my job.

Today, I work on a number of small company boards, which is different from a board like Ryland. I look for advisors for those small boards—not necessarily *Fortune* 500 experience, but I do search for business expertise that is directly relevant to the small company's challenges. We need a willingness to roll up the sleeves, take a very hands-on approach, and be a hardworking board member.

A lot of women are focused exclusively on public boards where the director compensation is attractive. I look for directors who want to do board work because they enjoy it—they want to learn from the experience and to build relationships and credibility. It's a great educational experience to work with a small business owner. It teaches you a lot that will help you run your own business.

Private company boards are smaller in size: 5 persons on average, compared to the 9 to 11 persons on average at a larger public board. I'd like to recruit more women, but it's tough to find them. I tend to stay within my network rather than recruit through professional search firms. But I do use recruiters when I have a particularly challenging assignment.

My experience is that women are not afraid of risk. As a potential director, you need to be sure that the company has good directors and officers' insurance as well as internal controls over accounting and business operations.

The management and the business plan need to be solid. I had to be willing to take on some risk when I joined the Ryland board at that particular time, as it was coming out of a turnaround situation and under new management. I was impressed by the quality of the people and the business opportunity. Five years later, Ryland was a tremendously successful business and well regarded by Wall Street. Today, even though the housing market is under severe pressure, the company is one of the better performers due to its strong management team and balanced, consistent business strategy. So, joining a board is not without its risks. The risks need to be carefully assessed.

LESSONS LEARNED

Ms. Frécon's first choice has not always been her final choice, but she has been willing to take measured risks because she has done the due diligence necessary to manage the chances she has taken.

- She left Smith for Stanford.
- She went back to business school at UCLA.
- She changed from an arts management major to a finance major.
- She left Bank of America to become manager of acquisitions at General Mills.
- She took on the ever-increasing assignments and financial responsibility at General Mills.
- She accepted a role as a senior executive at General Mills.
- She left General Mills to become an entrepreneur.
- She changed her business model from a strategy consultancy to a private equity investor.
- She started her private equity firm with seed money from friends, family, and associates.
- She took on the Ryland director role and became chair of the audit committee before Ryland had successfully completed a turnaround.
- She took an investment and a director position in six companies in her portfolio, plus another company in the Castle Harland portfolio.

Ms. Frécon built her private equity company upon a solid foundation of market research on her target sectors and the competition. She turned disadvantages into opportunities. LFE Capital developed a sound reputation in her niche market. Now, business opportunities come to her. And she reinvests in the next generation of entrepreneurs through her private company corporate board and management roles and by educating women in business in her many collaborative efforts.

Director Profile: Donna Frame Tuttle

Donna Frame Tuttle, age 60 at the time of our interview, came to her corporate board role as an investor in minor league sports and entertainment businesses and as an entrepreneur with government experience in the travel and tourism sectors. She is representative of the investment path because of her willingness to put her own money and business-building aspirations to work in a number of partnership experiences.

EARLY YEARS

Ms. Tuttle was born in Los Angeles in 1947 and has lived there her entire life except for the few years she worked in Washington, D.C. She is the middle of three sisters, all of whom attended the Marlborough School, an independent college-preparatory day school for young women located in Los Angeles.

Her father, Lester L. Frame, a regional manager of the Fuller Brush Company, would challenge her to become the president of her class or her sorority. From a very young age, she imagined herself running her own company. While she was in college, her father started a second business as owner of light manufacturing housing communities (Les Frame Mobile Home Enterprise), where she serves as CEO today.

Ms. Tuttle entered the University of Southern California the fall after the Watts Riots broke out in South Central Los Angeles in August 1965. She majored in black history in order to better understand U.S. race relations. After graduating in 1969, she went across town for graduate studies at UCLA's Department of History, where she received a secondary teaching credential.

SAMUEL GOMPERS JUNIOR HIGH SCHOOL

She applied for her first job at Samuel Gompers Junior High School, an all-black school in the Watts District of Los Angeles. The black vice principal there resisted hiring her at first, telling her that he had tried someone just like her who lasted only three months, quitting after her tires were punctured. Ms. Tuttle talked her way into the job, saying, "I'm not unrealistic about this; I'm trained for this. I understand it and want to be here. This is my choice."

That pattern of persuasion would be repeated at several other key steps in her professional life. She taught at one of the toughest schools in the Los Angeles area for the next five years (1970–1975). There were gangs, students roaming the school, and many fights, including an attack in her classroom. Her classroom was burned the day she was married, and she had to teach in the cafeteria for the rest of the year. Even so, she loved the experience. She was tough, disciplined, and respectful. She told the students she only wanted those who wanted to go to college. Her students responded. They voted her the best teacher during her second and third years there.

In 1972 she married Robert Holmes Tuttle, at that time co-CEO of the Tuttle-Click Automotive Group. With her older sister, Diane, she started a business buying, renovating, and reselling houses in 1976. She was astounded to realize that she could earn more in real estate in four months than she made teaching for a whole year. They continued this work until the 1980s, when the real estate market dipped.

Her two daughters were born in the late 1970s. She was involved in supporting the arts locally as a member of the Decorative Arts Council of the Los Angeles County Museum of Art and the alliance board of the Natural History Museum.

THE REAGAN-BUSH CAMPAIGN

When the housing market slowed, Ms. Tuttle turned to politics full time, working with her husband, supporting Republican campaigns. She began as finance chair for state races, learning everything on the job. She ran a speakers bureau for the Reagan-Bush campaign in 1978 at the state level and then expanded it to the national scale. Campaign organizers kept asking her to take on more responsibility.

She was put in charge of the Santa Monica Assembly District campaign for Reagan for president, for which she organized volunteers. Next, as the national chair of the Youth for Reagan program, she organized a mini-convention that ran parallel to the 1980 Republican convention in Detroit, the only woman among the campaign's 14 regional operatives responsible for organizing the event.

> I met a lot of people because of my father-in-law, Holmes Tuttle, who truly was the Kitchen Cabinet for Reagan. Holmes Tuttle was one of the most incredible fund-raisers. Since I, too, am addicted to politics, we had a lot in common. I had the benefit of seeing him work a crowd and represent the candidate. I met a lot of people. It was a great experience for me to be able to learn fund-raising on the job—something that I would repeat throughout my career.

When Ronald Reagan was elected president, Ms. Tuttle and her husband debated whether to go to Washington, D.C., or stay in California. She remained in

Los Angeles, first working on Assemblywoman Carol Hallett's Republican campaign for lieutenant governor and, later, Lieutenant Governor Mike Curb's Republican campaign for governor. The Tuttles relocated to Washington, D.C., in 1982 after the loss in the Republican primary. Mr. Tuttle was appointed a special assistant to the president, one of 10 people handling White House appointments under John S. Herrington. President Reagan appointed Ms. Tuttle to the board of trustees of the John F. Kennedy Center for the Performing Arts in September 1982. She resigned the following October when she was nominated as undersecretary of commerce for travel and tourism.

UNDERSECRETARY OF COMMERCE: TRAVEL AND TOURISM

The travel and tourism agency within the Department of Commerce had a long and troubled past, with high turnover of its leadership: 13 different undersecretaries or directors in the past 10 years. In 1980, President Carter had vetoed a national tourism policy bill that would have removed authority for travel and tourism from within the Department of Commerce, placing it more directly under the control of the travel and tourism industry. A new position of undersecretary of commerce for travel and tourism was created, and Peter McCoy was appointed in November 1981. Ms. Tuttle recalled, "Then Peter McCoy put his Washington house up for sale, and that was the sign that he was going to resign his post. We never talked, but when I thought the job would be open, I decided to try for it."

She went to the Library of Congress to learn everything she could about the position, spending the next three months reading and studying every report, every transcript, and every hearing on travel and tourism. She learned about every director and read all the industry comments and remarks. "I always do this. I always prep first. I always do research about the job because at least I'm smart enough to figure out whether or not I can be a success there. I want to understand why I think I could change it or what could I do differently."

She wanted to understand why the agency had not been successful, and why there had been so much turnover and so many restructurings. For a decade, the agency had focused only on the isolated components of the industry. When she viewed the statistics in those reports, she realized the travel and tourism industry had a significant impact on the economy. However, the Standard Industrial Code was not tracking the industry's overall performance. Airline data were reported under one sector, lodgings were in another, and agents/brokers were reported in yet another category. She realized that if the travel and tourism industry came together and presented itself as a cohesive whole, it would be the second-largest industry in the country. "I realized I would have done things differently. I thought I could make a difference."

Ms. Tuttle told her husband of her plan to apply for the position. He was not enthusiastic and told her she was shooting too high. He didn't think she would get the job. He said, "Obviously we can't talk about this anymore. You have to decide what you want to do, but I have to stay out of it." He signed a letter removing himself from any involvement in the matter.

In the preliminary round of questioning, her interviewers were astounded that she knew as much as she did about the agency, travel, and the tourism industry. Concluding that she was the most qualified candidate for the job, they forwarded her name to the White House for consideration.

Members of the travel and tourism industry objected to her nomination, fearing that she was just another Californian, another friend of the president, and another short-term agency head. The industry wanted someone from within their ranks: an airline or lodging CEO.

Ms. Tuttle understood their thinking, based on the agency's reputation, track record, and turnover. She told the White House appointments staff that she wanted to meet with the industry people. They objected strongly: the normal protocol was for a candidate to endure a "quiet period" before confirmation hearings were scheduled on Capitol Hill. Again, she had to persuade them that she would embarrass neither the White House nor herself. She wanted to meet with industry members to let them see that she knew the business and to quiet their objections.

The appointments staff finally agreed. She developed a list of 30 names of industry leaders. She first called the head of the union lobbyists, all of whom were Democrats.

> Typically, I am conservative in my thinking and actions, but I surprise myself with the risks that I take in my professional life. It was a huge risk for me to go down to Watts. It was a risk for me to do the mini-convention in Detroit. Both of those decisions could have been flops that might have ruined me. And this was another big risk.

She invited Bob Juliano, a union lobbyist, to lunch. They spent three hours talking about the industry. He was impressed by how much she knew. He said, "We've always had people close to the president, but they haven't been willing to fight for us. You'd be great for this job because you understand the industry—you believe in it."

She asked Mr. Juliano to introduce her to Senators Inouye, Hollings, and Laxalt. She won over the Democratic senators early on. Then the Republicans started coming on board. Three months later, she had taken all 30 people on her list to lunch, meeting with everyone and paying for every lunch.

Next, she traveled to Los Angeles and met with industry representatives such as Bill Edwards, the CEO of Hilton Hotels, and Peter Ueberroth, who was running the Los Angeles Olympics. She knew Mr. Ueberroth from the Young Presidents' Organization and from reading trade studies he had prepared for the agency. By the time her name came before the subcommittee, all the objections had been completely turned around. The industry people supported her nomination for the job.

Ms. Tuttle was undersecretary of commerce for travel and tourism from 1983 to 1988. During her tenure, the agency more than doubled its size and opened new offices all around the world. In February 1984, President Reagan signed the

National Tourism Week Proclamation, which launched a campaign focused on tourism as a trade issue, an "invisible export." The first U.S. global marketing campaign was unveiled to 100 of the top CEOs in New York City. It was the first time that a unified marketing advertising campaign had been organized by the U.S. government and paid for by the competing companies in the tourism industry.

DEPUTY SECRETARY OF COMMERCE

Secretary of commerce William Verity took over the department in 1987, after the death of Malcolm Baldrige, and was impressed by the briefing Ms. Tuttle gave him on the Office of Travel and Tourism. Secretary Verity proposed her name for nomination as the deputy secretary of commerce, the No. 2 position in the department. While deputy secretary (March 1988–1989), Ms. Tuttle read papers and reports daily on trade issues in every economic and industry sector. She learned about the global markets that interested foreign nations. She was exposed to top briefings that gave her in-depth knowledge and understanding of international trade.

The pinnacle of her career in government was the briefing session to President Reagan before his first trip to Russia. Ms. Tuttle was asked to sit in for Secretary Verity, who was on a trade mission to the Far East. The meeting with President Reagan "in the bubble of the White House" was led by Secretary Powell and attended by the heads of state and defense, the attorney general, and the FBI. Weeks before the scheduled presentation, she studied the Department of Commerce's reports in a notebook about five inches thick.

> For me, that was climbing to the top of the mountain. There has never been anything like that experience. And there won't be. It doesn't get any bigger than that. After the briefing, I walked out and said to myself, "You know, you've just done it. This means now you can do anything because you've just done the hardest thing that you'll ever do."

At the end of her governmental tour of duty, the travel and tourism industry, which had initially doubted her credentials, awarded her their top honors: she was named the Travel Industry Association of America's woman of the year and the National Tour Association's travel industry leader of the year. The American Society of Travel Agents inducted her into their hall of fame (1987).

ADVERTISING ENTREPRENEUR

Ms. Tuttle returned to Los Angeles in 1989 and opened her own public relations company, Donna F. Tuttle Inc., which developed press releases and marketing materials for clients in the hotel, travel, and tourism industries. One of her clients was the American Society of Travel Agents, for which she prepared a TV show for their national convention. Before long, N. W. Ayer approached her and asked her to run their office in Los Angeles. Ayer was the oldest advertising company in the United States. She knew the firm from when it worked with the Department of Commerce.

Since she had not come up by way of the ad world's corporate ladder, again, she was not an obvious choice to run a travel advertising agency. She did have extensive industry contacts and knowledge of the travel/tourism industry. Still, she had to prove to the people in Los Angeles that she knew advertising as a business. She repeated the techniques that had helped her in her earlier careers: she started reading everything she could and studying the ad industry in detail.

In January 1990, she was named head of the Los Angeles office of N. W. Ayer, which was renamed Ayer Tuttle, and she redesignated the western division of the international advertising firm. She remained chair and CEO until March 1992, when Ayer Tuttle merged with the independent Los Angeles shop of Gumpertz/Bentley/Fried.

COLLABORATIONS AND INVESTMENTS

The year 1992 marked the start of her most significant entrepreneurial investment endeavors. She joined with Lester Korn, a personal friend, to form Korn Tuttle Capital Group, a diversified investment company with an office in Century City. She became president, and Mr. Korn was CEO and chair.

Korn Tuttle Capital Group would take a minority stake in business opportunities. They invested in a children's television show, which was later revived by the BBC. When a baseball team investment opportunity came up, Ms. Tuttle opted to participate on her own based on her study of the sports entertainment industry.

Also in 1992, she joined David G. Elmore in establishing the Elmore-Tuttle Sports Group. Mr. Elmore had built the Elmore Sports Group as a diverse organization with companies specializing in sports, entertainment, and event management.

The entertainment industry was becoming a major economic force in the 1990s. I wanted to own my own company. I believed that entertainment might be my niche. I was so impressed when I went to my first minor league game: tickets were between $2 and $4 each. This was not the big-ticket entertainment business, where you paid $75 to see major league teams play. I thought, "This is affordable family entertainment. With all the high tech and computerization, there's bound to be some backlash. People are going to want to get away from their desks and their computers. They'll want live entertainment." Minor leagues are recession proof. I honestly would not have put these ideas together if I had not studied industry sectors while at [the Department of] Commerce. Because I knew the industry, I just knew I was right.

In 1992, Dave Elmore, who was living in Hawaii, asked Ms. Tuttle if she knew anything about the San Bernardino, California, market. The opportunity was just right: the minor league baseball team was close enough to manage and an opportunity for her to learn the business. She had been investing in the stock market for some time and her portfolio had done very well. She borrowed $700,000 on margin against her stocks and put up a 50 percent share in the single-A minor league team called the San Bernardino Spirit. Mr. Elmore bought the other half of the team. "It was a real financial risk for me and the first time I ever took out money on margin. I paid that back in a couple of years from the stock market. I did the same thing again to buy the Inland Empire 66ers hockey team, who have now won five league championships."

Ms. Tuttle was named the International Hockey League's executive of the year in 1997–1998. Ms. Tuttle and Mr. Elmore also co-own and co-chair Centennial Management, a company that specializes in managing arenas, stadiums, convention centers, and amphitheaters, and Diamond Creations, a concession company that manages banquets, concessions, and restaurants. Both Centennial Management and Diamond Concessions operate in Utah with the hockey team. Centennial manages other stadiums and amphitheaters. Diamond Concessions runs concessions for other events.

> I own the teams and am actively involved in running the teams, from designing brochures to managing the budgets. I talk to someone connected with the businesses every day. I know everything that's going on. I do more work with the baseball team than the hockey team. But it's all very hands-on.

EARLY GOVERNANCE EXPERIENCE

From 1992 to 2000, she was a member of the Marlborough School board of trustees and co-chair of the private phase of the school's Campaign for a New Era of Excellence. Her two daughters graduated from Marlborough in the mid-1990s, and she was named Marlborough's woman of the year in 2005. From 1992 to date, she has been a member of the Saint John's Health Center Foundation board of trustees in Santa Monica, California.

In 1992, she was named a director of Herschend Family Entertainment, a privately owned theme park and entertainment company, originally based in Branson, Missouri, and now located in Atlanta, Georgia. Herschend owns Dollywood, Silver Dollar City, and other Branson entertainment sites.

> Herschend was founded by two brothers who set up a board of five outside directors. That takes a lot of confidence to turn over the approval process of major decisions and acquisitions to outside directors. There are times when we don't agree with the brothers. It is amazing to see an entrepreneurial family believe in outside governance. The brothers retired early so they could help transition the company to outside management. It's a fabulous company, very well run and very successful.

HILTON HOTELS CORPORATION BOARD

She joined the board of directors of Hilton Hotels Corporation in 1992 as the first female director, ultimately serving as chair of the corporate governance and nominating committee. She had come to the attention of Hilton's CEO, Bill Edwards, as she was interviewing for the undersecretary position. They knew of her work for the administration and at the various travel and tourism associations. The company wanted to add a woman to the board because diversity was becoming a positive corporate issue, and the company was trying to change with the times; they were conscious that it was something they should do. The other board members were comfortable that she understood the industry from a business perspective.

> The value I brought to the board was, first, professionally, I had the advertising experience. Second, I had a lot of knowledge about the industry as a whole, not just the lodging part. I knew the other components that made the industry work: the convention business all across the country, how to operate in, and sell to, the foreign markets. I knew the buyers as well as the foreign tour operators. The people on the board at the time I got there were stronger in real estate and banking. I added the perspective of being from the industry.

The management knew that the first woman director would have to be someone with whom Barron Hilton would be comfortable. Mr. Edwards recommended Ms. Tuttle to him.

Ms. Tuttle said, with some pride, "Today, we have three women on the board. Christine Garvey has a strong financial background, and Barbara Bell Coleman has experience with the lodging industry."[1]

> When you add a female perspective, you just get a totally different context for opinions, beliefs, and experiences. There isn't a board that I sit on today where that doesn't come up over and over again. Women think differently: they're much more conscious about the amenities and security features in a hotel. I can look at a hotel and say that that's a great location, but I'll also ask if it looks right, if the amenities are right, if they're reaching out to women and minorities. For so long, hotels just appealed to the traditional businessman, their main bread and butter. Women just think differently, [they are] much more intuitive and sensitive.

PUBLIC COMMISSION APPOINTMENTS

Ms. Tuttle was named to several top business leadership positions in the Southern California market because of her unique combination of business and public roles. Mayor Richard Riordan named her chair of the Los Angeles Private Industry Council (1995–2001), where she went back to her Watts roots and distributed private funds for economic redevelopment. She became the chair of the Los Angeles Convention Bureau and served on the executive committee (1996–2001). In 2003, she was a member of Governor Arnold Schwarzenegger's economic recovery council and his transition team. Governor Schwarzenegger appointed her co-chair, with

Leon Panetta, of the base realignment and closure council, chartered with mitigating the adverse local impacts of military base closures (November 2004 to date). In 2006, she became chair of the California State Chamber of Commerce (and currently is its second vice-chair). Since 2000, she's been a member of the National Collegiate Athletic Association leadership advisory board.

LESSONS LEARNED

Ms. Tuttle demonstrates how investor experience prepares someone for public company boards of directors.

1. *Market research:* Investors may not always know the industry in which they involve themselves, initially, but they end up knowing it better than almost anyone else. She did the homework, the due diligence, that prepared her to deal with teaching in Los Angeles during the post–Watts Riots period, the disjointed market components that summed up to become a national travel and tourism policy, the advertising business, and the minor league baseball and hockey business.

2. *Persuasiveness:* Investors have to overcome others' natural resistance to change. She faced doubts at many turns but turned doubters into supporters. The principal of Samuel Gompers, Republican convention organizers, the White House appointments staff, the travel industry, and Democrats and Republicans on the nominating subcommittee are all examples of early skeptics who ultimately became business collaborators. She learned that knowledge was the key to power, and acquiring knowledge became a daily habit and exercise throughout her career.

3. *Partnerships:* Investors look for management teams that will ensure the success of the venture. She partnered with her sister, her husband, her friends and associates, and contacts from the industry and government not simply to rub shoulders, but to build new business opportunities.

4. *Risk:* Investors must be willing to put their own financial "skin in the game." She invested her own sweat equity in the homes that she and her sister renovated. She took measured risks as a campaign operative and leader in California, Detroit, and Washington, D.C. She borrowed on margin against her own equity investments to buy a partnership interest in two minor league teams. She continues to grow her investment portfolio through partnerships in businesses related to the sports entertainment industry.

Ms. Tuttle demonstrates that an investment entrepreneur, by encountering great challenges, creates a deep reserve of inner confidence: a feeling that there is almost nothing she cannot accomplish.

Maybe we all need some huge challenge in our life, some tall mountain to climb. I'm sure women who do get to the top and become CEOs of these companies must think something like that too. It's difficult to describe it— everyone has their own mountain, their own standard, their own height.

I love learning experiences. I think you spend your entire life learning. Boards of directors offer real-time experiences and the chance to make decisions that affect long-term strategies. That role is a challenging responsibility because your decision will affect the company for years to come. You don't very often get to do that in real life. In your own company, you are thinking short term. On a board, you're thinking strategy and vision. I can't find that anywhere else.

I notice how comfortable I am entering into new situations. It may have a new name, a new look, but basically it's all the same. I often think about how the skills I've acquired from my different experiences have equipped me to ask the right questions and handle so much information. It is the skills that you accumulate over a lifetime that contribute to your confidence and success.

DIRECTOR PROFILE: DEBORAH ANN COLEMAN

Deborah Ann Coleman, 55 at the time of our interview, became an investor after serving as CEO and chair of Merix Corporation, a firm she spun off from Tektronix, and after 11 years climbing up the ladder at Apple Computer Inc. as CFO, vice president of worldwide operations, and CIO during the hey-day of Silicon Valley's rise to prominence. She represents the new breed of directors who combine operational, technological, and financial experience, which she now brings to her highly collaborative venture capital firm.

EARLY YEARS

Ms. Coleman was born in 1953 in the "tiny, one-mile-square city" of Central Falls, Rhode Island. She grew up in Cumberland and Narragansett, the oldest of six children—three boys and three girls. Her interest in manufacturing came from her father, who worked at some small fabricating companies, and her grandfather, who worked at Owens Corning Fiberglas® Company. At an early age, she worked at part-time jobs, saving money to put herself through college. If there was a job she could do, she did it: bookkeeper, legislative intern, a server at a beach restaurant, supermarket checkout person, housekeeper, bartender.

She was fascinated by antimatter and wanted to study physics at UC Berkeley, but her parents would not let her attend such a "radical hotbed." Her next option was to study literature at New York University in the heart of Greenwich Village. They nixed that as being too "bohemian." She opted for Brown University in Providence, Rhode Island, because it had the "New Curriculum"—students didn't have to declare a major but could take several seminar classes instead. Courses were graded on a pass or no-credit basis, which appealed to her. She left Cumberland to go live on campus.

Ms. Coleman's introduction to technology—circuit boards for calculators—and large corporate operations was her summer job at Texas Instruments in Attleboro,

Massachusetts, in the Metals and Controls Division. It was a huge facility—the largest business she'd seen at that time. Texas Instruments "was not obsessed with rules or bureaucracy," she recalled. "It was more fly by the seat of the pants. You could be a maverick if you did something well."

She graduated from Brown with a BA in English literature in 1974 and found that a tough economy awaited her. OPEC oil price increases of 1973 and soaring Vietnam War expenses created unemployment, inflation, and a difficult job market for new graduates. She found a financial management training program at General Electric's Providence offices. There were required classes in accounting, finance, financial information systems, and auditing—almost a mini-MBA. During the two-year program, trainees were given four different assignments in operational areas. GE was her introduction to a large bureaucratic company. Everything was done "by plan, on plan."

She had applied and received deferred admissions to the business schools at both Stanford and Harvard. In June 1976, she had to choose between a three-year commitment to GE's audit team or business school. At 23 years old, she was ready to get away from home, so she opted for Stanford business school, on the other side of the country. She expected just to get her degree, come home, and work in product management at a consumer company somewhere on the East Coast. Then, between her two years at Stanford, Hewlett-Packard gave her a summer job developing materials for the corporate training department.

> I thought HP was the most terrific company I'd ever seen. It was profitable, still run by the founders, and had a tremendous commitment to the community and to the values that the company espoused. They didn't just talk these words; they definitely "walked the talk." The whole Silicon Valley in the late 1970s was like a candy shop of academic, business, social, and community opportunities—absolutely amazing. It was just on the cusp of the silicon, information, and technology revolution. I got hooked.

She earned her MBA from Stanford Graduate School of Business in 1978 and continued working for Hewlett-Packard for over three years. "I loved HP. There was no reason to leave. I was promoted there three times; I had wonderful friends, mentors and associates. I was 28 and must have been out of my mind because I decided to jump ship. It took about six months to convince me."

APPLE COMPUTER INC.

Ms. Coleman joined Apple Computer Inc. in Cupertino, California, as a controller for a skunk-works project called the special task force in the fall of 1981. It was a project for which she prepared the budget and forecasts against actual expenditures. That small group became the Macintosh group in June 1982.

> The second year I was there, it gained official status as a division. We finally published a P&L; we began to have departments within the division; we had general and administrative costs, some marketing costs, and a lot of product

development costs. We used the corporate systems but were still largely out-side of the mainstream. We definitely were the pirates of the organization.

We were trying to be truly innovative and believed that the technology we were putting in this little desktop computer was going to change the world. That's why we worked 90 hours a week. I thought it was the most exciting company and industry in the world, and I got a chance to work with Steve Jobs. Working with him was like working for the biggest vision-ary you could ever imagine—a Leonardo da Vinci for the 20th century—somebody who was equally obsessed with the technical and aesthetic as-pects of the product. It was fascinating and challenging. In effect, I made the right decision.

The mid-1980s at Apple were tumultuous. The Lisa workstation was announced in January 1983, with delivery five months later. John Sculley was brought on board from Pepsi-Cola as CEO and president in April. Steve Jobs convinced the Apple board of directors to replace the Carrrollton, Texas, manufacturing opera-tion with a technologically sophisticated $50 million production facility in Fre-mont, California, just 25 minutes from corporate headquarters at 10290 Bandley Drive in Cupertino. Ms. Coleman was controller of the division at the time the Macintosh computer was announced in January 1984 at the now-legendary Super Bowl XVIII halftime commercial—"the best commercial of the 20th century," she said.

Later that year, Apple merged the divisions for the two computers (Lisa and Mac) that used the Motorola 68000 microprocessor, redesigned the Lisa to run the Mac software, and changed the display output to square pixels. That last minor technical change was what gave Apple its historic lead in graphical applications. Ms. Coleman became the group controller of the newly merged division, deeply involved in the business planning for the division's product launch, the factory, and the information systems.

In May 1984, Ms. Coleman became manager of operations at the Fremont, Cali-fornia, Macintosh plant. Apple needed a new information system to support the Fremont plant's challenging "just-in-time" manufacturing processes. Ms. Coleman's team essentially created from scratch information system tools that companies like GM and IBM were investing hundreds of millions of dollars to develop. The Apple team took Tandem Computers, known for their fault-tolerant, transaction-oriented architecture; interfaced them with the factory's numerical control equipment; and adapted software from a start-up company to monitor the costs associated with building 1,000 to 2,000 Macintosh machines daily.

In June 1985, Ms. Coleman was named director of worldwide manufacturing. She was running several parts of the worldwide operations already: the printer factory, the keyboard and accessories factory, and a disc drive factory. She added responsibility for the new operations in Mexico City, Dallas, Ireland, and Singa-pore. The job became global and she spent weeks traveling all over to learn all about the operations.

Apple's co-founder, Steve Wozniac, left the firm in February 1985, and Steve Jobs left in September 1985 following a power struggle with John Sculley. Ms. Coleman ran worldwide operations from May 1985 to April 1987, when she was named CFO of Apple Inc., the youngest CFO in the *Fortune* 500. "John Scully once told somebody, 'The thing about Debi is that she was not just loyal to Steve or the Macintosh team. She was loyal to Apple Computer. That was her No. 1 priority.' I think that's why I became a big part of his executive team and helped turn the company around."

In 1987, Worcester Polytechnic University in Massachusetts gave her an honorary PhD in engineering for the work she had done in manufacturing at Apple. She was CFO from April 1987 to April 1989, during which time the firm grew from $2.6 billion to $5.2 billion. It was a dynamic and highly stressful time. She took a six-month leave of absence in 1989 to assess her options. She returned to the finance group and then, in early 1990, was named vice president of information systems and technology.

TEKTRONIX INC.

At the end of 1992, she was recruited by both Dell Computers in Austin, Texas, and some former Apple executives at Tektronix in Oregon. She was torn: the idea of moving to Texas wasn't entirely attractive, yet she wasn't sure about Tektronix's future. After interviewing in Portland during the fall, she "just fell in love with the place."

Ms. Coleman was named vice president of materials/operations at Tektronix Inc. and relocated to Oregon in November 1992. She was brought in to completely overhaul product operations, manufacturing, and administrative procurement. She thought it would be a brief assignment, after which she would return to Silicon Valley. She rented out her California home for two years.

MERIX CORPORATION

In late 1993, she wrote a memo to the Tektronix board suggesting a strategy to combine three operations and spin them off as a separate company that would manufacture interconnect solutions for use in electronic equipment. Together, they represented $60 million in total pro forma revenue: $20 million in revenues from inside Tektronix and $40 million in revenues from the merchant market outside the company, including Motorola, StorageTec, EMC, Teradyne, and Hewlett-Packard.

The board concurred and asked her to become CEO of Merix Corporation: MER stood for Merchant Market and IX represented the firm's roots at Tektronix. Merix went public in May 1994. Ms. Coleman was chief executive officer from March 1994 to September 1999, and chair from March 1994 through September 2001. In four years, Merix grew from $40 million in merchant sales to $200 million. Today, it's a $400 million firm. The Merix board of directors, from 1994 to 2001, limited her board participation to two outside boards, both of which had to be public.

> I learned our business was even more cyclical than semiconductor equipment manufacturing. There's a lot of high-technology know-how that goes into building these basic electronic circuits, but you still end up with commodity pricing. You were really whipsawed by customers, changing demand, and competition. I left Merix after I'd become interested in angel and venture investing.

EARLY ANGEL AND VENTURE CAPITAL EXPERIENCE

Ms. Coleman's became a more active director as a result of her interest in and experience developing electronic industry networks in Portland. Larry Neitling, president and COO at Merix, was very involved in establishing the Electronic Interconnect Conference, an annual, industry-wide technology and business meeting established in 1993 in Portland. He had a strong grasp of the industry and the important role of partnerships with customers, suppliers, and employees. She had seen the value of similar inter-networking conferences in the early Silicon Valley days at Apple. She and Mr. Neitling collaborated in broadening these relationships for Merix.

> We invited our suppliers and our customers to [the Electronic Interconnect Conference]; we had panels to get really honest feedback from customers; we gave really honest feedback to suppliers; we gave out awards; we had white paper technical talks; economists would talk about the high-tech industry and we had a few team-building exercises. They were highly successful.

Another member of Ms Coleman's so-called new girls' network was Josie Mendoza, who left Hewlett-Packard to work at Apple as a technical procurement executive. Her husband, Hugh Mackworth, was another Stanford business school alumnus. "Hugh is a real serial entrepreneur and the one who persuaded me to be more actively involved in angel investments. Hugh completely stirred and shook up the angel capital industry here in Portland. He was a catalyst."

Mr. Mackworth founded the Oregon Entrepreneurs Forum's Portland Angel Network, a network of private investors that reached almost 200 members in 1998 before scaling back due to the dot-com economic downturn then revived in 2004. Mr. Mackworth also founded the Angel Oregon Conference, an annual gathering organized by the Oregon Entrepreneurs Network, drawing start-ups and would-be angels.

EARLY BOARD ROLES

Ms. Coleman's earliest board role was at a small financial joint venture between Apple and Benetton in Italy, dealing with leasing and factoring receivables for distributors in Europe. When she became Apple CFO in 1987, she was selected to serve on that board. Next, she was named to the board of Claris, Apple's software subsidiary, which had been spun off and headed by Bill Campbell from 1987 to 1991. "I was very honored to be on that board."

The next two company boards came her way by the new girls' network. The network was not simply women gathering together. The women who recommended her knew her credentials through an association at Stanford business school, they worked with her professionally at Apple or Merix, or they knew her by reputation as a valued and technically savvy business leader. They could count on her performing well in the positions for which they recommended her.

SOFTWARE PUBLISHING CORPORATION BOARD

Gaye Krause, wife of Bill Krause (the first president of 3Com and a leader in the commercialization of Ethernet), was a principal at a middle school in Mountain View. When Ms. Coleman was vice president of information systems at Apple, Ms. Krause invited her to be principal for a day. Ms. Coleman continued to be very involved in the school, helping the students and supporting their science fair. Much later, Gaye and Bill Krause were having dinner with Fred Gibbons, founder of Software Publishing Corporation, the San Jose PC graphic software company best known for Harvard Graphics. When Mr. Gibbons mentioned that he really would like to get a qualified woman on the board, they suggested he consider Ms. Coleman. The company was transitioning from a board of venture capitalists to one with more corporate experience. She served on that board from November 1991 to 1994.

Earlier, Ms. Coleman had been on the Harvard Business School board of trustees (1987–1993), and so continued her academic trustee board roles: she was on the Corporation of Brown University board of trustees from 1994 to 2000 and Stanford business school's business advisory council from 1994 to 2000, and a Marylhurst College trustee from 1994 to 2002.

She said,

> I respect these academic institutions tremendously. I had no idea academic boards worked as hard as they do, working with the administration. I learned how important the committee structure could be, especially the audit committee, and due diligence before going on a board. I thoroughly enjoyed it.

VMX INC./OCTEL COMMUNICATIONS INC. BOARDS

Her next public board was at VMX Inc. in San Jose, California, which provided integrated messaging and call processing systems to PBX business users. It was another new girls' network connection. VMX Inc. wanted someone to serve on the audit committee. Mary Pat McCarthy,[1] the auditor of VMX Inc. and a partner at KPMG LLP, recommended Ms. Coleman. A year later, VMX was purchased by

Octel Communications Inc. Ms. Coleman served on the audit committee at the Octel board from 1994 through 1997, when it was bought by Lucent Technologies Inc. She recalled:

> The head of Octel, Bob Cohn, also went to Stanford business school. We really hit it off. He was a brilliant and visionary leader who saw the potential for voice over the Internet way back then. I was really delighted to be a director of that board. I learned so much. I was thrilled to be exposed to what goes on in a young high-technology public company just as Merix was going public. We were trying to be "best practices" in everything.

SYNOPSIS BOARD

In November 1995, Ms. Coleman joined the board of Synopsys, a world leader in semiconductor design software, intellectual property, manufacturing solutions, and professional services that companies use to design systems-on-chips and electronic systems. Synopsis was a natural fit with her 20 years of experience with the semiconductor industry.

When she joined the board at Synopsys, she was welcomed by chair Harvey Jones: "We're excited about adding someone with Debi's enthusiasm and dedication to constant learning and excellence to our board. We think she can help guide the company to a higher degree of operational efficiency."[2]

APPLIED MATERIALS INC. BOARD

The new girls' network was at work again when she joined the Applied Materials Inc. board in 1997. James "Jim" C. Morgan, chairman and CEO of Applied Materials, was looking for younger corporate board members. His wife, Becky, was a classmate at Stanford whom Ms. Coleman had recommended to be the president of Joint Venture Silicon Valley, a public-private partnership with a goal to revive Silicon Valley, starting in 1990. Becky Morgan returned the favor.

Jim Morgan welcomed Ms. Coleman to the Applied Materials board with these words:

> We are very pleased to have as accomplished an industry leader as Debi Coleman join our board. Debi's unique manufacturing and operations expertise will be important resources for Applied Materials' global activities. Her experience in rapidly introducing new computing technologies and products to market will provide a unique perspective as Applied Materials pursues its purpose of enabling the Information Age.[3]

WOMEN'S NETWORKS

Another referral from the new girls' network came from Henrietta Holtzman Fore, acting administrator of the U.S. Agency for International Development and designated acting director of U.S. foreign assistance, whom Ms. Coleman knew through their membership in the Washington, D.C. International Women's Forum and the Chicago-based Committee of 200 (C200). Ms. Fore nominated Ms. Coleman, at 44 years old, as a Henry Crown fellow for the inaugural class (1997) of the Aspen Institute. "Henrietta is a wonderful woman," said Ms. Coleman, "with an amazing global business background. The Crown fellows are a group of incredibly talented, committed people. Many of them are much younger than I am—you're going to see them lead very large boards of all kinds."

Ms. Coleman has been a member of Women's Forum West (the northern California affiliate of the International Women's Forum) since 1987 and a member of C200 since 1988. She sees C200 conferences as "top-level executive development and training" and describes the International Women's Forum as focused on global issues of human rights, the environment, health care, and women's positions in the world. The mission and charter of both groups are focused on developing women for leadership, unlike the venture investment networks or the Crown fellows, which provide connections to private equity and the business world. "Both groups have fellowships for women graduate students, which I think is terrific. You get out of these organizations what you put into them."

CURRENT VENTURE FUNDS

Ms. Coleman has been a limited partner and has served as an adviser to three venture capital funds: Utah Ventures in Salt Lake City, Utah; PacRim Partners in Menlo Park, California; and Alexander Hutton Ventures in Seattle, Washington.

She and the funds' other advisors are responsible for evaluating the investment potential of companies and reviewing the fund's progress once or twice a year. Her angel investments taught her how stand-alone venture investments differed from the corporate venture experience she had had at Apple. Her first fund was Utah Ventures, where she was a limited partner in the late 1990s. She invested in fourteen companies as an angel investor between 1995 and 1999. Ms. Coleman is a member of the advisory board of PacRim Venture Partners, which merged its $25 million fund with SmartForest Ventures' $75 million fund in October 2005. Alexander Hutton Ventures is a fund with which she and her partner participate in investments across Oregon and Washington state boundaries. She sees the relationships as a way to keep her connected, knowledgeable about new technologies and investments, and able to tap new venture capital business opportunities.

SMARTFOREST VENTURES

Ms. Coleman is managing partner of SmartForest Ventures, a fund that she co-founded with technology colleague Hugh Mackworth in October 1999 as an SBIC-licensed,[4] $75 million venture capital firm that is focused on early-stage high-technology firms (semiconductor food-chain and information technology) located primarily in the Portland metro area. SmartForest has received $6.5 million since 1999 from the Oregon Growth Account, an investment fund that gets its money from the Oregon Lottery, with returns going back to Oregon's common school fund.

SmartForest invested in 19 companies in its initial round of investing. Two firms were sold successfully. Teja Technologies Inc. was sold to ARC International. TechTracher was sold to CNET Networks in San Francisco. The firm has nine companies still under active management. Ms. Coleman is on the board of six private companies: Neopad, Phoseon, Kryptiq, Teseda, ConceroGroup, and Reply!

Ms. Coleman knows that venture capital is not for the faint of heart:

> Four of our investments went bankrupt or had fire sales. In Silicon Valley, a bankruptcy is a badge of honor. We're just beginning to build a cadre of serial entrepreneurs in the Portland area, and they're also starting to show up in the Seattle/Puget Sound area. Some entrepreneurs there were among the early folks at Microsoft who then went on to RealNetworks, and now they're on their third company. Just like in Silicon Valley, they just keep going at it until they become very successful venture capitalists.
>
> Finatus was our second venture investment in 2002, and I was the leader. I loved the product: a Web-based way for small- to medium-sized businesses to track their environmental health and safety issues, to give training to employees, [and] to do their automated reporting to state, local, and federal authorities. But we just could not get the right sales model. We tried direct sales, telephone sales, we just couldn't make money, so it folded in August 2003. We had a great product, a great market, but no cost-effective way of a selling through channels. And we had an inexperienced CEO.

LESSONS LEARNED

These are all the experiences that have made Debi Coleman qualified to serve on public company boards of directors. At Stanford Graduate School of Business, Ms. Coleman met many other like-minded individuals, men and women, who became part of Silicon Valley's dynamic emerging technology marketplace and a part of her extended network of business partners and collaborators.

Her experience began in finance at such notable firms as Texas Instruments, General Electric, and Hewlett-Packard, then she ended up at tiny Apple Computer, where she worked on a project that was more vision than reality—at that time. She grew her responsibilities from finance to business planning to operations. She became a C-level leader at Apple's manufacturing operations and then took charge of information technology by agglomeration—adding to her portfolio of challenges and accepting responsibilities that stretched her talents to a global and worldwide scale of operations.

She was the youngest at some stages in her career (as CFO at Apple) and the oldest at others (as a Henry Crown fellow). She gave the board at Tektronix a proposal to build a new business, they put her in charge, and she grew it up to five times its original size.

Next, she became a venture investor fostering deal flow from California to Washington, and serving as a leader on the board of six companies, each of which would like to emulate the Apple corporate success trajectory. While essentially a technology person (software, networks, hardware), Ms. Coleman is even more a people person. "As an executive, I'm a great fan of hiring people who are smarter than you because they always make you look good if you treat them well."

She is proud of the people with whom she has worked and how well they succeeded. "Every single one of my staff from information systems and technology at Apple went on to become vice president [or] CIO or to even better jobs at significantly larger companies. They were the most incredible group of people, and they all did very well."

She sees that there are many top executive women in the pipeline, today. She cites her own C-level experience as a crucial factor in her selection as a director for major public company boards. "First, you have to prove your worth, your value to the company."

Second, she says that director candidates need to sustain their great networks and stay in the "business loop" within their industry. She points to women who have been out of the workforce for four or five years who suddenly decide to consider a board role. "We could have a lot more women on boards if, earlier in their careers, women thought about what it takes to get nominated."

Ms. Coleman says she very much enjoys working on the audit committee issues. "Not a lot of people like the audit role. I love working on strategic planning. I've taken a lot of training in corporate governance. Initially, I was a little unsure about the new Sarbanes-Oxley requirements, but now I am converted. I'm an advocate."

Finally, Ms. Coleman dispels the myth that a woman director will sit quietly in the corner of the boardroom, waiting for permission to speak her mind.

> The longer I spend on corporate boards, the more I don't sit around and wait for somebody to ask for my advice. I am very creative. I can generate more ideas and approaches [by brainstorming] in 20 minutes than most people can do in 20 years. I always try to come up with creative approaches and to look at obstacles as opportunities.

She takes her work as a director very seriously and has turned down other board offers in order to keep the time commitment to all her board roles at manageable levels. She is proud of the companies where she serves: "They are firms with very high integrity and great reputations. And that means a lot to me."

Han Solos: The Entrepreneurial Path

George Lucas described Han Solo, one of the heroes in his epic film *Star Wars,* as "a loner who realizes the importance of being part of a group and helping for the common good."[1] The women who followed the entrepreneurial path into the boardroom also struck out on their own and built their companies as a viable ship for their ambitions, while also recognizing the importance of being a rebel within an alliance.

Entrepreneurial women pursue a consulting dream and build a business entity themselves. The evidence shows they are equal-opportunity business partners, creating diversity-based growth- and profit-oriented enterprises rather than simple small, self-contained "go it alone" entities.

RELATIVE IMPORTANCE

The entrepreneurial path is a significant path to a board role: 43 women (23% of the experience cited, as shown in table 6.1) mentioned they created one entrepreneurial enterprise or more. Some built more than one business entity, while others created a company plus an investment vehicle.

DIVERSE EXPERIENCES

The women directors surveyed had options available to them within the entrepreneurial path. One typical strategy was to collaborate with others: either family members or partners from their professional field of expertise. Other women created consulting businesses as an extension of their interests, while still others created angel or venture investment vehicles through which they could fund business activities as a reflection of their own investor preferences.

Table 6.1
Entrepreneurial Path: Experience of Women on Corporate Boards of California *Fortune* 1000 Companies

N	G	A	I	E	C	Name	Company
				E	C	Marilyn A. Alexander	New Century Financial Corporation
				E		Nancy Hellman Bechtle	Charles Schwab
N				E		Angela Glover Blackwell	Levi Strauss & Co.
			I	E	C	Mariann Byerwalter	Pacific Life
				E	C	Janet Morrison Clarke	Gateway
				E	C	Adelia A. Coffman	Qualcomm
			I	E	C	Deborah Ann Coleman	Applied Materials
				E		Barbara Bell Coleman	Hilton Hotels
			I	E	C	Kathleen A. Cote	Western Digital
			I	E		Patrice Marie Daniels	CB Richard Ellis
	G	A		E		Diana Lady Dougan	Qualcomm
				E		Donna Dubinsky	Intuit
				E	C	Judith L. Estrin	Walt Disney
				E	C	Doris F. Fisher	Gap Inc.
			I	E	C	Leslie Myers Frécon	Ryland Group
	G			E		Linda Griego	Granite Construction
				E		Mary R. Henderson	Del Monte
				E	C	Patricia A. House	Levi Strauss & Co.
				E	C	Penelope L. Hughes	Gap Inc.
	G	A		E		Anita K. Jones	Science Applications Inc.
		A		E		Janet E. Kerr	CKE Restaurants
			I	E		Catherine M. Klema	Watson Pharmaceuticals
			I	E		Catherine P. Lego	Lam Research, SanDisk
			I	E	C	Linda Fayne Levinson	Ingram Micro, Jacobs Engineering Inc.
	G			E		Monica C. Lozano	Walt Disney
		A		E		Claudine B. Malone	Science Applications Inc.
				E		Cynthia H. Milligan	Wells Fargo
	G		I	E		Roslyn B. Payne	First American Corporation
				E		Lucille S. Salhany	Hewlett-Packard
			I	E		Naomi O. Seligman	Oracle, Sun Microsystems
				E		Jane E. Shaw	Intel, McKesson
				E		Linda J. Srere	Electronic Arts
				E		Charlotte St. Martin	Ryland Group
				E	C	Rebecca A. Stirn	Safeway
				E	C	Mary Alice Taylor	Autodesk
				E		Rosemary Tomich	Occidental Petroleum
	G		I	E	C	Donna Frame Tuttle	Hilton Hotels
				E	C	Jacquelyn M. Ward	Sanmina-Sci
		A		E		Kathy Brittain White	Mattel

Note: N = Nonprofit; G = Government; A = Academic; I = Investment; E = Entrepreneurial; C = Corporate.

1. *Partnering with Others:* Eleven women collaborated with others (typically men) in their professional field to establish new business entities.

   - Adelia "Dee" A. Coffman was one of seven founders of Qualcomm in San Diego, California.
   - Donna Dubinsky co-founded, with Jeffrey Hawkins, Handspring Inc. to commercialize the personal communication device in June 1998. She is one of only a few women entrepreneurs about whom a business case study has been written.[2]
   - Patricia A. House co-founded, with Thomas Siebel, Siebel Systems Inc. to provide e-business application software (initially called sales management software, later customer relationship management software).
   - Rebecca A. Stirn co-founded Aesthetic Sciences Corporation with Gary S. Petersmeyer (chair and CEO) and Edward E. Schmitt (chief scientific officer) to develop innovative medical products dealing with facial aesthetic treatments and incontinence.
   - Jacquelyn M. Ward co-founded Computer Generation Inc. in 1968 and served as its president, CEO, and chair until its sale for $245 million to UK-based Intec Telecom Systems USA in December 2000.
   - Janet E. Kerr founded the Geoffrey H. Palmer Center for Entrepreneurship and Technology Law at Pepperdine University, where she serves as executive director. She was one of five co-founders of X-Laboratories, a technology company formed to evaluate and commercialize technologies emerging from the Caltech Jet Propulsion Laboratory.

2. *Co-founders with Family:* Six women collaborated with family members to create or enhance a business either with their spouse or through family inheritance.

   - Nancy Hellman Bechtle was chief financial officer of the firm J. R. Bechtle & Co., a European-centric management consulting firm originally founded by her husband, Joachim R. Bechtle. She is chairman and director of the Sugar Bowl Corporation, which is owned by limited shareholders, including the Hellman family.
   - Doris F. Fisher founded Gap Inc. in 1969 with her husband, Donald G. Fisher, who credited her with the name "Gap" in his self-published autobiography.
   - Anita K. Jones, with her husband, William A. Wulf, co-founded Tartan Laboratories Inc., which specialized in software to optimize compilers for high-level programming languages, such as ADA, for military/defense applications. Dr. Jones was vice president of Tartan Laboratories until she and her husband returned to academia after selling their firm to Texas Instruments.
   - Monica C. Lozano is publisher and CEO of *La Opinión,* the largest Spanish-language newspaper in the United States, which was founded by her grandfather, Ignacio E. Lozano Sr.

- Rosemary Tomich owns and operates three family-owned firms (a construction company and two cattle/farming businesses), and co-founded a private bank in Palm Springs, California.

3. *Personal Consulting Firms:* Another dozen women built their own entrepreneurial consulting firms either after a successful career or between career stages. Three women provide business or marketing consulting services as individuals.

   - Marilyn A. Alexander created Alexander & Friedman LLC in Laguna Beach, California, to provide general and financial management consulting services to senior executives of corporations and not-for-profit entities.
   - Barbara Bell Coleman formed BBC Associates LLC, a Newark, New Jersey, consultancy service for corporate and philanthropic organizations.
   - Mary "Nina" R. Henderson founded Henderson Advisory, a food industry consultancy, after capping her 30-year career as corporate vice president of global core business development for Bestfoods Inc.
   - Penelope L. Hughes started Hughes Business Consultancy to develop her portfolio of interests after a successful career as the head of Coca Cola UK.
   - Claudine B. Malone established Financial and Management Consulting Inc., a general and strategic business consultancy in McLean, Virginia, after nine years as an assistant and associate professor at Harvard Business School.
   - Cynthia H. Milligan's firm, Cynthia Milligan and Associates, in Lincoln, Nebraska, delivers financial industry consulting services.
   - Jane E. Shaw's company, the Stable Network, is a biopharmaceutical consultancy she started after retiring as CEO and chair of Aerogen Inc., a specialty pharmaceutical corporation.
   - Charlotte St. Martin founded Charlotte St. Martin Enterprises after a 28-year career with Loews Hotels in Dallas, Texas, and New York.
   - Linda J. Srere became a marketing and advertising consultant after a career in corporate advertising, including CEO of Young & Rubicam.

Women who came to a board role primarily by way of the entrepreneurial path were likely to have some investment experience—founding or co-founding an enterprise based on their investment skills and interests. Many of those women who came to a board role by the entrepreneurial path also rose through the corporate ranks with finance, technology, legal, or retail/marketing expertise.

MYTH BUSTING

A commonly repeated myth is that venture capital investors and corporate buyers are not interested in doing business with women-owned companies. Research supported by Babson College shows two possible ways of viewing the women-investment challenge. Patricia Greene, Candida Brush, Myra Hart, and Patrick Saparito concluded in 1998 that "the flow of venture capital investment to women-owned businesses has been much more meager than their number and force in the economy would suggest appropriate."[3] They suggested that the small share of investment in firms led by women, while increasing from 2.4 percent in 1957 to 4.1 percent in 1998, might be explained by three fundamental factors: structural barriers (i.e., women have different networks and are not socialized to compete), human capital (i.e., occupational segregation keeps women out of fundable business sectors), and strategic choice (i.e., women prefer control over growth).

Another study led by Candida Brush reported that, by 2000, women-led firms received 5 percent of institutional venture capital although they represented 39 percent of all U.S. firms.[4] Their focus was on the demand side: how women-led firms might or might not seek out venture capital. Brush et al. found that women-led firms that *received* venture capital did behave differently:

- They tapped the advice of attorneys and company board members (not just accountants).
- They operated in manufacturing, Internet, and information technology business sectors.
- They were better educated (60% had a graduate degree).
- They had a long-term growth perspective (specifically, an exit strategy).
- They were younger.
- Their firms had higher sales.

Their research pointed to the factors that contributed to the success of women entrepreneurs: new sources of advice, ambitious strategic goals, and aspirations for growth.

They concluded that when female and minority entrepreneurs matched their business needs to the preferences of venture capitalists, they were successful in finding funding: "Women-led ventures more likely to receive funding are those in early stage financing, located in the West and Northeast, and in computer hardware/software business sectors."[5]

LESSONS LEARNED

The very strong growth in the number of entrepreneurial women-owned businesses nationwide creates opportunities to expand the supply of female director candidates if women-owned businesses grow to investment scale. The U.S. Small Business Administration estimated there were 6.5 million majority-owned women-led businesses in 2002. Another 2.7 million businesses were jointly owned by men and women, producing a combined total of 9.2 million firms partially or wholly owned by women. Majority-owned firms led by women entrepreneurs increased 19.8 percent since 1997.[6]

Women-owned businesses that earned revenues of $1 million a year or more represented just 1.8 percent of the total (about 117,000 firms). The Center for

Women's Business Research estimated that 13.3 percent of these (about 15,600 firms) had a board of directors. The many more businesses that earned less then $1 million a year (6.4 million firms) reported that barely 4.6 percent of them had a board of directors. Even so, that meant almost 300,000 smaller firms with boards of directors or advisors.[7] Thus, the great potential of the entrepreneurial path into the boardroom could be enhanced if women-owned businesses heed the advice to enter viable industry sectors, pursue growth markets, tap partnership potentials, and grow their business through teamwork with employees and capital investment. In addition, successful women-owned businesses can benefit from the creation of a board of directors or advisors to help them chart the course into strategic growth.

The women directors in our sample created firms in fields that were of interest to businesses: technology, biopharmaceuticals, finance, marketing, media, and strategic planning. Some of the companies they founded or co-founded became recognized leaders in the marketplace. Other women extended and enhanced the value of family company assets they inherited. Still other women formed companies that were an extension of their own strategic career planning or re-prioritization. These are the some of the key reasons the women were tapped as corporate directors.

THE WOMEN INTERVIEWED

The women entrepreneurs who were interviewed are Judith L. Estrin and Lucille S. Salhany, the former a high-tech Silicon Valley start-up expert and the latter a media/entertainment entrepreneur.

The entrepreneurial path into the boardroom offers women in any field a chance to define and develop skills, relationships, and markets that they identify in those other settings. Women-owned businesses constitute one of the fastest-growing segments of the economy. Women can also create governance boards for their own businesses, where they can tap the talent pool of experienced women to help create viable and thriving top publicly held companies.

Director Profile: Judith L. Estrin

Judith L. Estrin, age 53 at the time of our interview, came to her board roles as a "serial" entrepreneur in the classic Silicon Valley tradition. She co-founded four high-technology companies, the last of which was a company in the business of building innovative companies. As an entrepreneur, she has unique insight into the different roles that directors perform at various stages of corporate development. Today, she is a public company director at FedEx and Disney, and a director of two small private technology firms.

EARLY YEARS

Ms. Estrin was born in 1954 and grew up in Southern California, the middle of three sisters, each highly accomplished in science and technology. Their parents are leaders in computer science and biomedical research, both professors emeriti in the Computer Science Department in the School of Engineering and Applied Sciences at UCLA. Her father, Gerald "Jerry" Estrin, was an academic advisor to two leaders in the Internet revolution: Vinton Cerf and Paul Baran. Her mother, Thelma Estrin, has a PhD in electrical engineering and was an innovator in the field of brain research and an early advocate of medical informatics—the application of computers to medical research and treatment. Judith Estrin said:

> Both of my parents were very strong role models and not just in terms of computer science. My mother was a built-in role model as a strong professional. My father was equally exemplary in the way he treated my mother. All three sisters were raised in an environment where we could assume there were no limits to what we were going to do as females.

Ms. Estrin began her career as a computer scientist and technologist then migrated into the business world. She received her BS in math and computer science from UCLA in 1975. She went to Stanford University for her master's in electrical engineering and computer science (1977) and worked with the same Vinton Cerf who was leading the development of the basic Internet protocols. Mr. Cerf said of Ms. Estrin: "She has been able to translate technical concepts and ideas into practical business models."[1]

Ms. Estrin told *IEEE Spectrum: People,* "What I liked about math and computer software was the problem-solving aspect—which may be what I like about business. It's also about taking large problems and figuring out how to break them into pieces and solve the pieces to get you to an end result."[2]

She had job offers from Hewlett-Packard, Intel, and Xerox Office Systems Division, large organizations that produced and sold office products and equipment. She chose Zilog Corporation in Campbell, California, because she thought the opportunities for growth were greater: "Zilog was a small company [about 50 employees], where I got a taste of the excitement and innovation of a small organization. From the very beginning, I was very interested and involved in the local area network market, which was just beginning to develop."

From 1976 to 1981, Ms. Estrin worked on the architecture for next-generation chips and early LAN technology. She became engineering manager there, reporting to general manager Bill Carrico, who joined the firm in 1979.

> Initially at Zilog, I was a technical contributor then quickly went into management, where I found that I really liked leading and managing people steeped in the technology and in the technology business. I discovered that I was more interested in the people side than sitting in front of a computer all day.

Her boss and a group of other engineers left Zilog to found Ungermann-Bass to develop computer networking systems for large-scale clients. Zilog was sold to Exxon Office Systems in 1980, and a year later Ms. Estrin joined the team at Ungermann-Bass.

BRIDGE COMMUNICATIONS INC.: START-UP 1

She worked there for about five months. When Bill Carrico left Zilog, she decided to join him to start their first corporate venture, Bridge Communications Inc., an "internetworking" company to support their idea of gateways: hardware and software connecting different LANs over Ethernet. As they were putting the business plan together, they decided to bring on the initial engineering management as they went after venture capital. They founded Bridge Communications Inc. in November 1981, with Ms. Estrin as the vice president of engineering, very much on the technical side. They invited Eric Benhamou, who had worked for her at Zilog, to join them as vice president of software, and a fourth founder, Jean-Pierre Boespflug, as the vice president of hardware.

Bridge Communications was their first experience starting a company and their first time going after venture capital. They had two rounds of venture capital and one mezzanine round before the company went public in 1985. Two years later, the company was profitable at $70 million in annual revenues and 450 employees, selling communication servers, internetworking routers and bridges, and competing successfully against more established competitors. Ms. Estrin was executive vice president and Mr. Carrico was CEO. They were married that year.

> Our experience at Bridge was both incredibly stressful and incredibly exciting. When the company went public, I had a sense of responsibility—making our stock available to lots of people we didn't know. We were profitable and had a sense of commitment to continue to make it successful.

Personal computers were becoming a major force in the market. They knew that Bridge had to quickly scale up by either entering the PC-connectivity market or merging with another company. She had known Bob Metcalf, the founder of 3Com, when they were at Stanford. Bridge and 3Com negotiated a merger whereby 3Com could expand their business, and Bridge's investors could either own part of the larger company or gain liquidity. Bridge was acquired by 3Com in September 1987. Ms. Estrin moved over as head of the Bridge Communications division, while Mr. Carrico became president of 3Com, positions they held until 1988. She recalled, "The merger did not turn out as we had hoped either from a personnel or a strategy perspective. After about nine months, Bill Carrico and I decided it would be better for us to move on."

NETWORK COMPUTING DEVICES INC.: START-UP 2

In February 1988, a group of engineers who had developed a prototype of an X-terminal (a graphically oriented terminal that runs applications on the network of a shared server) formed Network Computing Devices in Mountain View, California. Ms. Estrin and Mr. Carrico were tapped as executive vice president and CEO, respectively. Together, they successfully pursued some of the same Silicon Valley venture capital interests that had supported the creation of Bridge Communications. Two years later, in June 1992, Network Computing Devices went public, and the following year, she became CEO, while Mr. Carrico became chair.

> When you do something the second time, it's never exactly the same. The timing and markets were different. We knew what to do and what to expect. Our son was born in 1990, right in the middle of all this. We took him on all of the trips for the road show—probably the only two-year-old to go on an IPO road show. Not to the presentations, though.

Network Computing Devices was doing well, but by the time it went public, the remaining growth in the market was not enough to generate returns for their investors. "It was a humbling experience. [Network Computing Devices] started out very strong, but it was not a success over the long term. We began to branch out into software and e-mail through acquisitions. In September 1994, I needed a break and replaced myself as CEO."

For the next two quarters (September 1994–March 1995), Ms. Estrin was a computer industry consultant on her own. "We took about six months off. During that time off, I discovered that I wasn't very good at retiring."

PRECEPT SOFTWARE INC.: START-UP 3

In March 1995, Ms. Estrin and Mr. Carrico incorporated Precept Software in Palo Alto, California, with $7 million in start-up capital. Precept was one of the very early video-streaming providers for corporate intranets and the Internet. She was president and CEO.

Precept's new technology product, based on multicast, was interesting to Cisco because it gave their customers reason to upgrade their infrastructure. In the third quarter of 1996, Cisco took a minority share in the company and agreed to re-sell its multimedia networking software products. Cisco acquired the remaining shares of Precept Software in March 1998. Ms. Estrin became chief technology officer and senior vice president. John Chambers, president and CEO of Cisco, welcomed her with these words:

> Judy Estrin is one of the great entrepreneurs and leaders in Silicon Valley, and we are thrilled to have her join us. She brings a unique blend of technical knowledge and business skills which will help maintain Cisco's leadership as we move into the next generation of integrated voice-data-video networking.[3]

As CTO, she was responsible for oversight of mergers and acquisitions, legal and governmental affairs, and client-oriented consulting engineering groups, as well as guiding long-term research and development and driving the company's strategic technology investments. She said:

> I had never worked at a big company before. On the one hand, it was a fascinating experience. From 1998 to 2000 they grew from 18,000 to 20,000 people. They were one of the stars of the bubble. I was responsible for looking forward in terms of the long-term R&D. For the last year I was there, I also ran their centralized software organization. It was a fascinating job.

PACKET DESIGN LLC: START-UP 4

Ms. Estrin said, "I had committed to John Chambers that I would work at Cisco for at least two years, thinking that I would stay longer if it felt like the right fit. But after two years, I decided that I wanted to go back to my own company, building my own culture, rather than working in someone else's."

Packet Design LLC, in Mountain View, California, was established in May 2000. Mr. Carrico was chair, and Ms. Estrin was president and chief executive officer. This time, they decided to build a new and different company, something similar to a high-tech incubator.

We decided we didn't want just to start another product company. We wanted something that would look a little farther out—what I called medium-term innovation—so we created an organization with researchers and developers to work on a portfolio of different technology projects. The idea was to spin out different companies to product-ize the technologies. It was an interesting experiment in a business model.

Their company would conduct serious medium- to long-term research on emerging Internet technologies, match up researchers with development engineers to maximize the real-world product orientation of their analyses, build close relationships with potential clients, and build and spin-off projects into separate entities that could be sold. Two sister companies were established, which is how most venture firms are set up. Packet Design LLC, the limited liability company, held the assets and equity. Packet Design Management Company LLC employed all the staff. The combined enterprise began with $24 million in funding from Foundation Capital, individual investors, and their own resources. Sun Microsystems Inc. invested another $5 million in November 2001.

Packet Design LLC started with six projects dealing with different aspects of Internet technology and spun off three corporations to which they transferred intellectual property and products while retaining ownership positions and continuing to assist them in their development, funding, and management of common services. The three spin-offs were Vernier Networks (March 2001; now Automatic Designs), PrecisionI/O (March 2003), and Packet Design Inc. (March 2003).

"I consider Packet Design [Inc.] to be the most successful of the three spinouts," she said. "We started in 2000, focusing on the networking businesses, but the bottom fell out of the market in 2001 and 2002."[4] Packet Design LLC was dissolved in 2007, and the assets were distributed back to the investors. Ms. Estrin bought out Packet Design Management LLC and renamed it JLABS in November 2008. It now serves as the vehicle through which she consults, speaks, and writes.[5]

FEDERAL EXPRESS CORPORATION BOARD

Ms. Estrin joined her first corporate board, that of Federal Express Corporation, in 1989 while heading her first entrepreneurial venture, Bridge Communications.

When you are a venture capital start-up, your initial board consists of your investors. In the early days of Bridge, our venture capitalists were on our board. Later on, we brought on more independent board members, including Jim Barksdale, who at the time was COO at FedEx. He was a terrific selection.

Fred Smith, head of FedEx, was looking to add a woman to his board but wanted someone with a strong technology background and an entrepreneurial perspective. Jim Barksdale recommended Ms. Estrin to Mr. Smith. "When I came on the FedEx board," she said, "not only was I the only woman, but also I was

20 years younger than the other directors. It was a very different experience. There wasn't another woman added until 1999, when Dr. Shirley Ann Jackson came on board."

Ms. Estrin currently chairs the information technology oversight committee, which was created at Mr. Smith's initiation in collaboration with Ms. Estrin and Dennis Jones, the firm's chief information officer.

ROCKWELL INTERNATIONAL BOARD

Ms. Estrin joined her second corporate board at Rockwell International in Seal Beach, California, while she was at her second startup. Donald R. Beall, the CEO of Rockwell, invited her onto the board, where she served from September 1994 to 1998, at which time the company merged into the Boeing Company. She was a member of the science and technology committee.

> Initially, I declined because I thought I was too busy. But Don Beall flew up to persuade me. Rockwell at the time was a structurally different company: they were more diverse than they are today and had some interesting things going on in the communications chips business. I thought it would be an interesting experience. After the company restructured and spun off its semiconductor-related businesses, I had less value to add to the company. And I was getting busy.

SUN MICROSYSTEMS INC. BOARD

In August 1995, Ms. Estrin was invited to join the board of Sun Microsystems Inc. by Scott McNealy, the CEO, and John Doerr, a Sun director and general partner in the venture capital investment firm Kleiner Perkins Caufield & Byers. She was starting up her third firm, Precept Software. She was the only woman director at Sun until 1999, when Naomi O. Seligman, another technology industry expert, joined the board. Ms. Estrin was on the audit committee until June 2003 then left the board in November 2003, as Sun had invested in her fourth enterprise, Packet Design LLC, and she felt it was better not to be on the Sun board.

WALT DISNEY COMPANY BOARD

In 1998, Michael Eisner was just beginning to try to redo his board at Walt Disney Company in response to criticism that there were too many insider directors. George Mitchell, who knew Ms. Estrin from the FedEx board, suggested her as a director candidate. She met with Mr. Eisner and the other directors and was invited to join the board. She chaired the compensation committee for five years and currently serves on the governance and nominating committee. Today, she is one of three women (with Susan Arnold and Monica Lozano) on a board of 12 directors.

ARCH ROCK CORPORATION BOARD

Ms. Estrin became a director at Arch Rock in March 2005 because she knew Dave Cullar, co-founder and CTO of the firm, and helped them get their start-up financing. Roland Acra, president and CEO since December 2005, also worked with her at Cisco and started his career in America as an intern at Bridge. Arch Rock is a systems and software company that builds products and technology for wireless sensor networks with funding from Intel Capital, Intel's venture capital organization; Shasta Ventures; and New Enterprise Associates.

LESSONS LEARNED

Today, through the vehicle of JLABS LLC (formerly Packet Design Management LLC), Ms. Estin continues to serve as a board member and advisor in addition to speaking publicly. Her book, *Closing the Innovation Gap: Reigniting the Spark of Creativity in a Global Economy* (New York: McGraw-Hill, 2008), discusses innovation from the business perspective while presenting her insights into "What are the fundamentals for creating innovative cultures and leading innovation organizations? It also deals with the broader national issues of policy, education, and investment in research."

For three years starting in 1998, Ms. Estrin was named to *Fortune* magazine's list of the 50 most powerful women in American business. In 2002, she was inducted into the Women in Technology Hall of Fame in Encino, California.

> There are two types of honors or lists. The women's organizations honor and highlight role models for other women. Those are positive things to do. The lists that rank women are rather arbitrary. They are nice to be on, but you're eligible only if you manage a certain size of budget. When I was at Cisco, the budget I managed was sufficient [for] me [to be included]. As an entrepreneur or a board member, I wasn't eligible to fit on those lists. There are many talented individual women who are not included on those lists. I think the lists help the companies. They really don't make me a different person.

Judith Estrin is a role model as a collaborative business builder. She's started businesses, taken them public, merged them with larger firms, rolled them back, and handed them off to new management. Each experience has provided her with valuable insight for the next round of entrepreneurial challenge.

The small company exposure gave her, as a technologist, early hands-on management experience. Her start-ups taught her that sometimes businesses must prime their own pumps; that is, they must install networks to create demand for the innovative products the company really wants to sell (bridges, routers, or multicast video). She learned the importance of selecting a successful strategy (PCs versus communications, consumer versus enterprise target market). Her ability, with Bill Carrico, to tap venture capital was unparalleled, yet she learned that when a bubble bursts, everyone is affected. Venture capital helped kick-start their great product ideas, but only timing, competition, and great management can keep great businesses going.

Her board roles came to her, first, because she has impressive technical insight in her areas of expertise (networks, innovative IP platforms, and products) and, second, because she has the wealth of experience with the ups and downs of real business ownership—to which only a select few entrepreneurs can lay claim.

Ms. Estrin is a technology leader who became an entrepreneurial business leader by building businesses in one of the most competitive marketplaces: network products and systems.

> I think it is very important that I have always thought of myself not as a woman board member, but as a person with diversity of perspective and diversity of thought. I think I am a valued director more for the diversity of my thinking, not so much for the specifics of gender or experience. On a board, I am not there to focus on women's issues. I am there to be a full board member looking at all of the issues of the company.

Director Profile: Lucille S. Salhany

Lucille S. Salhany, age 61 at the time of our interview, came to her board roles after a long career as an "intra-preneur"—an entrepreneur inside the corporate entertainment and television media world. She is a director at Hewlett-Packard, having transitioned from the corporate board of Compaq Computer Inc. when it merged into Hewlett-Packard. She is on the board of Echo Bridge Entertainment, an independent film distribution company that she co-founded with Michael Rosenblatt.

EARLY YEARS

Ms. Salhany was born in 1946 in Cleveland, Ohio, where her parents owned a small grocery store. She has one older sister. "Mom worked with Dad in the store," she recalled. "We all lived the business at home. There were conversations all the time over the dinner table about business and politics. My mother was a tremendous influence on me. We were very close."

Ms. Salhany's family came from Lebanon and, as in other "old world" families, girls were not pushed to get an education. Her parents suggested that she go to a nearby college so they could keep an eye on her. She went to Kent State University, majored in elementary education, and became active in several campus activities—she was vice president of her dorm and the first freshman on the campus-wide advisory council. "I was into every organization, and sometimes I went to class. I was a typical 18-year-old: sure that I knew everything and that I didn't really need school."

The lack of attention was evident in her grades. After her first year, she returned to Cleveland. "Why go back to school? I'll just get married and have kids," went her thinking. "I was married in 1967. I was very young, three days shy of my 21st birthday—just a baby myself." But she loved working and decided she wanted a career, so took on a number of secretarial/clerical jobs.

WKBF-TV

Over the next eight years, she worked her way through entry-level positions in the television industry. Her first job was at a UHF station in Cleveland, working for Art Hook, the program manager of WKBF-TV. After two-and-a-half years, she left and became a production assistant at a "barter music show" (*Scene 70*). Next, she did publicity, promotion, and marketing for Children's Theater. At Art Hook's suggestion, she returned to WKBF-TV to work on promotion under Mel Harris, the new program manager. She began as an assistant copy writer for Sandy Hamer, who reported to Mr. Harris as head of publicity and production and who was the only woman in management. When Ms. Hamer left that position, she recommended Ms. Salhany as her replacement. Then Ms. Salhany took over as WKBF's program manager after Art Hook was transferred to WLVI-TV in Boston and Mel Harris became general manager.

During this period, Ms. Salhany transformed herself from a 21-year old who thought she was going to "just get married and have kids" into a professional woman who acquired experience and confidence through working hard at what she liked, while absorbing the know-how available from the people whom she admired.

> Art and his wife, Shirley, were so instrumental in my getting ahead. Not long after I started working for Art, I told him that someday I was going to have his job. It was the '60s, when women were not yet considered management material. I had to learn the production business by just taking things over.
>
> I was cocky and bossy when I first met Mel Harris. He asked me what I wanted to do with my life. I said, "I don't know. Maybe I'll just stay at home, watch soap operas, and eat bonbons." He flared his nostrils and then challenged me: "Oh no, you won't. Now sit up and listen to me." I listened, and we've been best friends ever since.
>
> After I became program manager, I'd pretty much turned into a bitch on wheels—bossy, someone who didn't listen to anyone, someone who thought she knew everything. In reality, it was a defense mechanism, because there was still a lot I didn't know. It was pretty hard—there were no other women managers. Shirley Hook gave me the book *The Feminine Mystique* to read. I thought, "This is me, this is it." I felt as if I had come home—after reading that, I was much more comfortable with myself.

That also was the end of her first marriage after seven-and-a-half years. "I decided not to change my name because I believed I was established in the business. It turned out that I was just at the very beginning of my career."

Mel Harris left as general manager, and WKBF-TV was sold in 1975. She tried for his position, but it was too big a stretch for the company to consider. As an alternative, they gave her a position as program manager at the Boston station. The general manager there did not recognize her capabilities and declined her request for a promotion to head public affairs. She realized there were no more opportunities for her there. "I was told, 'You don't want the job, you just want the title.' I realized they still looked [at] me as just a secretary. I wanted to get ahead, but there were no more opportunities at the station. It was just a reflection of the times."

JOHN POLCARI AND THE BOYS

She met John Polcari after she transferred to the Boston station in 1975. He owns the Boston Restaurant Association, an "authentic Old World Italian restaurant." They were married in 1979, just two weeks before she moved to the Taft Broadcasting Philadelphia programming office. She commuted back to Boston on weekends. "That was the beginning of my married life. But we've been together for 31 years. I married someone who was 15 years older than I am. We adopted two boys from Beirut in the middle and late 1980s. They are 23 and 20 years old today, and they are marvelous."

TAFT BROADCASTING COMPANY

Kent Replogle, another friend from Metromedia, recommended her for a job as general manager at Taft Broadcasting's Philadelphia station. But Taft only hired women as program assistants and secretaries, not full directors or managers. Another strike against her was her background in programming, not sales. Network management didn't believe that creative staff could run the business end. When Ro Grignon of Taft interviewed her, he said as much. Then he offered her a staff job as head of programming. "I liked Ro—he seemed very straightforward. I thought that might be interesting, so I accepted."

Ms. Salhany became vice president of television programming at Taft Broadcasting in 1979 and for the next six years significantly expanded its program offerings. Taft grew into a major station group through initiatives that she spearheaded. She persuaded Taft to join the New Program Group, with representatives from all the major station owners: Metromedia, Gannett Broadcasting, Hearst Broadcasting, and Storer Communications. The New Program Group was created to produce programming because the stations could not get enough original material from the studios.

> The [New Program Group] was thinking about doing something with a daytime talk show starring a woman on ABC in Chicago: Oprah Winfrey. I thought she was phenomenal, wanted Taft to syndicate the show in all our markets, and had to pursue the syndication rights through King World for weeks. They finally relented.

She committed Taft markets to airing the show before anybody in the company ever saw it live. Many Taft station managers were upset. They thought the program would bomb because the star was not as attractive as the other talk-show hosts. Some managers called Mr. Grignon, her boss, yelling furiously, "Who does she think she is, cramming this down our throats?" Her boss stood behind her.

The first episode of *AM Chicago* starring Oprah Winfrey aired January 1984. Ms. Salhany locked down the King World agreement in the winter of 1984. Taft stations began syndicating the show in September 1985. And the rest is history. "I was a hero at Taft, but by the time the show aired, I had left to go run Paramount TV in Los Angeles. But I kept close ties with everyone."

PARAMOUNT DOMESTIC TELEVISION

She had progressed from general manager of Taft's Providence station to being in charge of cable, and then the company opened an office for her in Boston. She finally moved back home, where she and her husband had adopted their oldest son. She began to get job offers from New York and Los Angeles. Mel Harris, now president of Paramount TV, invited her to become president of Paramount Domestic Television, running the syndication arm in Los Angeles. "Mel and his boss, Frank Mancuso, took a tremendous risk on me. No woman had ever been hired for that position before. No one had ever come from the creative side or from the station side to head program syndication. It was unheard of."

She and her husband talked it over. A New York job meant she'd have to find housing outside New York City to raise their son. The Los Angeles offer meant she could have a home closer to work, and their son could have something of a normal life. The real pressure would be on her husband.

> John said, "What difference does it make if I take a plane to New York or to Los Angeles? I think you've got to do it, because if you don't, you won't be happy for the rest of your life." I thought that was unbelievable and liberal for an old Italian guy. I think we both liked the idea that the LA offer was from Mel and Ruth, whom I had known for so many years. And I had a lot of friends out there. So, I moved again to Paramount TV in Los Angeles. And for the next 13 years, my husband commuted to see us.

Ms. Salhany was president of Paramount's domestic television group from 1985 to 1991. She reported to Mel Harris, who reported to Frank Mancuso (president of Paramount's film division within Gulf + Western).

"At Paramount," she said, "they allowed our division to do things that no other TV group had done. We were so successful. Then, suddenly there was this sea change at Paramount." In March 1991, after a bad year of movies, Paramount's Martin Davis told Frank Mancuso that henceforth he would report to Stan Jaffe, the new president and COO of Paramount Communications.[1] Mr. Jaffe brought in Brandon Tartikoff (former NBC Entertainment chair) to take over as head of Paramount Pictures, the film entertainment group.

> Frank is one of the finest people I ever met in my life—a great boss. Stanley was tough, but also terrific. Even though I liked Brandon, I didn't think he

was right for that position. I was afraid he was going to try to squeeze Mel out, which bothered me a lot. I began talking to Barry Diller over at Fox.

Those years were like a game of musical chairs among TV and media ownership interests. She knew Barry Diller when she syndicated programming for Paramount stations and he was chair of Paramount Pictures. Mr. Diller moved to Twentieth Century–Fox in 1984. The following year, Fox was acquired by Australian newspaper mogul Rupert Murdoch.

TWENTIETH TELEVISION

Barry Diller had given her a standing invitation to join him at Fox anytime she wanted. Negotiations went on for about three months. The offer was for a bigger job than Mel Harris's and more freedom than she had had at Paramount. In May 1991, she joined Fox as chair of Twentieth Television, a division of Fox Broadcasting Company (the production and syndication arm of Fox Inc.).

Barry Diller was a tough boss and mercurial, but I thought he was great because he was a man of his word. Honoring your word is very important to me. Barry would say, "If you commit to something, bad or good, you better live with it." I believe that Barry started the Fox network and made it what it was.

Both Barry Diller and Rupert Murdoch were titans whose egos often clashed. Mr. Diller left Fox in April 1992 to take over as chair and CEO of QVC. Ms. Salhany now reported directly to Mr. Murdoch. She was prepared to move on to another network when Mr. Murdoch asked her to run the Fox network. In January 1993, she became the first woman to manage an American broadcast TV network when she was appointed chair of Fox Broadcasting Company (a subsidiary of Rupert Murdoch's Fox Inc.).

We got a tremendous amount accomplished in the year and a half that I was at Fox network. We went from four to seven nights of programming. I told Rupert that we'd better do it or Paramount would get those nights because I had laid the groundwork for that while I was there.

Next, we launched *The X-Files* and *Party of Five*. When I had been at Twentieth Television, we produced *The X-Files* with Peter Roth, head of programming there. After I moved over to Fox network, I bought it. *X-Files* was the most financially profitable program in the history of the company, except for *The Simpsons*, today.

I learned a lot from Rupert. He was a real visionary who put his money behind his words.

UNITED PARAMOUNT NETWORK

There was a clash of wills and personalities between Ms. Salhany and Mr. Murdoch. Each became disenchanted with the other. She resigned from Fox in

June 1994 to become president and CEO of the newly formed United Paramount Network (UPN). It premiered January 16, 1995, with a two-hour episode of *Star Trek: Voyager* and special-interest situation comedies like *Moesha*.

> I love television. It is an amazing medium. Free over-the-air television was the great equalizer that entertained everybody, whether rich or poor. It offered a national consensus. When *Johnny Carson* or *Laugh-In* was on the air, the next day everyone at the watercooler would be talking about the show. How many other countries could watch Neil Armstrong walk on the moon? I tried to never underestimate the audience. Some people in the business from New York or LA might say they just fly over the Midwest. But growing up in Cleveland as I did, I think I learned to respect the audience in the middle of the country.

In December 1996, Viacom (Paramount's parent company) began buying up UPN, an acquisition that was completed in 2000. After 13 years of long-distance commuting to Los Angeles, Ms. Salhany resigned from UPN to return to Boston in May 1997. "I didn't want to stay at the network under Viacom control. My husband had been sick in 1995 and 1996. My oldest son was going into the seventh grade. I had done everything. It was time to come back home."

JH MEDIA

Ms. Salhany now transformed herself from someone who operated independent business units within the corporate entertainment and television media world (an "intra-preneur") to a genuine entrepreneur in charge of her own business enterprise. Her employment contract at UPN had been with Chris-Craft Industries, which had a controlling interest in UPN. When she returned to Boston, she started her own consulting firm (JH Media, named after her two sons, Jake and Hal) with an 18-month media consulting contract with Chris-Craft beginning in October 1997. She also consulted with Macy's to help them negotiate with the networks for coverage of their Thanksgiving Day parade. And she advised NASA on how to market its content to the media industry.

LIFE F/X INC.

Ms. Salhany recalled:

> I met Michael Rosenblatt on an airplane trip: I was going to a board meeting in Los Angeles, and Michael at the time was running Atlantic Entertainment. It turned out that I used to sell Michael's movies when he was doing deals with Paramount. We had a number of mutual colleagues and became instantaneous friends.

Several years later, Michael Rosenblatt approached her with a technology that he wanted to build into a company. The software technology created photorealistic 3D digital human faces (avatars) for the Internet. They raised investment money together and took the company public in December 1999. She joined him as CEO, co-president, and a director on the board, while he became chair.

LifeF/X could not get funded after the dot-com market slide and closed down in March 2002. Running a public company and being on the other side of the board as a director was an interesting perspective for me. It was an amazing experience for me to see all that the CEO of a company has to go through with shareholders, with people trying to get inside information, and with the games that investors try to play with your stock. It was an education.

ECHO BRIDGE ENTERTAINMENT

Ms. Salhany and Michael Rosenblatt collaborated again in creating Echo Bridge Entertainment, a firm in Newton, Massachusetts, that they co-founded in February 2004 to distribute independent films. Michael Rosenblatt is now the managing partner, while Ms. Salhany serves on the board. She is responsible for evaluating independent film libraries for prospective acquisitions. The value she brings to the firm includes her experience in product selection, marketing, and management. The company is looking to become more involved in television production and recently won financial backing from J. P. Morgan.

EMERSON COLLEGE TRUSTEESHIP

Ms. Salhany knew Jim Coppersmith, the chair of the board of trustees at Emerson College, from her Boston TV station days. The board was looking for new trustees with business experience. They invited her to speak to the graduate school's commencement ceremonies. Afterwards, they gave her an honorary doctorate of humane letters and invited her to become a trustee of Emerson in 1992. The following year, Emerson invited Jacqueline "Jackie" Liebergott to become the first woman president of Emerson College.

In 2003, Emerson announced that a scholarship had been created in honor of Ms. Salhany's parents to promote media education opportunities for a more diverse population: "Emerson College has received a gift of $200,000 from Compaq Computer Corp. in honor of Lucille Salhany, a member of the Board of Trustees of Emerson College and a member of the Board of Directors of Compaq Computer. This gift will be used to create The Hal & Tillie Mady Scholarship."[2] Said Ms. Salhany, "My goal was to create more educational opportunities for the truly creative people who make the entertainment industry the success it is today."

EARLY BOARD EXPERIENCE

Ms. Salhany's earliest board experiences at Los Angeles area academic and nonprofit groups followed from her role as the leader of major television and entertainment organizations. She joined the executive committee of the UCLA School of Theater, Film and Television; the dean's advisory board at UCLA; the board of directors of the Academy of Television Arts and Sciences; and the board of directors of Hollywood Supports.

When Ms. Salhany was a member of top management at Taft, Paramount, Fox, and UPN, she worked with their boards of directors, giving presentations and discussing strategies. She was on the board of B.R.A. Corporation (her husband's family owned restaurant business) from 1996 to early 2000. She remained on the board of UPN after returning to Boston in 1997, and she's been on the UPN operating committee since 2000.

COMPAQ COMPUTER CORPORATION/ HEWLETT-PACKARD INC. BOARDS

Joining Compaq Computer Corporation in Houston, Texas, was a significant step up for her as a corporate director. An executive search firm recruited her to interview for positions on three boards: Bank of America, Gap Inc., and Compaq Computer.

Compaq was looking for advertising and marketing expertise; they wanted to be cutting edge and more oriented toward the young consumer. They saw that I had that experience from Fox. But, also, I was of the right gender, and I think that that weighed into their deliberations.

Ms. Salhany became the first woman director of Compaq Computer in March 1996, when Eckhard Pfeiffer was president and CEO and Ben Rosen was chair of the board. She became a member of the human resources committee and of the nominating and governance committee. She chaired the latter committee during the last 18 months before Compaq was merged into Hewlett-Packard in 2002.

I was not part of the special committee involved in the merger with HP. There were other board members that knew the technology side of HP better than I and who were more qualified to deal with the merger. I became very close with Michael Capella, who had taken over as head of Compaq in September 2000.

She moved over to the HP board and served alongside two other women directors: Patricia Dunn and HP president/CEO Carly Fiorina (until September 2006 and February 2005, respectively). Today, Ms. Salhany is a member of the human resources committee and the audit committee. She chairs the nominating and governance committee, which brought Sari M. Baldauf onto the board in 2006. Ms. Baldauf served as executive vice president and general manager of the network business group of Nokia Corporation, a communications company in Finland.

AVID TECHNOLOGY INC. BOARD

When Ms. Salhany moved back to Boston, she was contacted by the board of Avid Technology Inc., a maker of digital media creation tools for film, video, animation, games, and broadcast professionals in Tewksbury, Massachusetts. They sought her out to help them expand their contacts among stations and for advice on how to grow their business. She served on the Avid board for two years (January 1998–December 1999).

AMERICAN MEDIA INC. BOARD

While she was at Fox, she was invited to join the board of American Media Inc. in Boca Raton, Florida, the publisher of national tabloid publications in "the celebrity journalism and health-and-fitness categories." Roy "Copi" F. Coppedge III, the managing director of Boston Ventures—a major investor in American Media— thought her knowledge of the media industry would be of value to the firm. Initially, she declined the offer because of the possible cross-interests: Boston Ventures had invested in News Corporation and Metromedia. After returning to Boston, she joined the AMI board in 1998. The next year, the company went private through a merger into AMP Acquisition Corporation, with David Pecker as head of the firm. He formed his own investment board.

COTY INC. BOARD

She went on the board of Coty Inc. in New York City as they were preparing to go public in 2000. Two other directors from Compaq (Peter Larson and Kenneth Roman) were on the Coty Inc. board and wanted outside directors in anticipation of the firm going public. The IPO did not proceed, and the board was disbanded.

iMEDIUM INC. BOARD

iMedium Inc. in Wayne, Pennsylvania, developed visually interactive software to improve Internet sales effectiveness. She was on the iMedium board briefly during 2000 when Safeguard Scientifics Inc. (their equity partner at LifeF/X) was looking for independent directors in anticipation of going public. iMedium was able to secure two rounds of funding but ultimately did not go public; the board was disbanded.

ION MEDIA NETWORKS BOARD

She was a director of ION Media Networks (formerly Paxson Communications Corporation) in West Palm Beach, Florida, from June 2006 to January 2008. She knew the chair of the company, Larry Patrick, who was looking for an outside board member with network experience. In May 2007, the company went private with a reverse stock split and was bought by the private equity fund CIG Media LLC, an affiliate of Citadel Investment Group LLC.

LESSONS LEARNED

Ms. Salhany pioneered the pathway for women in the television broadcast industry. From a secretary at a tiny UHF television station in Cleveland, she rose to program manager positions in Boston and Philadelphia. Then she became the first woman in positions of ever-increasing responsibility at Taft Broadcasting, Paramount TV, Twentieth Television, Fox Broadcasting, and United Paramount Network. After being an entrepreneur within these huge corporations (an "intrapreneur"), she established her own consulting business at JH Media, followed by collaborative and creative partnerships at LifeF/X and, most recently, Echo Bridge Entertainment.

Serving as a director of Compaq Computer, followed by Hewlett-Packard, was equally challenging.

> It took me a long time to understand the board thing because it was such a different kind of business to me—non-entertainment, non-creative, a consumer hardware business. At first, it was very hard to grasp. It took about two years [for me] to begin to scratch the surface of understanding, and I worked very hard at it. In some ways, it was an awakening for me. I tell the story about when I first got on the board, I thought Black-Scholes [a complex mathematical model used in options pricing] was a writing team.
>
> You have to be prepared to work twice as hard and learn everything from the ground up. There were terrific people on the board, in fact the whole board, who helped me learn and to feel comfortable there. The depth of technical expertise that was needed was far from what I had experienced up to that time. But I would sit next to Dr. George Heilmeier, and I'd lean over to him and ask him to explain it to me in English. He was very helpful. Tom Perkins was also very bright. I tapped into their technical expertise and knowledge of business strategies. We have all remained very good friends.

As current chair of the nominating and governance committee, Ms. Salhany agrees that companies always are looking for talented director candidates, women, minorities, and geographic diversity—meaning people with international business experience.

> With a company as large as HP, generally you look at sitting CEOs or COOs, and there are not as many women in those positions. Or, if they are, they sit on a number of other boards, which becomes a limiting factor. We have two women out of eight, which is pretty good. We work with executive search firms, like Russell Reynolds. We always look for technology people but need to avoid conflicts like competing companies or companies with whom we do business. Sari Baldauf from Nokia is terrific: she matched so many of our selection criteria, and she is so savvy.
>
> Sitting on a board these days is not what you might call fun. It's very hard work; you're really in the spotlight. I enjoy it because I feel that I can identify with a shareholder. I think boards more and more are thinking about shareholders—what they want and expect. As a director, you cannot be all things to all people: you can't necessarily meet all of their expectations.

Shareholders don't have the vast amount of information that directors have. But I think you can ask, "How would a shareholder feel about this decision?"

I'm not on the board to have fun. It's interesting. It's stimulating. I learn something new [at] every board meeting. I think I contribute something, a lot actually, in each board meeting.

LADDER CLIMBERS: THE
CORPORATE PATH

Four out of 10 of the women directors in our sample built a career within the traditional corporate framework, with strong credentials and experience in the technology, finance, law, and retail sectors, demonstrating again that the issue of women on boards is a matter of experience, expertise, and, above all, competence.

RELATIVE IMPORTANCE

Seventy-five women (40% of the experience cited, as seen in figure 7.1) followed a corporate career path, the largest share of all. There were five subcategories within the corporate path, the corporate path (see table 7.1). Four out of every 10 women took advantage of the dramatic growth of career and senior leadership opportunities in the technology field. Another 3 out of 10 came by way of a financial background. Twelve women were in the retail field, and nine in law. Three women came from other fields: Two from oil and gas production and one from health-related fields.

One of the most important credentials for a board member is the ability to understand the challenges and risks faced by the leadership of the enterprise. This is a primary reason why boards tend to search for sitting or former CEOs. Women who have risen to top executive positions at large organizations (including heads of international operations or major manufacturing centers) find they are high-value candidates for a director role. Contemporary business enterprises have presented women with more opportunities than ever before to develop and demonstrate their leadership capabilities.

DIVERSE EXPERIENCES

1. *Technology:* Emerging technologies have created an equal-opportunity playing field where women executives thrive. Thirty director seats were held by 26

Figure 7.1
Corporate Sub-paths to the Boardroom.

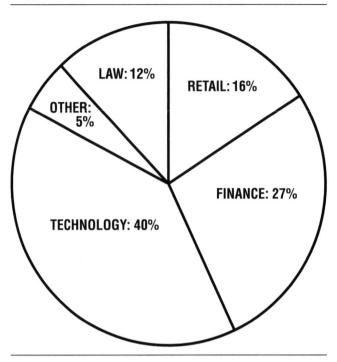

Source: Tabulations from proxy statements and research conducted by Technology Place Inc. covering backgrounds of women on California *Fortune* 1000 boards.

individual women who came to their board roles at California *Fortune* 1000 firms by way of the corporate technology path (more than any other route into the boardroom). (See table 7.2.)

The women directors gained experience at some of the top technology companies of the past three decades, from Apple and Autodesk to Zilog and Zyan. The businesses were in computer hardware, software, printing, networking, broadband and wireless telecommunications, medical and bioscience technologies, dot-coms, and a wide variety of electronic business and customer services across several industry sectors.

Women demonstrated true leadership at technology companies. Eight of the women currently hold positions of executive chair, chair, CEO, president, or combinations thereof. They include:

- Carol A. Bartz, executive chair, and previously president and CEO of Autodesk Inc., a design software company, and CEO of Yahoo! as of January 2009.

Table 7.1
Corporate Sub-paths: Experience of Women on Corporate Boards of California
Fortune **1000 Companies**

	Corporate Sub-paths	# Occurrences	Percent
C-O	Other	4	5.3
C-L	Law	9	12.0
C-R	Retail	12	16.0
C-F	Finance	20	26.7
C-T	Technology	30	40.0
	Total Corp. Sub-paths	75	100.0

- M. Michele Burns, chair and CEO of Mercer, a leading global human resource consulting, outsourcing, and investment firm owned by the Marsh & McLennan Company.
- M. Christine Jacobs, chair, president, and CEO of Theragenics Corporation, the leading manufacturer of radioactive isotopes used in prostate brachytherapy (a seeding technology for the treatment of prostate cancer).
- Dawn G. Lepore, president, CEO, and chair of drugstore.com, inc.
- Patti S. Hart, chair and CEO of Pinnacle Systems, a leading provider of digital video solutions for beginners to broadcasters, and previously chair and CEO of Excite@Home, which provides residential broadband services; chair, president, and CEO of Telocity; and president and COO of Sprint Corporation's long distance division.
- Michelle Guthrie, CEO of Star Group Limited, the Asian media and entertainment entity that is a wholly owned subsidiary of News Corporation.
- Safra Catz, co-president of Oracle Corporation.

Even more women are former CEOs, chairs, or presidents and have held top corporate leadership positions in major public and private high-tech corporations.

- Penelope L. Hughes was chair of the technology investment incubator Web-Angel plc. Before that, she was president of Coca Cola UK and Ireland.
- Mary Alice Taylor was chair and CEO of Webvan Group Inc. and its predecessor, HomeGrocer.com.
- Betsy J. Bernard was president of AT&T. Previously, she was president and CEO of AT&T Consumer.
- Gale S. Fitzgerald was president and CEO of QP Group, a procurement solutions company. Before that, she was chair and CEO of Computer Task Group Inc., an international information technology services firm.
- Judith C. Pelham was president and CEO of Trinity Health, a national system of health care facilities created through the merger of the Holy

Table 7.2

Corporate Technology Path: Experience of Women on Corporate Boards of California *Fortune* 1000 Companies

Paths into the Boardroom						Name	Company
					C-T	Sari L. Baldauf	Hewlett-Packard
					C-T	Carol A. Bartz	Autodesk, Cisco, Network Appliance
		A			C-T	Sara L. Beckman	Building Materials Holding
					C-T	Betsy J. Bernard	URS
			I		C-T	Safra Catz	Oracle Corporation
			I	E	C-T	Deborah Ann Coleman	Applied Materials
			I	E	C-T	Kathleen A. Cote	Western Digital
					C-T	H. Paulett Eberhart	AMD, Solectron
				E	C-T	Judith L. Estrin	Walt Disney
					C-T	Gale S. Fitzgerald	Health Net
					C-T	Sharon D. Garrett	Ross Stores
			I		C-T	Maureen E. Grzelakowski	Broadcom
			I		C-T	Michelle Guthrie	VeriSign
					C-T	Patti S. Hart	Spansion
				E	C-T	Patricia A. House	Levi Strauss & Co.
				E	C-T	Penelope L. Hughes	Gap Inc.
					C-T	Martha R. Ingram	Ingram Micro
					C-T	M. Christine Jacobs	McKesson
					C-T	Dawn G. Lepore	eBay
					C-T	Carol Mills	Adobe Systems
					C-T	Judith C. Pelham	Amgen
				E	C-T	Rebecca A. Stirn	Safeway
					C-T	Susan G. Swenson	Wells Fargo
				E	C-T	Mary Alice Taylor	Autodesk
			I		C-T	Carolyn M. Ticknor	Clorox
			I		C-T	Elizabeth Vanderslice	Xilinx
				E	C-T	Jacquelyn M. Ward	Sanmina-Sci

Note: N = Nonprofit; G = Government; A = Academic; I = Investment; E = Entrepreneurial; C-T = Corporate Technology.

Cross Health System and Mercy Health Services. She was president and CEO of Mercy Health Services and, before that, president and CEO of the Daughters of Charity Health Services.

- Elizabeth Vanderslice was general manager of Terra Lycos Inc., an Internet access and interactive content provider. Before that, she was president and CEO of Wired Digital Inc. (acquired by Lycos).

- Carolyn M. Ticknor has over three decades of global technology expertise, with 24 years at Hewlett-Packard, during which time she served as president and general manager of Hewlett-Packard's imaging and printing systems and their LaserJet Solutions Group.
- H. Paulett Eberhart was president of the Americas for Electronic Data Systems Corporation, an information technology and business process outsourcing company.
- Carol Mills was president and CEO of Acta Technology, a company that sells software for collecting and organizing data for enterprise resource planning applications.

Two women currently hold positions as executive vice president or chief operating officer in charge of technology or technology firms:

- Sharon D. Garrett is executive vice president of enterprise services at PacifiCare Health Systems. Before that, she was CEO of Zyan Communications; senior vice president and CIO of the Walt Disney Company; and deputy director of UCLA Medical Center.
- Susan G. Swenson is chief operating officer for New Motion Inc. Previously, she was COO of Amp'd Mobile Inc.; CEO of T-Mobile USA; president and CEO of Leap Wireless; and president and CEO of Cellular One.

2. *Finance:* Just as technology advancements during the early 1980s and the late 1990s created mini-booms of economic opportunities, the passage of the Sarbanes-Oxley Act, with its increased requirements of auditor oversight and internal controls and heightened executive accountability, created a host of economic opportunities for women following a financial career. Nineteen women (holding 20 director positions) had significant financial careers (representing 27% of all the experience in the corporate sub-path, as shown in table 7.3).

Women who came by the financial path today hold the topmost chair/vice-chair and equivalent positions at a wide variety of companies.

- Linda Fayne Levinson is the chair of Connexus, an Internet marketing platform. She was a senior advisor to the venture capital firm GRP Partners and was an independent investor and advisor to professionally funded, privately held ventures such as Overture Services (now a Yahoo! company), lastminute.com, Cybersource, Homestead, and I4 Technologies.
- Barbara L. Rambo is vice-chair and former CEO of Nietech Corporation, which serves financial institutions and payment processors, and former president and CEO of Openclose.com, a subsidiary of Mortgage.com, a member-based mortgage service for brokers and lenders.

Two women currently hold the top CFO positions at major corporations:

- Melissa Lora is CFO of Taco Bell Corporation, a subsidiary of Yum! Brands Inc.

Table 7.3

Corporate Finance Path: Experience of Women on Corporate Boards of California
***Fortune* 1000 Companies**

						Name	Company
Paths into the Boardroom							
				E	C-F	Marilyn A. Alexander	New Century Financial Corporation
					C-F	Sandra N. Bane	Petco
	G		I		C-F	Kathleen Brown	Countrywide Financial
					C-F	M. Michele Burns	Cisco
			I	E	C-F	Mariann Byerwalter	Pacific Life
				E	C-F	Adelia A. Coffman	Qualcomm
	G				C-F	Linnet Frazier Deily	Chevron Corporation
			I	E	C-F	Leslie Myers Frécon	Ryland Group
					C-F	Christine Garvey	Hilton Hotels
					C-F	Nancy H. Handel	Broadcom
			I		C-F	Marie L. Knowles	McKesson
					C-F	Heidi Kunz	Agilent Technologies
			I	E	C-F	Linda Fayne Levinson	Ingram Micro, Jacobs Engineering Inc.
					C-F	Melissa Lora	KB Homes
			I		C-F	Marjorie Magner	Charles Schwab
					C-F	Anne Mather	Google
					C-F	Nancy S. Newcomb	DirecTV Group
					C-F	Barbara L. Rambo	PG&E
	G		I	E	C-F	Donna Frame Tuttle	Hilton Hotels

Note: N = Nonprofit; G = Government; A = Academic; I = Investment; E = Entrepreneurial; C-F = Corporate Finance.

- Heidi Kunz is CFO and executive vice president of Blue Shield of California, responsible for accounting, corporate finance, treasury, analytics, actuarial services, internal audits, facilities, and information technology. Previously, she was executive vice president and CFO of Gap Inc., CFO of ITT Industries Inc., and treasurer of General Motors Corporation.

Four women are former chair, CEO, president, or head of a global financial operation. Among them are:

- Christine Garvey, a senior financial services executive with commercial and industrial real estate expertise, and global head of corporate real estate and services for Deutsche Bank AG.
- Sandra N. Bane, a retired audit partner from KPMG LLP with 24 years at the firm, during which time she held positions including head of the

western region's merchandising practice and partner-in-charge of the western region's human resource department.

- Nancy S. Newcomb, a former senior corporate officer of risk management at Citigroup Inc.; a customer group executive of Citicorp; a division executive of Latin America; and the CFO of Citicorp, responsible for liquidity, funding, and capital management.

Many of the women are former CFOs. They include:

- Dee Coffman, who was CFO of Qualcomm for nine years.
- Nancy H. Handel, former CFO and senior vice president of Applied Materials Inc., a supplier of equipment and services to the global semiconductor industry.
- Marie L. Knowles, the former executive vice president and CFO of Atlantic Richfield Company, a large U.S.-based integrated oil company acquired by BP.
- Anne Mather, former executive vice president and CFO for Pixar, responsible for finance, administration, business affairs, investor relations, and human resources, and previously executive vice president and CFO at Village Roadshow Pictures, within the Walt Disney Company.

Corporate boards today look for financial experts, directors with hands-on experience dealing with contemporary audit and accounting challenges under Sarbanes-Oxley and exchange regulations. Just as real-world technology expertise provides boards with insight into internal corporate controls, financial acumen is valued when it comes from firsthand experience.

3. *Retail:* Many expect the retail path to be a dominant route to corporate leadership for women. Twelve women directors (16% of all experience in the corporate sub-path, as shown in table 7.4) followed careers along the corporate retail path.

Women directors are leaders at major consumer corporations, holding positions as chair, CEO, president, or vice-chair and group leadership positions.

- Linda A. Lang is CEO and chair of Jack in the Box and previously was its president and COO.
- Susan E. Engel is chair and CEO of Lenox Group Inc. (formerly Department 56 Inc.), a designer and marketer of tabletop giftware and collectibles. Previously, she was president and CEO of Champion Products Inc., the athletic apparel division of Sara Lee Corporation.
- Janet E. Grove is corporate vice-chair of Federated Department Stores Inc. and former CEO and chair of Federated Merchandising Group, a division of Federated Department Stores Inc.
- Julia A. Stewart is president, CEO, and COO of International House of Pancakes Corporation. With over three decades of experience in the restaurant business, she has been marketing manager for Carl's Jr., Burger King, Saga Corp., Taco Bell, and Applebee's.

Table 7.4

Corporate Retail Path: Experience of Women on Corporate Boards of California
***Fortune* 1000 Companies**

Paths into the Boardroom						Name	Company
				E	C-R	Janet Morrison Clarke	Gateway
					C-R	Susan E. Engel	Wells Fargo
					C-R	Janet E. Grove	Safeway
					C-R	Doris F. Fisher	Gap Inc.
					C-R	Miriam L. Haas	Levi Strauss & Co.
			I		C-R	Jeanne P. Jackson	William-Sonoma
					C-R	Linda A. Lang	Jack in the Box
					C-R	Jan L. Murley	Clorox
					C-R	Paula A. Sneed	Charles Schwab
					C-R	Julia A. Stewart	Avery Dennison
					C-R	Pamela Thomas-Graham	Clorox
					C-R	Margaret C. Whitman	eBay

Note: N = Nonprofit; G = Government; A = Academic; I = Investment; E = Entrepreneurial; C-R = Corporate Retail.

- Paula A. Sneed is group vice president and president of e-commerce and marketing services at Kraft Foods North America. She has a 30-year career with Kraft and General Foods Corporation.
- Jan L. Murley is the former CEO of the Boyds Collection Ltd. (designer and manufacturer of whimsical gifts and collectibles).

Some of the women brought additional expertise beyond their marketing competence, combining technical, financial, or entertainment industry expertise with solid retail backgrounds, like these two:

- Jeanne P. Jackson is the former president and CEO of Walmart.com, the online retail presence of Wal-Mart Inc. Previously, she was president and CEO of Gap Inc.'s direct business and president/CEO of Banana Republic.
- Pamela Thomas-Graham is a former group president of better and moderate apparel for Liz Claiborne Inc. Previously, she was chair of CNBC, executive vice president of NBC, and president/CEO of CNBC.com.

The women directors with retail experience lead major entities or subsidiaries that are as large as entire corporations in other sectors of the economy. Today, retail requires competencies in technology, finance, and international markets. These are exactly the skills for which boards are searching.

4. *Law:* Just as corporations are limiting the outside board roles of their CEOs, companies today are placing greater demands on their internal corporate counsel. Eight women holding nine director positions (12% of the experience in the

Table 7.5

Corporate Law Path: Experience of Women on Corporate Boards of California
Fortune **1000 Companies**

Paths into the Boardroom					Name	Company
				C-L	Margaret G. Gill	Con-Way
				C-L	Anne B. Gust	Jack in the Box
				C-L	Maryellen C. Herringer	ABM Industries, PG&E
G				C-L	Aulana L. Peters	Northrop Grummond
				C-L	Patricia Salas Pineda	Levi Strauss & Co.
				C-L	Colleen Pouliot	Adobe Systems
				C-L	Judith M. Runstad	Wells Fargo
				C-L	Laura Stein	Franklin Resources

Note: N = Nonprofit; G = Government; A = Academic; I = Investment; E = Entrepreneurial; C-L = Corporate Law.

corporate sub-path, as seen in table 7.5) followed the corporate-law path into the board room.

Two women currently hold top corporate legal positions of responsibility:

- Patricia Salas Pineda is group vice president of corporate communications and general counsel for Toyota Motor North America Inc.
- Laura Stein is senior vice president, general counsel, and corporate secretary of the Clorox Company.

Other women directors are former partners of major law firms, including:

- Margaret G. Gill, the former senior vice president in charge of legal external affairs and corporate secretary of AirTouch Communications, a wireless communications company acquired by Vodafone plc.
- Aulana L. Peters, a retired partner of the law firm of Gibson, Dunn & Crutcher who spent four years as a commissioner of the U.S Securities and Exchange Commission.

Three other women are former corporate general counsel and/or corporate secretaries:

- Anne B. Gust is the former executive vice president and chief administrative officer, general counsel, and corporate secretary to Gap Inc., where she oversaw human resources, legal, corporate administration, corporate architecture and construction, global compliance, real estate, corporate communications departments, and the Gap Foundation.
- Maryellen C. Herringer is the former executive vice president, general counsel, and corporate secretary to APL Limited, an intermodal shipping and rail transportation company.

- Colleen Pouliot is the retired senior vice president of special projects for Adobe's CEO and previously was senior vice president, general counsel, and corporate secretary at Adobe Systems Inc.

The legal expertise required of corporate boards today is not litigation so much as an in-depth understanding of the tougher new regulatory environment, the ability to put sound governance processes into place, and the capacity to judge the areas in which the corporation faces heightened risk, domestically and internationally.

5. *Other:* Two women specialized in the operation of oil/gas distribution facilities— very nontraditional paths for women in leadership. A third woman was the first woman in leadership at a major U.S. health insurance company. (See table 7.6.)

- Margaret A. Dano has a mechanical-electrical engineering background from the General Motors Institute and rose through the ranks to become vice president of Worldwide Operations of Garrett Engine Boosting Systems, a subsidiary of Honeywell Inc.
- Rebecca Ann McDonald was president of Gas & Power at BHP Billiton, a leading global resources company until her retirement in October 2007.
- Betty Woods is the former president and CEO of Premera Blue Cross, with 26 years of experience as a leader in health care. She was the first woman in the nation to lead a Blue Cross Blue Shield organization.

Corporate boards want directors who have invested a substantial amount of time acquiring experience in the same corporate world that boards seek to govern. Boards are looking for directors with top-level executive experience. The women directors demonstrate the wide variety of ways that women have and can acquire leadership skills.

MYTH BUSTING

One of the myths dispelled by these findings is that a strong math, science, or engineering background is a prerequisite for women directors coming from a technology or computer science career path. The reality is that technology today

Table 7.6

Corporate Other Path: Experience of Women on Corporate Boards of California *Fortune* 1000 Companies

Paths into the Boardroom						Name	Company
					C-O	Margaret A. Dano	Fleetwood Enterprises
	G				C-O	Rebecca Ann McDonald	Granite Construction
					C-O	Betty Woods	Beckman Coulter

Note: N = Nonprofit; G = Government; A = Academic; I = Investment; E = Entrepreneurial; C-O = Corporate Other.

represents a wide-open path into top leadership roles and responsibilities because technology now infuses all areas of business operations.

Board members are searching for candidates with a solid understanding of new economy business. Many of the companies tapped women with network/telecommunications expertise or business process or outsourcing capabilities, followed by bioscience technology or medical technology applications. These competencies all fall well within the definition of the new economy. Only a handful of the women were chief technology or information officers—most were general managers or were responsible for oversight of the operational coordination among technology business units or their financial performance; they were not limited to the "geek" side of traditional hardware, software, or network specialties.

The financial path into the boardroom favored those who are or were CFOs, but again the number and variety of their financial responsibilities offer women candidates many career options. Nine of the 19 women with financial expertise were either a CEO or head of a major bank or financial arm or were an audit partner or principal.

Mary S. Metz and Linda Griego are examples of those who acquired their financial expertise on the job. Many women said that serving on the audit committee of a corporate board gave them, as directors, unique insight into the nuts and bolts of the corporation. Women directors often said they were willing to volunteer for the audit committee role on their board. Forty-five percent of the women directors in our sample serve on the audit committee, 43 percent on the nominating and governance committee, and 28 percent on the compensation committee.

The independence of the audit committee is a highly valued governance attribute that can positively influence firms' shareholder valuation.[1] Sarbanes-Oxley has put tremendous pressure on companies to improve the ways they ensure that directors are independent. That involves looking for the most talented financial analytical expertise available, individuals with a track record of managing internal financial controls and improving financial and reporting technologies from within the corporation. That is exactly the talent these women possess.

In a reversal of another historical trend, legal positions in academia and government are facing greater competition from legal positions in business and corporations. There has been a plateauing of the number of women law deans, professors, judicial clerks, and government lawyers as more women choose other legal career options within the corporate marketplace: general counsel, corporate secretaries, chief administrative officers, and partners capable of dealing with domestic diversity as well as overseas trade and contract vendor issues.

Linnet Frazier Deily mentioned that her skills and experience as a financial deal maker in the international community are more valuable than a background in litigation. That is exactly the kind of legal experience for which boards are searching today.

The global economy and international competition require the use of more diverse business strategies, techniques, and partnerships, and a heightened awareness of international interdependencies. The women directors surveyed have experience in oil pricing, manufacturing controls at outsource vendor locations, and international labor law compliance, as well as merger and acquisition legal requirements in Europe, Asia, and Latin America. It is this global diversity of experience that boards value today.

LESSONS LEARNED

Some writers suggest that women tend to either "opt out" or take side steps in their career trajectories. The women directors who follow the corporate path, and all its various sub-paths, are more like long-distance endurance runners. They do not get out entirely. Like Aulana L. Peters, they take on a new and bigger challenge (as a Securities and Exchange commissioner), excel there, and then return to a successful private corporate securities practice. Donna F. Tuttle took on the position of undersecretary of commerce for trade and tourism, followed by a stint as deputy secretary of commerce. After her public service, she continued her work in the private sector as a logical application of that business knowledge.

The women identified complementary activities to extend their expertise and stretch their talents into new areas of challenge where they could continue to excel and contribute. The women did not "go it alone" or work in isolation. They acknowledge the contribution to their success made by superiors, peers, and subordinates. They collaborated with professional men and women more often than with friends or family. They took responsibility for their own success and learning experiences yet gave credit when and where it was due to individuals whose work enhanced or complemented their efforts.

The women were not afraid to deal with the messy part of cleaning up and rebuilding a broken business entity. Linda Griego headed Rebuild/LA and the Community Reinvestment Bank during their very challenging years. Linnet Frazier Deily headed the restructuring of the private Texas Bank. Roslyn B. Payne was president/CEO of the Federal Asset Disposition Association, responsible for thrift workouts, before it was replaced by the congressionally chartered Resolution Trust Corporation. Jan L. Murley made the decision to take the Boyds Collection Ltd. into bankruptcy. Linda Fayne Levinson, Judith L. Estrin, and Deborah Ann Coleman have endured the ups and downs of several new technology ventures. Kathleen A. Cote was in charge during the closing days of Worldport Communications, and M. Michele Burns was named chief restructuring officer in charge of bringing the Mirant Corporation Inc. out of bankruptcy. Mary S. Metz was on the board of PG&E while it worked its way out of energy crisis–created bankruptcy.

THE WOMEN INTERVIEWED

Three women were interviewed concerning their experience along the corporate path: Janet Morrison Clarke, Judith M. Runstad, and Kathleen A. Cote. These women represent a diverse spectrum of corporate interests: technology, real estate, finance, publishing, and resort/recreation industries. They have held positions as law partner, CEO, investor, and entrepreneur. Just focusing on these few individuals who came up the traditional business ladder should convince us that it is impossible today to generalize or stereotype women directors. They just don't fit into the tight, neat little boxes that once characterized women on boards. This should make it interesting and exciting for young women today to consider all the options and opportunities that are available to them as they pursue their own personal career paths to leadership tomorrow.

Director Profile: Janet Morrison Clarke

Janet Morrison Clarke, age 55 at the time of our interview, is president of Clarke Littlefield LLC, a firm she founded to provide strategic consulting to corporations with an emphasis on marketing technologies. Ms. Clarke came up the corporate ranks at R. R. Donnelley & Sons Company, Citibank, and Young & Rubicam. She has experience in sales, operations, marketing, and general management at top U.S. corporations. Today she sits on two public and four private company boards.

EARLY YEARS

Ms. Clarke was born in 1953 in Springfield, Massachusetts, and grew up in Worcester, the oldest of five girls. Her father was an entrepreneur who founded his own lumber company. She developed her sense of business as his right-hand person, helping prepare invoices, tally inventories, and pay the bills from their home office on evenings and weekends.

Both of her high-energy, athletic parents encouraged their daughters to work hard, get good grades, volunteer in the community, and play sports. Her mother was an avid golfer and high school tennis coach. Her father was a former Ivy League football player. Ms. Clarke played field hockey and softball in high school, taught tennis and archery, and coached softball in the summers. At college, she co-founded the women's ice hockey team and played on several coed intramural sports teams. Said Ms. Clarke, "I'm a big believer that team sports build character and teach you about fair play; they prepare you well for the rough and tumble world of business. Sports actually helped a lot in my career and continue to help me in the business world today."

EDUCATION

Her two favorite subjects in high school were art and math—a novel mix of interests for a teenage girl in the 1960s. She won awards for her drawings and was a member of the math team. That combination, and Ayn Rand's book *The Fountainhead,* led to her interest in architecture as a possible career path. In the fall of 1971, she entered Princeton University, a college that had been all male for nearly 225 years and had begun admitting women only two years earlier.

She took a year off after her sophomore year because her father's business experienced a serious financial setback. She returned home to help with the family business and to work full time at a local engineering firm. Returning to Princeton in 1974 with a full financial aid package, Ms. Clarke shifted into an entrepreneurial role, earning money as a graphic designer, then graduated with a bachelor's in architecture and urban planning in 1976. She received a graduate teaching fellowship to the University of Nebraska–Lincoln College of Architecture but spent only one semester there before dropping out. When she returned to Worcester ready to work again at her father's business, he told her she could do better elsewhere "after all that high-priced education."

EARLY CAREER

Heffernan Press, a local printing firm in Worcester, hired her at $10,000 a year as a sales rep covering southern New England and New York. The owner liked her "fancy Ivy League education," her graphics experience, and the uniqueness of hiring a female in a dominantly male field.

She soon realized she needed a better-paying job to pay off her college loans. Science Press, a small company in Ephrata, Pennsylvania, asked her to become their first saleswoman at a whopping salary of $15,000 a year and the promise of a small commission. She joined the New York City office and discovered she enjoyed sales—going to publishers and journals to pitch Science Press's printing processes and occasionally bid on composition, layout, and typesetting services. She became skilled at understanding the equipment, binderies, labor, time, and material requirements of her clients.

R. R. DONNELLEY & SONS COMPANY

Purchasing agents at her client companies told her that she could make a lot more money working on straight commission for a major firm like R. R. Donnelley & Sons Company in Chicago, the world's largest printer of books, magazines, catalogs, and telephone directories. But those same agents speculated that Donnelley would never hire a "woman salesman."

Naturally, she was intrigued and pursued a number of channels. R. R. Donnelley finally invited her to interview for a new sales position in a new group that would market all the services of the huge firm: Group D, nicknamed Group Dog by insiders because it was considered such a tough and risky assignment.

In December 1978, Ms. Clarke joined them as a trainee, taking a pay cut, but vowing to herself to get back on commission as quickly as possible. Sales reps were assigned very specific sales territories, so as a trainee she had to sell to her customers in "stealth mode."

While still in training in 1980, she met and married Fred Clarke, a very successful Donnelley salesman. She considers him a mentor who helped her navigate through the many tough battles and issues she faced daily inside the large, structured corporation.

She saw that by focusing on products, Donnelley's sales reps were missing out on enterprise jobs—sales opportunities at major corporate businesses in New Jersey and New York. She started calling on the bigger firms like Exxon, Prudential, AT&T, and IBM, all of which became her customers. Her big break came in 1983, at the IBM corporate headquarters in Armonk, New York. She mentioned that her husband had just purchased the new IBM personal computer and that it was going to be a hot high-volume seller. She asked about the user manuals bundled with the computers. They told her it was all handled by an IBM "skunk-works group doing their own thing" in Boca Raton, Florida. Through her associates in Armonk, the Boca Raton purchasing agent contacted her to set up a meeting. She caught the next plane from New York to Florida and met with a team of very secretive engineers and designers working under Don Estridge of the IBM entry systems division.

She told them, "I work for one of the biggest printing companies in the world. We can partner with you and keep it confidential. We'll help you understand the printing business, and you can teach us about the disk duplication business. We can create a dedicated facility for you in Indiana."

John "Jack" B. Schwemm, R. R. Donnelley's CEO and chair, talked about how this perky 30-year-old woman sold the company's biggest contract ever: initially over $50 million. Follow-up implementation meant around-the-clock work for the next several years. "It was three years without a vacation," she recalled, "but the rewards were worth it."

In 1984, she was named T. E. Donnelley salesperson of the year. She traveled around the globe working exclusively with IBM, finally benefiting from straight commission sales. "Commission sales are gender blind," she said. "Your pay is your own report card, and nobody can take that success away from you."

She rose through the ranks at R. R. Donnelley from sales representative to manager of national accounts and then vice president and director of the OEM sales division. In 1988, she was named vice president; two years later, she became the firm's youngest senior vice president of sales, overseeing all the computer industry-related printing and establishing a new business unit to provide printing solution strategies for top companies such as Hewlett-Packard, Apple, Digital Equipment Corporation, and Sun Microsystems.

By 1992, IBM and Microsoft were going head-to-head with announcements of new competing operating systems: OS/2 (IBM) and Windows (Microsoft).

Ms. Clarke proposed that R. R. Donnelley pursue the disk duplication business for both new products. "I told our CFO, Frank Jarc, that it was risky, but if we could lock down enough raw media and duplication equipment to accommodate both jobs, then the financial rewards would more than outweigh the risk of expanding production."

He supported the idea, and the payoff was handsome: the business unit achieved its annual objectives in one quarter. Ms. Clarke was asked to name her reward.

ADVANCED MANAGEMENT PROGRAM AT HARVARD

Her career, to that point, was "all sales, all the time" with little formal business education. She suggested that R. R. Donnelley send her to the Advanced Management Program at Harvard Business School, a three-month intensive business program for mid-career executives.

> That was a big turning point. For years, I had worked hard in sales on behalf of the customers, built successful sales teams, and ... encouraged and promoted a number of promising men and women. Then I realized that it was time to disengage from all that in order to do something more developmental.

For 12 weeks ending November 1992, 121 men and 8 women worked, studied, collaborated, and became very close friends at Harvard. Ms. Clarke later told James "Jimmy" R. Donnelley, vice-chair of R. R. Donnelley and a member of the founding family, that that program was "the greatest gift that Donnelley ever gave me."

One of the many program participants who became her lifelong friends was Gordon Bethune, a Boeing executive until 1994, when he joined Continental Airlines as chair and CEO, managing one of the most dramatic business turnarounds of that decade. Another was Judith Haberkorn, who held a variety of top management positions at Bell Atlantic and its predecessor, NYNEX.

An early challenge for Ms. Clarke was all the new jargon in the finance class. She approached Samuel L. Hayes, the program's finance professor, telling him that the class material seemed over her head. Dr. Hayes held a pre-class oriented to those who were unaccustomed to financial statements, bringing them quickly up to speed on corporate financial basics. "He was brilliant and a terrific mentor who could explain complex financial concepts very clearly."

After she completed the Advanced Management Program, R. R. Donnelley and Ms. Clarke agreed to broaden her scope of responsibilities from sales and marketing to operations and management. They promoted her to senior vice president of manufacturing for the financial printing services group, headquartered in New York, with plants in Singapore, Hong Kong, London, and a dozen U.S. cities. She went from managing a highly profitable sales unit of 60 people to running a sizable business segment with 2,200 employees and six vice president/plant managers, with technology and human resources support staff. Within two years, she moved into another unit as senior vice president of Donnelley's digital division, information services group, and then senior vice president of the information technology sector.

EARLY GOVERNANCE EXPERIENCE

Her first board experience was as a director of R. R. Donnelley's newly formed venture capital group, 77 Capital Corporation, which made investments in new business opportunities for the firm. Three of their successful investments were Multex.com Inc., Desktop Data, and MapQuest. "They gave us complete autonomy to invest $25 million a year in new start-up businesses," she said. "We funded over a dozen different ventures in three years, some more successfully than others. It was fascinating."

Through the 1970s and 1980s, Ms. Clarke took on roles at not-for-profit boards such as the YMCA and became more involved with Princeton, where she was named to the advisory board for the Center for Computing and Information Technology. She was the first chairwoman of the school's annual giving effort. In 1993, Ms. Clarke won a four-year elected position as alumni trustee of Princeton University and, shortly thereafter, was invited to co-chair Princeton's 250th five-year capital campaign. When her first term as alumni trustee ended in 1997, Princeton appointed her to a 10-year term as a charter trustee. Today she remains very active at Princeton and is a member of the advisory board for the Center for Economic Policy Studies there.

Leading corporate businessmen viewed her as a peer because of her board-caliber committee experience at Princeton and her top-level business contacts packaged together with her process-oriented education and team-building sports exposure.

STANHOME CORPORATION BOARD

In 1994, she was elected to the board of Stanhome Corporation, a *Fortune* 500 public company in Westfield, Massachusetts, that made and distributed home and personal care products, imported and distributed porcelain figurines and other giftware, and sold giftware and collectibles. Stanhome was a precursor to the Mary Kay home-oriented marketing concept.

Their headquarters were in the Springfield suburbs, with businesses extending throughout the Midwest and the South. Ms. Clarke's New England background provided one connection for the firm, which also wanted someone with a sales and marketing background from a national company. The CEO, Alejandro "Alek" Diaz Vargas, had attended the Harvard Advanced Management Program, as had another Stanhome director, Judy Haberkorn, who served on the organization committee responsible for searching for director candidates. Ms. Clarke became the third woman on their board (joining Anne-Lee Verville and Alla O'Brien) and was a member of the audit and organization committees.

COX COMMUNICATIONS INC. BOARD

A year later, Ms. Clarke was elected to the board of a second public company: Cox Communications Inc. Her nomination was presented to the company by Korn Ferry International. Samuel Hayes, her finance professor at the Advanced Management Program, was instrumental in preparing her for the board interview by reviewing the complex merger agreement involved when Cox Enterprises (the Atlanta-based TV and newspaper company) acquired the cable assets of Times Mirror Corporation.

She became a director at Cox Communications when the company went public, listing on the New York Stock Exchange in March 1995. She chaired the audit committee and was a member of the compensation and executive committees. Nine years later, she chaired the special committee on Cox Communications' $8.5 billion privatization proposal, which ended her service as a director the following year. Her nomination to the Cox board gave her a solid foundation in governance and corporate oversight. Her successful leadership of the special privatization review committee put her "on the map as a director." She joined the board of the acquiring firm, Cox Enterprises, in 2007 and today chairs its compensation committee.

CITIBANK

Even though her responsibilities at Donnelley were broadened after she completed the Harvard Advanced Management Program, Ms. Clarke realized that it was time to move on.

I stepped back and took a hard look at myself: three senior vice president titles but I wasn't seeing a promotional opportunity to president. I didn't quite fit the structured culture of the company and, after careful thought, decided to test myself in the outside marketplace.

She had two offers within the financial services industry, one from AIG and the other from Citibank. Both opportunities were in the marketing area, and both offered a substantial increase in pay. In interviews she was convinced that Citibank was the better fit. Citibank's leaders wanted a fresh set of eyes to look at their internal technology processes and someone who could tap some of their key people, put together a small staff of experts, and develop an enterprise-wide client interface system (building a global database strategy and systems) so the bank could cross-sell to their more than 100 million customers in 62 countries.

From May 1997 to February 2000, Ms. Clarke was managing director for global database marketing of Citibank in New York. "That position was one of the best roles I have ever had—I learned so much and loved the challenges. When the merger between Travelers and Citibank occurred, I decided that I had to move on. I realized I was more of a 'numerator' person, rather than a 'denominator' type: I like to grow businesses, not cut them back."

YOUNG & RUBICAM

The following year, Ms. Clarke became executive vice president of Young & Rubicam Inc. and chair and CEO of KnowledgeBase Marketing Inc. She was recommended by Linda Gridley, CEO/president and co-founder of Gridley & Co. LLC, a Manhattan investment banker who had been involved in the formation and sale of KnowledgeBase Marketing Inc. to Young & Rubicam in 1999. Within a year, Young & Rubicam was sold to WPP. "I had been through two changes of control in less than two years," she said. "I wanted more control over my own destiny, so I decided to start my own company."

CLARKE LITTLEFIELD LLC

She formed the consulting firm Clarke Littlefield LLC in February 2001 as a vehicle to provide strategic consulting to the financial services industry with an emphasis on marketing technologies.[1] Her first clients came through her prior contacts at Young & Rubicam. With her own company, Ms. Clarke now had the flexibility to add more boards to her growing portfolio. In rapid succession, she joined the boards of three spin-off companies. eFunds Corporation (now EFD) came through a search firm, while Forbes.com and ExpressJet Holdings came through personal connections.[2]

She has remained president of Clarke Littlefield except during a nine-month assignment (September 2002–June 2003) as chief marketing officer and senior VP of operations at DealerTrack Inc., a provider of Web-based financing tools for the automotive retail industry in Long Island, New York. "I was able to apply the automobile industry technology experience that I learned while at DealerTrack to the Asbury Automotive Group and Cox Enterprise boards. You try to learn something from every experience."

ASBURY AUTOMOTIVE GROUP INC. BOARD

Ms. Clarke joined the board of Asbury Automotive Group Inc. in New York City, one of the largest automotive retail and service companies in the United States. Asbury chartered Tom Neff, chair of the executive search firm Spencer Stuart, with finding independent directors to fill vacancies created by the retirement of two directors, one of whom could qualify to serve on the audit committee. Ms. Clarke's background was perfect for one of these openings.

President and CEO Kenneth B. Gilman welcomed Ms. Clarke in April 2005: "Janet is an expert at integrating data-driven marketing and customer relationship management, and should bring a valuable perspective to the board."[3]

Ms. Clarke, as a member of the nominating committee and the sole woman on the board, was proud of Asbury's addition of another woman, Juanita James (a fellow Princetonian and former trustee), to their board two years later in October 2007.

You sit on a board and try to bring forward more nominations of women, but it doesn't always happen. The challenge is to find the right match on a number of areas: specific business or industry experience, committee experience, culture, fit, and chemistry. Sometimes it's hard to explain these multiple criteria to women who are seeking a director role.

GATEWAY COMPUTERS INC. BOARD

In May 2005, Ms. Clarke joined the board of Gateway Computer Inc., a company in Irvine, California, that provided PCs and related products to consumers, businesses, government agencies, and schools. Richard D. Snyder, chair, welcomed Ms. Clarke to Gateway with these words:

> Janet brings a wealth of business experience in the financial sector, as well as expertise in brand development through the use of leading-edge technologies, which will provide the Board and Gateway senior management with a fresh and valuable perspective as we continue to define avenues for further growth.[4]

Ms. Clarke was a member of the audit committee and chair of the corporate governance and nominating committee. She was on the CEO search committee that brought in J. Edward Coleman as Gateway's chief executive officer. She was on the board through September 2007, when Gateway sold its professional services unit business line to MPC Corporation (formerly Micron Electronics Inc.) and the rest of the company to Acer Inc. in Taipei, Taiwan.

> Gateway was a tough set of circumstances. I learned a lot and chaired a nominating and governance committee, which was a first for me. We had a lot of challenges—executive turnover, acquisitions, hedge fund activists—but in the end the results were very positive.

MIMEO.COM BOARD

Linda Gridley, who had introduced Ms. Clarke to Young & Rubicam, also recommended her as a director to Adam Slutsky, the CEO of New York–based Mimeo. com, the online on-demand digital printing company. They debated whether she would advise the company through Clarke Littlefield or whether she would join the board. In June 2006, she took the board seat because Mimeo.com was a private company with outstanding prospects for growth.

She brought insight from her experience at Donnelley, which, in the summer of 1995, had struggled with its own nascent digital division and the question of whether digital printing was a new business model or just a new way of printing. Did it belong somewhere inside the huge $5 billion printing behemoth or should it venture off into the strange new world of the Internet? This question and others had been presented in a Harvard Business School case study.[5] Eleven years later, Mimeo.com addressed many of the same challenges within a significantly more mature online electronic publishing industry. She recalled, "Mimeo.com gave me the chance to be around top-tier venture capitalists from the East and West Coasts. It was an opportunity to get back in touch with the private equity world."

Mr. Slutsky publicly welcomed her to the board: "In addition to her outstanding board experience, she provides a unique perspective as a past senior marketing and sales executive in the print industry."[6]

EDUCATIONDYNAMICS LLC BOARD

In 2008, Ms. Clarke joined the board of EducationDynamics LLC, a portfolio company of Halyard Capital, a New York–based private equity fund. Education-Dynamics, located in Hoboken, New Jersey, provides marketing and student affairs technology tools to facilitate student recruitment, enrollment, and retention at higher education institutions. What interested EducationDynamics' CEO and founder, Steven R. Isaac, and members of the investment team was the trifecta of her retail, governance, and database marketing experience and her deep commitment to education.

LESSONS LEARNED

In late 2007, Ms. Clarke was a director on four public and two private boards of directors. In just a year an a half, by early 2009, two of the public companies were sold, and Ms. Clarke now sits on two public company boards (ExpressJet and Asbury Automotive) and four private boards (Cox Enterprises, Forbes Media LLC, Mimeo.com, and EducationDynamics). Even though she began her career in the art and design world, today she is recognized as a director with technical, operational, sales, and marketing experience with significant governance and deal competencies drawn from the depth and breadth of her board roles. "People tell me I'm a nonlinear thinker. That probably comes from an architectural education that taught me to think about processes and structures."

She came up the corporate ladder at R. R. Donnelley, Citibank, and Young & Rubicam, yet the route was neither a straight line nor traditional. She began as a salaried then a commissioned sales rep and then became an executive and senior officer at three large corporations. Today she is a highly regarded, financially savvy business executive who runs her own small company.

Ninety-eight percent of any board role is numbers: data, measures, metrics, and processes. If you can't understand the financials, you're going to have a really hard time on a board. Even though I come from a sales and marketing background, the continuous exposure to business plans, spreadsheets, and financial analyses creates a capability, acquired through experience, which builds on itself.

Other lessons Ms. Clarke gathered from her trek up the corporate path:

- Make your own destiny: Generate your own revenues through commissions, find your own value in the marketplace, and create your own professional entrepreneurial image.
- Build teams: This she did in Princeton sports and trusteeships; in the Harvard Advanced Management Program; and through ongoing collaborations with executive search, banking, and venture interests.
- Constantly learn: She listened to and learned from the Donnelley sales reps and her husband; she sought out Professor Hayes for the pre-class financial training and the Cox debriefing; she asked for the Harvard Advanced Management Program opportunity; and she asked several search, banking, and venture colleagues to help find her value in the marketplace.

Ms. Clarke represents the new breed of women directors who are business-school educated with a diverse corporate background and trusteeship experience; they are equally at ease with technology and finance, entrepreneurial, and investment savvy; and they have a willingness and almost a sense of adventure in seeking out business solutions and strategies.

Director Profile: Judith M. Runstad

Judith M. Runstad, age 63 at the time of our interview, came to her board roles as a partner in a law firm—a collaboration of 30 years during the most dynamic period of federal and state environmental land-use regulations and policies. She took on leadership roles at public and private financial, land-use, and development-related organizations, where her skills and capabilities caught the attention of corporate boards.

EARLY YEARS

Judith Rundstad, born in 1944, grew up with one older brother in Fruitland, Idaho, a tiny town located outside Boise. "There were so few people in our town who went to college that it's amazing that I went at all," she recalled. "Both my parents put a strong emphasis on education, self-reliance, and succeeding."

> My parents and grandmother expected great things of me. My mother was valedictorian of her high school class [and] started at the University of Idaho but left to get married after her sophomore year. She wanted to be sure that I was prepared to make my own living, that I'd always have a good source of income and never assume that someone else would support me.

Her grandmother had political ambitions for her, telling her stories about an uncle who was secretary of the Republican National Congressional Committee in Washington, D.C., and a staff assistant to Senator William Borah of Idaho, who was "quite a character himself."

EARLY EDUCATION

Ms. Runstad followed in her mother's footsteps to the University of Idaho in Moscow, ran college-level political campaigns, and worked summers in the

Washington, D.C., office of Senator Len Jordan. She earned a BS in 1966 and a master's degree the following year, both in political science. She was married in 1966; they moved to Seattle, and she started teaching high school.

LAW SCHOOL

She applied to law school while teaching but didn't follow through because she could not figure out how to pay for it. In the early 1970s, a national recession became known in the Seattle area as the Boeing Bust because declining air travel had such an adverse impact on the aerospace giant. Two local real estate agents rented a billboard and posted the message: "Will the last person leaving Seattle turn out the lights?" Voters rejected bond proposals for the school district where she was teaching, and she was laid off. Then she received a letter from the University of Washington Law School accepting her into the class starting in the fall of 1971. "I couldn't believe it. Somebody had taken my application out of the pile and decided, 'Why don't we give this woman a shot at it?' I immediately wrote back accepting."

The law school saw that she had scored well on the LSATs; her undergraduate grades were excellent; and she had received the Top Ten Senior Award in college and was named to Phi Beta Kappa, Phi Kappa Phi, and Mortar Board—all academic honors. Universities were trying to recruit more women into professional schools, and the 1970s saw the first big push, when enrollments of women reached 30 percent. Today, law schools average 50 percent women or more. She received her JD from the University of Washington Law School in 1974 and was named executive editor of the law review.

THE KINGDOME

Ms. Runstad was a summer intern for the prosecuting attorney in the civil division of King County, Washington, during her early years at law school. "Work was both an economic necessity and a way to fight off boredom" she said. "Law school is disciplined, like boot camp: they're teaching you a way to think. Work made law school interesting and fun. It was a heady time, and I was right there at the start of the environmental movement."

Congress passed the National Environmental Protection Act (NEPA) in 1968, requiring environmental impact statements for new public construction. Washington State passed its own State Environmental Policy Act (SEPA) in 1971. Her mentor in the prosecuting attorney's office, Norm Maleng, let her help brief the issue and sit at the counsel table during the litigation proceedings as King County defended the environmental impact study for the Kingdome, Seattle's new football stadium, arguing that there would be few adverse effects on the nearby Asian community. When they won the lawsuit and gained the necessary land-use approvals for the Kingdome, Mr. Maleng gave her the honor of retrieving the building permit from the city of Seattle.

FOSTER PEPPER

Ms. Runstad's ambition was to enter private practice. She landed a job with Foster Pepper, a regional Pacific Northwest law firm with an impressive stable of real estate clients, after working there during her later years at law school. No one in the firm was familiar with the burgeoning field of land-use and zoning law. Foster Pepper provided a platform for her to practice "the art of rainmaking"—generating opportunities and clients and spreading influence in the growing branch of land-use and environmental law.

> I joined them full time after graduating in 1974 and have been there all these years. I love the firm and the people and could not have accomplished everything I've done in my career without the support of my firm. I believe that my work has reflected positively on the firm. It's been a great collaboration.

She met Jon Runstad in 1973 while she was a summer intern at Foster Pepper. He had just formed a real estate development company, Wright Runstad & Company, with Howard S. Wright. Foster Pepper was their legal counsel when Wright Runstad undertook its first major project in Seattle, the Northgate Executive Center. She had followed NEPA and SEPA cases closely after her experience in the King County prosecuting attorney's office. Since the courts had required environmental reviews for public projects like the Kingdome, she expected they also might require environmental impact studies for private developments. She told the client, Jon Runstad, and Tom Foster, the firm's senior partner, that an environmental assessment might be required because the project might have impacts on a nearby creek.

> It was not the conventional thinking at the time. Tom Foster looked as if he were going to throw me out of his office, that I didn't know what I was talking about. He was embarrassed that somebody would be saying such silly things to a client struggling to start this company and who certainly didn't need roadblocks from [his] attorneys.

In the summer of 1973, the Washington State Supreme Court ruled that SEPA in fact did require environmental assessments as a precondition for private construction permits. The Seattle City Council placed a moratorium on commercial development permits until it could figure out how to react to the court's decision.

> I got some money from the client to hire someone to do a basic environmental assessment. I took the report to the superintendent of buildings, who asked, "What do you want me to do with this?" I suggested he initial it, file it, and give me my permit—which he did. That was the beginning of our land-use practice. After that, it just exploded with all the new rules and regulations.

New laws were being passed almost daily to deal with the land-use issues. She was the sole attorney practicing zoning and state environmental policy at the firm.

The practice was growing rapidly, but it was lonely. I went to one of the other attorneys and suggested we create a new land-use group. He agreed. Our group started with one lawyer, increasing to over 20 attorneys today in land use, environmental sustainability, growth management, zoning, shoreline management, and related regulatory matters. Creating that unit is one of my proudest achievements. Today our practice in the field is one of the strongest in the Pacific Northwest.

Ms. Runstad became partner at Foster Pepper in just four years. She founded and chaired their land-use group (1974–1989) and was co-managing partner (1988–1990). She is now attorney of counsel with Foster Pepper PLLC. "I was a hard-charging career woman who didn't want children. When I married Jon in 1977, he was a package deal: two stepdaughters and one surrogate daughter, who, together, now have eight children. It's been a wonderful experience, and I'm very lucky."

GUBERNATORIAL COMMISSIONS

Ms. Runstad was one of just a handful of experts deeply involved in environmental law from its earliest days. As Washington State established commissions to interpret the various environmental regulations, she was in the right place at the right time and was invited to serve on a total of six gubernatorial commissions.[1] The first three were direct extensions of her expertise and a natural outgrowth of her positive reputation as an environmental advisor: the Washington State Environmental Policy Act Commission, the Puget Sound Water Quality Authority, and the Washington State Growth Strategies Commission.

She had been a long-time friend and supporter of Governor Gary Locke, who formed the Washington Competitiveness Council to deal with the state's regulatory environment. At the time, it looked like Seattle had lost the Boeing headquarters and might also lose the Boeing Dreamliner. Other businesses were facing similar problems. "We came up with concrete recommendations to streamline the regulatory morass; many of our ideas were implemented through legislation or administrative orders. The council had terrific staff, and I do think we changed the business climate in the state."

Governor Chris Gregoire succeeded Governor Locke and followed a slightly different tactic, focusing on how Washington State could be more competitive in the international marketplace rather than vie against other states. Governor Gregoire emphasized education strategies, ports, and strategic global challenges. Ms. Runstad headed her Global Competitiveness Council for two years.

PROFESSIONAL AND COMMUNITY INVOLVEMENT

Ms. Runstad was introduced to governance through her early involvement in professional groups at the national and state bar associations. She was selected by her peers to be a member of the American College of Real Estate Lawyers. Shortly after joining Foster Pepper, she became a director (then chair) of the Washington State Young Lawyers Division and a director on the boards of the continuing legal education and the environmental and land-use law sections, all within the Washington State Bar Association.

> When I first moved to Seattle, I did all the grassroots things: I rang doorbells, working for political candidates. My work often put me in front of the city council, speaking publicly. I was a woman, which was a little bit unusual. People would hear about me; as a result, I kept being asked to do things.

Her volunteer work included fund-raising and leadership positions at the YWCA, the Seattle Art Museum, and local theater groups. "If you go on a committee," she said, "I believe you commit to working hard. If you work hard, people tend to want to make you chair. I was a serial volunteer, but I think I'm getting over that—it's like a disease."

DOWNTOWN SEATTLE ASSOCIATION

Ms. Runstad gravitated toward the business community, focusing her attention on the Downtown Seattle Association, an organization that Foster Pepper had joined because its business clients had interests in downtown projects. In the mid-1980s, Seattle was considering an initiative to limit new development. Ms. Runstad co-chaired a committee to help the city develop a comprehensive plan for an alternative to growth controls. She became the first female chair of the board of trustees of the Downtown Seattle Association. Later, she chaired the Seattle Chamber of Commerce, where she led the chamber's study mission to China during the SARS epidemic, broadening her exposure to global business issues.

UNITED WAY OF KING COUNTY

She faced the biggest challenge of her nonprofit career as the first woman chair of the King County United Way general campaign.

> A major national battle was brewing in 1988 when Catholic Community Services decided it did not want Planned Parenthood to be a United Way agency because of the abortion issue. Women's activist groups from all over the country became involved. The King County United Way board was dragged into the argument and voted to oust Planned Parenthood. Our fund-raising campaign was just getting started in September when the headlines hit: "United Way Kicks out Planned Parenthood." Seattle, which is a very liberal city, responded by boycotting the United Way campaign. For awhile, it looked like we were going to raise only $15 million (less than half of that year's $35 million goal). It was a hellacious experience, a nightmare, just heart rending. I had visited all the charitable agencies, and it looked like

we were going to have to cut their budgets in half. It was one of those experiences where every morning you had to just reach down into the very depths of your soul to figure out how you were going to get through the day.

Ms. Runstad hit the speaking trail, getting the word out at the downtown Rotary and at corporations throughout Seattle. "I said, 'We cannot let this happen. We have to spread the word about all of the innocent people who would be hurt. You need to persuade your companies to dig deeper.' Can you imagine? As the first woman? That was probably my biggest challenge."

To their credit, the corporations came through: the campaign raised the same amount as it had the previous year. Business interests in Seattle saw that Ms. Runstad was willing to stand up, speak out, and not lose sight of the larger goal. Some of the corporations that invited her onto their boards saw her rise to that occasion.

SAFECO MUTUAL FUND/SAFECO CORPORATION BOARDS

The Safeco Mutual Fund in Seattle was her first public company board (1982–1990). She met Dick Lange, a major Safeco Mutual Fund shareholder, at a social event. "He really wanted to promote women. I'm sure he picked up the phone and called the CEO at the time and said, 'You need a woman on your board. I just met this very professional lawyer, and you need to consider her for your board.'"

After nine years on the mutual fund board, Ms. Runstad was asked to join the board of Safeco Corporation, the major property and casualty insurance company. "They had seen the way I had handled the United Way campaign, where Safeco was a major supporter. I think they were pleased. And I'll give them credit: they were looking for a woman."

PUGET POWER BOARD

John Ellis, a former United Way campaign chair who knew her as a peer director of Safeco Corporation, invited her to join Puget Power Board in Bellevue, where he was CEO. She soon realized that there was a possible conflict of interest. Puget Power occupied a building owned by Jon Runstad's company, and they were entering into negotiations. Ms. Runstad sensed that the situation might be untenable and told Mr. Ellis she would resign. Her intuition at that time would be considered a sound governance judgment call in today's tougher Sarbanes-Oxley environment.

FEDERAL RESERVE BANK BOARD

The Seattle branch of the San Francisco Federal Reserve asked Ms. Runstad to join their board in 1989, where she soon rose to chair. Next, the San Francisco Bank board invited her to become deputy chair and then chair.[2] The Federal

Reserve looks for people active in the community. By law, they are required to have representation from the professions, labor, and industry, among other stakeholder categories.

> There I was: (a) a woman, (b) a professional, and (c) fairly active in the community. Even though I never majored in economics, I was fascinated by fiscal and monetary policy. It was a wonderful opportunity to interact with the other district board members, the Fed governors, and the chairman.

Once a year, the chair and deputy chair of each of the 12 Federal Reserve banks meet for a two-day conference with the board of governors and the chair of the Federal Reserve in Washington, D.C. She was named chair of the Conference of Chairmen in 1997. "The chair conducts the meeting where each district chair reports on the economic happenings in each district," she said. "The governors and the chair of the Federal Reserve listen quite attentively: it was fascinating."

WELLS FARGO BANK BOARD

Ms. Runstad met Paul Hazen, chair of Wells Fargo Bank while she was on the San Francisco Federal Reserve Bank board. "Paul was very blunt; he said, 'Frankly, I'm looking for a woman, and it's not easy to find women to go on a board.' I was stunned and probably should have been offended."

At her second board meeting at Wells Fargo, Mr. Hazen announced the proposed acquisition of the firm by Norwest Corporation of Minnesota. Wells Fargo quickly transformed itself from primarily a West Coast bank into a national financial behemoth. In May 1998, Ms. Runstad became one of 5 women among 14 directors at Wells Fargo. Of the other 4 women—Reatha Clark King, Cynthia Milligan, Susan G. Swenson, and Susan Engel—3 came from the board of Norwest.

For most of her years as a Wells Fargo director, Ms. Runstad served on the audit committee. As a lawyer, the value that she added was her in-depth understanding of changing trends in the regulatory arena. "I'm not a banking lawyer or a corporate lawyer, but I understand the regulatory environment. That truly is my forte."

Recently, she rotated onto the finance and credit committees, positions she had requested based on her strong interest in economic trends as a result of her Federal Reserve experience.

> To this day, I read speeches and news articles from the Fed. It changed the way I think about things. I feel that I can add value by helping the bank structure the ways it watches credit trends. Directors are not involved at the operational level: it's a huge, extraordinarily well-run bank. The board committees are, however, involved in policy and strategy. Little did I realize I would be asking to go on the credit committee when the world credit situation started to deteriorate. It's a more interesting time to be on that committee, because our job is to ask the probing questions.

POTLATCH CORPORATION BOARD

In 1999, Ms. Runstad became a director at Potlatch Corporation, the forest products company in Spokane, Washington, with timberland in Idaho, Arkansas, and Minnesota. It converted to a timberland real estate investment trust (REIT) in 2006.

> Potlatch was another case of the good old boys knowing the good old girls. I was deputy chair of the San Francisco Federal Reserve when the chair was Gary Michael, who was then CEO and chair of Albertson's, the grocery store. He knew Potlatch as the largest private label supplier of tissues to Albertson's. He heard that Potlatch was looking for a woman director and recommended me.

As a manufacturing and forest products company, Potlatch meant new challenges for her financial services background. Ultimately, her expertise in land use, real estate, and environmental regulations became a valued resource.

> The board's interest in transitioning to a timber REIT was a logical change, but difficult to implement, mechanically. Under the REIT rules, non–real estate income is limited; so the company had to spin off several businesses. That was a complicated process, and management is to be credited with doing a splendid job by creating a lot of value for shareholders, especially because of the tax structure. It also enabled us to recruit new management. Overall, it has been an extraordinary success story. Today, lumber is not doing well because of the housing crisis, but timber is a crop that renews itself every 50 years. Timber land is highly desirable, as are carbon credits.

Originally, Ms. Runstad was a director at Potlatch with Vivian W. Piasecki and Toni Rembe. Both have retired, and Ruth Ann M. Gillis was added to the board in 2003. "The board already had one woman, Toni Rembe, a lawyer who had been with the law firm of Pillsbury Madison & Sutro LLP (now Pillsbury Winthrop Shaw Pittman LLP) even longer than I've been with Foster Pepper. She chaired the nominating committee, and I'm pretty sure she had a lot to do with my being invited to join their board."

Ms. Runstad is chair of the nominating and corporate governance committee and a member of the executive compensation and personnel policies committee at Potlatch. She was involved in identifying Ruth Ann Gillis as a director candidate. "Ruth Ann is terrific: what a find! I really wanted another woman on the board. We had a great headhunter who was very persistent. Ruth Ann is a marvelous operational person with great common sense who adds a lot of value to our board."

INVESTING IN EDUCATION

Education has been a major interest of Ms. Runstad's ever since she was a high school teacher. A number of organizations supporting the Seattle school district had sprung up during the 1980s, with the help of local business interests. In 1995, they consolidated the separate groups under the Seattle Alliance for Education, a nonprofit organization, "to serve as a catalyst for change, a convener of community leadership, and a conduit for directing private resources—both dollars and expertise—toward critical needs in Seattle Public Schools"[3] She is a past chair.

She served as a participating mentor at the Albers School of Business and Economics at Seattle University and as a trustee on their board of directors. She chairs the audit committee of the Seattle Foundation, a large community foundation (which is run by a woman with whom Ms. Runstad has served on corporate boards, Phyllis Campbell).

Ms. Runstad serves on the advisory board of the Michael G. Foster School of Business at the University of Washington in Seattle. A friend approached her and her husband to create a center for interdisciplinary real estate studies to bring together students from the business school, the college of architecture, the college of urban design, and the law school to teach them how to collaborate and understand the real estate process from each others' perspectives. In June 2000, the University of Washington announced that the Runstad Center for Real Estate would begin accepting the first class for an masters' degree in 2009.

> With all of my years in land-use battles, if I had been able to deal with planners who understood financing of projects, it would have made life so much easier. If only architects had a better grasp of land-use and zoning issues. If only developers had the perspective of urban planners. Our whole mantra is that this center will be interdisciplinary. We are so excited about it.

Jon Runstad, in April 2005, as a gift for his wife, organized the Judith Runstad Discovery Lecture Series at the University of Idaho. They expanded an existing interdisciplinary lecture series through a $15,000 honorarium for speakers to visit and talk with the students.

Many of the accolades Ms. Runstad has received are due to her highly effective fund-raising work. Other recognitions are from peer attorneys who acknowledge her outstanding contributions as a distinguished law professional. Women's organizations have provided her accolades as the first woman in many leadership positions. An award that she values highly is being named an honorary member of the local chapter of the American Institute of Architects in 2004, a recognition she shares with her husband.

LESSONS LEARNED

Like many women directors, Ms. Runstad has tapped the growing talent pool of competent and experienced women at the top tiers of public companies.

> I don't agree that it's not easy to find qualified women to serve on a corporate board. That might have been the case back when boards were looking only for sitting CEOs. In the old days, it was a case of only "the good ol' boys" and

"who do you see on other boards?" It became self-perpetuating. Today, the world has changed: a board of only CEOs would not be a good policy, just like having a board composed of only lawyers would not be advisable.

There are so many good women in the marketplace today.... *Corporate Board* magazine just published their [issue of] fifty women to watch in the tech world—truly outstanding women, some of whom everybody would know, but also some of whom are not well known and do not yet appear to be on any board. We have to constantly keep focused on women and minorities to make sure we all don't fall into our old habits of tapping the same familiar names.

Many boards now look for women in the professions, women who head up a line of business: CFOs, COOs, CIOs. Boards have become much more creative in searching for women director candidates.

Boards and headhunters are becoming more professional about how they search for new directors. As the use of headhunters to recruit directors is no longer seen as a second-class way of doing things, then we will get better at recruiting diverse talent. It is incumbent upon the chair of the nominating committee to make sure that the headhunters do more than simply tap their old rolodex [and] use [resources] like the Internet to find new talent.

Ms. Runstad participates with her company in advising women how to advance their careers and how to prepare themselves for governance service. Her advice is a reflection of her own career.

Be willing to take risks. Be willing to learn from your mistakes. I certainly made mistakes along the way. Every time you give a speech, every time you put yourself on the line on some business transaction, or anywhere that you could make a fool of yourself, you have to take risks. Perhaps women, for whatever reason, have been less willing to take those risks. I think that is changing now. We can learn a great deal from our mistakes.

Develop expertise in negotiating. I learned negotiation in the school of hard knocks. I never had classes in negotiating skills. I relied on my intuition. I always felt that the value I [brought to] the client was to understand what the public wanted in a project and then to walk that fine line between the public's policy goals and the developer's need to create a profitable project. To do that, you had to recognize what each party needed. Really good lawyers do that in almost all areas of the law. That's something that Tom Foster drummed into me from the day I walked into his office. Always figure out how to get the deal done. What does each party need? Figure out how to get there. Be a deal maker rather than a deal breaker. To this day, I hear his words echoing in my head.

Be willing to do more homework. Women have to be almost better on a board then men. They have a lot of catching up to do. In my board meetings, I'm probably better prepared than half of the people there. I work very hard to make sure I am on top of issues and materials.

Learn how to speak up in the boardroom. Women have to take the risk to speak up [and] state what's on their minds. At the same time, they cannot be noisy or confrontational either. It's a very fine line, but women cannot be reluctant in the boardroom.

Be willing to serve. There are many women in the marketplace today who would be viable director candidates. Willing[ness] is another big issue. Sometimes, the ones who are willing aren't the ones you want on the board. And the ones you want on the board are not always willing. The liability issues and the time commitment today are very different from 10 to 20 years ago, when I first went on a board. There are some real issues there that keep good people from going on boards.

The women who are CEOs of major corporations probably already know a lot of this, because it comes from experience. When I look for board candidates, I look for people who have been successful in their endeavors. That will give me a successful board member.

DIRECTOR PROFILE: KATHLEEN A. COTE

Kathleen "Kath" A. Cote, age 59 at the time of our interview, has over 30 years of executive management experience in emerging technology companies and large multinational technology organizations. She currently is an advisor and board member to four companies where she provides strategic, operational, and organizational expertise.

EARLY YEARS

Ms. Cote was born in Southbridge in 1949 and raised in Sturbridge, both small towns in south central Massachusetts. Her interest in history was sparked when she played with the children of workers at Old Sturbridge Village, New England's largest outdoor American history museum, where visitors experience a live re-creation of the 1800s.

Like other members of her family (her mother, two sisters, and a brother), she worked at a pharmacy in town, learning about business at the entrepreneurial level: inventory control, buying products, stocking the shelves, and dealing directly with customers. Her father worked at American Optical, a large business in Southbridge. Her family did not set any limits on what she might become, but a small town provided young women with little exposure to role models other than teacher, nurse, secretary, or librarian. The financial burden of a legal or medical career put those options out of reach for her family.

Thus, a natural career path was to study at the University of Massachusetts, Amherst, to become a history teacher. She practice-taught at a school in East Longmeadow, Massachusetts, and considered working there after graduating in 1971 with a BA in history. By then, she was married and so tried to find work closer to her husband's employment in Boston.

CTI CRYOGENICS CORPORATION

Ms. Cote scanned the papers for clerical positions and found an ad for an inventory control clerk, at just $100 a week, at CTI Cryogenics in Waltham, Massachusetts (now Brooks Automation Inc. in Chelmsford). CTI was so small that she interviewed with the president of the company as well as the heads of inventory, production, control, and human resources.

The only other women at CTI were the head of HR and two secretaries. I was just 21. My boss, Bob Armstrong, head of production control, was twice my age. He asked, "Do you know how to type?" Before I could answer, he said, "Don't answer that. If you know how to type, don't ever tell anyone. If you don't know, that's fine with me." He took me under his wing, taught me the ropes, and put time and energy into mentoring me. Production control was done manually in those days—just paper and pencil. We'd pour over blueprints describing the processes. There were no inventory management systems.

She loved the business world but soon realized that she needed a better foundation in accounting, marketing, organization, and business management. She decided to go to graduate school at Babson College in Wellesley, Massachusetts, studying for an MBA at night for the next five years while working full time at CTI.

Her focus was on her work and her studies, not on her relationship, which soon took its toll. She and her husband separated and divorced in the late 1970s. Working in the male-dominated world of manufacturing was a challenge on its own merits. CTI was a specialized low-technology machine works that fabricated infra-red scanning devices for the B-52 airplanes that were deployed to Vietnam or for laboratory instrumentation. Slowly, she earned more responsibilities and the confidence of initially skeptical male shop workers. But sensing that she would always be the clerk and not the MBA, she left CTI for a small engineering company in Gloucester, Massachusetts, where she worked for about a year before CTI invited her back with an offer to head one of their business units. Ultimately, she ended up running all of CTI's operations, gaining valuable experience in engineering prototyping, production drawings, and tight-tolerance, low-volume manufacturing. Still, she realized that if her career was going to go anywhere, she would have to get into high technology, a field that was just beginning to blossom.

MFE CORPORATION

In Gloucester, she had met Basil Dixon, who later became head of operations for MFE Corporation (now Memtec Corporation) in Salem, New Hampshire. He invited her to become manager in charge of all production for their 250-man operation. MFE produced chart recorders for heart monitoring and laboratory equipment and was just starting up a disk drive assembly operation, running a high-volume production center with state-of-the-art technology. She took over a much larger staff of assembly personnel—markedly different from the craftsmen she had supervised at CTI.

> I was pretty tough in those days. I thought I knew a lot. It was great. There's nothing like working in a manufacturing environment where at the end of the day you can count up exactly what you got done. There's a lot of satisfaction in terms of who the people are: no nonsense, no egos. We knew what we accomplished every day. Manufacturing operations is a very performance-based environment, very little politics.

WANG LABORATORIES

MFE also had limited growth potential. By 1979, Wang Laboratories in Lowell and Tewksbury, Massachusetts, was looking for new blood to fuel its rapidly expanding growth. Wang's head of human resources invited her for an interview, and she was brought in to run a group of six people doing final assembly and testing of their small desktop systems, reporting to vice president Joe Klemintovich. Within two months, she was running their entire printed circuit board testing area.

Wang was adding sophisticated new equipment for automated circuit board testing, but the technical person who brought the concept to Wang was not as good a manager. Mr. Klemintovich asked Ms. Cote to take over the group, where she was put in charge of all high-volume sub-assembly production work. Wang next asked her to manage the start-up and operation of a million-square-foot highly automated production plant at Pawtucket Boulevard in Lowell, Massachusetts. Because of her success with the Pawtucket Boulevard plant, she was invited by vice president of operations Jon Kropper to start up another unique plant in nearby Holyoke.

> I set up goals for the plant to have a highly diverse and involved workforce. My management approach, style, and ambitions meshed well with this particular effort. Wang was grooming me to have my own plant. It was a great opportunity—that plant was my baby, so to speak. I was there from 1983 to 1985, but then the computer market recession hit in 1985–1986. Wang had to pull back to the headquarters operation in Lowell. After all that effort and energy to build it up, I had to downsize the Holyoke plant.[1]

She returned to Lowell, worked on a few minor projects, and then was named head of all U.S. manufacturing for Wang and asked to consolidate the Tewksbury facilities back into Lowell. "There were these cycles of growing things and then consolidating them," she said. "I had wonderful experiences both ramping businesses up to deliver high-volume output and figuring out ways to do more with less, followed by the more difficult tasks of consolidating, restructuring, reducing, and making the very hard decisions around people, layoffs, and keeping the remaining staff motivated. I learned a lot through it all."

PRIME COMPUTER/COMPUTERVISION

Ms. Cote knew that Wang would never give a woman the chance to head an international assignment. When Prime Computer called her about a position, she realized their huge operations might provide the international experience that was missing in her background. Discussions with several people at Prime continued over the next six months. Their vice president of operations had both manufacturing and services under him, and he finally hired her to take over manufacturing.

Prime Computer's headquarters, in Natick, Massachusetts, had issued a press release announcing her arrival. When she started on the job at the manufacturing plant in Framingham in November 1986, some men were reading the newspaper clipping posted on the plant bulletin board. She overheard one of them say to his friends, "Can you believe they hired a woman to run manufacturing?"

Within two years, Prime merged with Computervision (February 1988), a major competitor in the computer-aided design/manufacturing (CAD/CAM) software market. She became part of the team responsible for consolidating the manufacturing operations of the two firms. Prime had plants in Puerto Rico and Ireland. Computervision brought in many more international operations: Germany, France Hong Kong, and Japan. Her job was to rationalize these two different cultures and eliminate domestic plant redundancies. "It was a very large and complex merger/ acquisition and a whole new experience for me. Being a woman in manufacturing was quite an anomaly. Out of that evolved the position of head of global manufacturing for the combined companies, reporting to Mel Friedman, senior vice president of operations."

The newly combined company soon became a target of a hostile takeover attempt by Bennett LeBow, a financier who owned a competing small computer maker, MAI/Basic Four. Mr. LeBow began buying up Computervision stock in 1988 to force their board into merger/acquisition negotiations. "That really put us into a state of turmoil," recalled Ms. Cote, "and we became very inwardly focused. My boss left in the middle of it all, so I reported to the new CEO, Tony Craig, who was trying to defend us from this hostile takeover."

Anthony Craig took over as CEO in October 1988. He had been a chief executive of the Information Services division of General Electric Company after 17 years at IBM. Computervision's management believed that it would be a better opportunity for the firm to find a white knight. Ms. Cote became part of the team dealing with investors, public relations companies, and venture capital companies, making strategic pitches to sell the company to outside interests and persuading them that there were opportunities to streamline the business further.

A buyout was organized in 1989 by J. H. Whitney & Company, a venture capital firm, but due to the heavy leverage required, Computervision inherited $1.5 billion worth of debt. J. H. Whitney principals were brought in to run the company and to downsize the firm beyond what had been accomplished with the merger.

They asked Ms. Cote to step out of manufacturing and take over the services arm. From 1989 to 1995, she was president and general manager of PrimeService, which was its own P&L (profit and loss) and a $500 million-plus business that supported all of the Computervision and Prime hardware and software. They believed it could be the cash generator for the company.

Don Ackerman, one of the J. H. Whitney principals, worked closely with me and developed a great strategy. He'd come in every six weeks or so with his list of priorities we had to focus on to get the business to be more profitable. So, now I was running a P&L, it was very process oriented, and it was international. It was a great opportunity for me to build on all my prior experiences.

The company realized it had to restructure and focus more strategically on the software side because the hardware business had now become more competitive and was beginning to standardize around a few operating systems. Russ Planitzer, a former partner of J. H. Whitney, stepped in as CEO to take the company through that restructuring and strategy refocus. Mr. Planitzer asked her to become vice president of marketing and services of Computervision in 1994 to take over software, streamline marketing, and get the company out of unproductive segments.

We had to get out of Prime's old computer hardware business while still preserving our clients' investments. We started up some new value-added services in systems integration and networking, offering new levels of business consulting, systems, software, and network services to replace other declining businesses.

I was taking on some of the most difficult high-profile activities in the company. I was successful at anything that was thrown at me. I got the jobs done. I had a lot of visibility. The services business became the financial backbone of the company: I demonstrated how we could reduce costs, improve margins, and create new businesses that could grow quickly.

In one of my courses at Babson, they had us map out our career in five-year increments. Way back then, my master plan was to be a CEO making over $50,000 by the time I was 50 years old. When the president/COO position opportunity came up, it was the acknowledged stepping stone; it was an opportunity for me to compete for the next level. The president/COO job was mine to lose. I knew the company; it was in a lot of turmoil.

In quick succession, she took over as president and chief operating officer of Computervision in November 1995 and then a year later was elevated to president and CEO, where she spent the next two years. She co-led the corporation's restructuring with Russ Planitzer, who was now chair of the board.

It wasn't the best position to be in as a new CEO, not an easy time. Any new outside CEO might have had even more difficulties. It was a trial by fire in a market that had some very tough competition. I can remember being anxious, very stressed—there were no easy answers. The company, the board, and the management all were under tremendous pressure. We had to continually downsize the company. Russ Planitzer and I evolved a strategic process of divide and conquer. I was chartered with the day-to-day operations, focused on keeping operations moving and the company together so there would be something of value to sell if we could find a strategic party. Russ took the time to talk with companies about strategic relationships or a merger/acquisition.

The market was in huge turmoil, with tremendous pressure from Wall Street. We did create some things that had lasting value for the market and for the successor organization. For example, we were using the Internet in the early 1990s for our services business because one young man who worked for me, Ravi Ravindra, kept talking about the possibilities it created. We did some of the very earliest implementations on the Internet.

There were positive things from that experience: I helped to solidify an internal and market strategy around product life-cycle management. We bought a company that had a Web-based data management system. Because of those efforts, Parametric Technology was able to follow the lead we established to branch out beyond CAD/CAM engineering seats to the beginnings of Web-based applications in the product life-cycle management space.

In January 1998, Computervision Corporation was acquired by Parametric Technology Corporation. "When we were acquired, that was the time for me to go. It didn't make any sense for me to stay. I fared well: we had employment agreements. Now I could pick and choose what I wanted to do."

EARLY GOVERNANCE EXPERIENCE

Ms. Cote's early board roles gave her even more insight into the tumultuous change inherent in the high-technology marketplace. Mergers, acquisitions, sale, resale, restructuring, and rebranding all characterized the four small public and private company boards that she joined in the late 1990s.

- Ms. Cote was named to the board of directors of Computervision in July 1996, while she was president/COO of the firm.
- She joined the board of WellFleet Communications (later WellFleet/Bay Networks) in Billerica, Massachusetts, in August 1996 at the request of Russ Planitzer, who was leaving that board.
- Her next board was an academic board. In 1996, Don Ackerman (formerly of J. H. Whitney) invited her to become a director of Walden University, "the university without walls" (now Laureate Education), in Minneapolis, Minnesota.
- She was recruited by an executive search firm to join her third outside board, MediaOne, joining Janice Peters as a director.
- In December 1999, another search firm recruited her for the board of Vtel Inc., a videoconferencing equipment manufacturer in Austin, Texas.

The company changed its name to Forgent Networks Inc. and later Asure Software.

Ms. Cote served on the audit committee of MediaOne, Walden University, and WellFleet/Bay Networks and continues to chair the audit committee for Asure.

SEAGRASS PARTNERS

In January 1998, Ms. Cote founded Seagrass Partners as a consulting firm to provide expertise in business planning and strategic development. She served as president of Seagrass through May 2001.

I had the severance package from the Parametric Technology acquisition, plus some shares from the Bay Networks sale. Now that I had achieved all of my goals, I had to decide what to do with my life. I was too young to do nothing. I contemplated taking another CEO job, but after looking around, I realized that most of the available CEO opportunities looked like more of the same: come in, the company has problems, help us restructure the firm. I wanted a CEO position with a start-up in the newer technology space, but no one believed that I was capable of doing anything except the big company stuff, as I had been doing over the past dozen years. My interest was in working with start-ups in what was becoming the hot new place: the Internet. Also, my goal was to have more flexibility in my life: to be able to pick and choose the projects rather than jump into a situation where I had to make a significant long-term commitment. I formed Seagrass Partners as the vehicle for investments and start-up activities, while also continuing with my board work.

Through Seagrass Partners, she was able to jump into situations where she could get an equity position, take on a mentor role, and advise entrepreneurial CEOs who had a lot of vision but needed help creating business plans, defining their strategies, putting together an operation and organization, or getting out in front of investment companies.

I didn't work full time with the companies in which we invested. I filled holes for them when they needed it in terms of staffing. Seagrass Partners was my company through which I tapped my network of people who could move in and add expertise that the company needed: human resources, financial, marketing, or legal, depending upon the requirements.

WORLDPORT COMMUNICATIONS INC.

Ms. Cote became a director of WorldPort Communications Inc. (originally in Kennesaw, Georgia) from July 2000 to June 18, 2003. She was asked to join the WorldPort board by one of its directors, Andy Sage, a former board member at Computervision.

Michael Heisley, a former CEO who became chair of WorldPort, explained his reasons for naming Ms. Cote chief executive officer in May 2001:

> I hand over the position of CEO of Worldport with complete confidence that Kathleen Cote is the ideal person to leverage the recent acquisition of *hostmark* and drive Worldport to the next level of strategic growth. Her invaluable international and operations experience coupled with her experience in enterprise and Web-based applications and services render her uniquely suited to establish Worldport as a powerful competitor in the Internet solutions market.[2]

Hostmark was a Web-hosting and professional services provider through which WorldPort acquired Internet solution centers in the United Kingdom, Sweden, and Germany to expand services throughout European cities. Ms. Cote's track record managing international operations centers was very attractive.

> The board said, "Our strategy is not working; would you step in and figure it out?" I was invited to come in as CEO; I relocated to London. Our focus was European—we had a huge infrastructure operation in Ireland and were developing others in France, Germany, Sweden, and London. It soon became evident that the market was not shaping up as people had thought. The board and I realized that if we didn't do something dramatic, quickly, we were going to run out of money. We started the process, again, of downsizing and streamlining, trying to figure out if there was a business. It became clear that the business was going to elude us. Several other companies were going under because the market was just not evolving as predicted. The only way for this kind of business to succeed at that time was to reinvent itself by acquisitions of cheap assets. It was too late for us.

The company ceased all active business operations in early 2002. Heico Companies repurchased the outstanding shares at a discount in 2003. She stayed on as CEO until June 18, 2003. A shareholder derivative class-action lawsuit was filed against the company and its two executive officers on March 12, 2003. It was settled in August 2004.

> The lawsuit at Worldport was unfortunate, but a great learning experience. It emphasized the importance of establishing a sound governance process as a board of directors. It also demonstrated the reality that whatever you do as a board must be founded on solid business principles, that decisions must be made in good conscience and in the best interests of the shareholders. Because I have experienced various lawsuits in my career, I am cognizant of the reality that litigation is part of the business system and that anyone can find a reason to sue.

WESTERN DIGITAL CORPORATION BOARD

Ms. Cote became a director of Western Digital Corporation, the Lake Forest, California, provider of high-volume computer storage devices, in January 2001.

Thomas E. Pardun of MediaOne became the chair of the board and recommended her. "I didn't know Tom well at MediaOne—he just knew about me." Mr. Pardun's welcoming statement revealed how her reputation preceded her: "We are very pleased to have someone with Kath Cote's deep technology and high-tech manufacturing experience join the Western Digital board. Her insights and experience make her an outstanding addition."[3]

RADVIEW SOFTWARE LTD. BOARD

Another board search found her for the directorship of RadView Software Ltd. in Tel Aviv and Burlington, Massachusetts, in May 2001. Ilan Kinreich, RadView founder, CEO, and president, announced her arrival with these words: "For many years, Kathleen has been instrumental in building world class organizations and helping to lead companies to increased levels of profitable revenue growth and market share."[4]

Recalled Ms. Cote: "RadView was a very small start-up. The company made performance-monitoring software for Web applications. It went public but never had enough money to get going." She resigned from the board in April 2006 as the company prepared to take on new leadership following the close of a definitive financing agreement with Fortissimo Capital Fund GP LP.

BOSTON COMMERCE VENTURES

In 2003, she briefly rejoined the investment world as a managing partner of Boston Commerce Ventures, a private equity company providing expertise in strategic, operational, and organizational assessments; financial assistance; and access to capital. Charlotte Walker, Jim Kelley, Dennis Shepard, and Ms. Cote co-founded Boston Commerce Ventures. Mr. Shepard had spent 25 years in senior management at Wang Laboratories. Boston Commerce Ventures was primarily a replacement of Seagrass Partners through which they collaborated on assignments together through 2005.

WORKSCAPE INC. BOARD

In January 2006, Ms. Cote became a director of Workscape Inc., a private company in Marlborough, Massachusetts, that provides outsourced benefits and compensation services. Tim Clifford, president and CEO of Workscape, said, "Kathleen Cote's proven leadership skills—especially her operations expertise—will be instrumental to our global expansion. She is proficient in creating highly productive teams and leveraging internal resources to address external complexities."[5]

The head of human resources of Workscape worked for me back in the Wang/Holyoke days, and he recommended me to their board. On some level, the value I bring is strategic and financial, but to a greater degree, it's my operational experience: they want me to look at their operating costs and processes. They have a large services organization. In order to improve their bottom line, they're trying to streamline how they use technology to deliver services to their customers.

VERISIGN INC. BOARD

In February 2008, Ms. Cote was appointed to the board of VeriSign Inc. in Mountain View, California, which provides Internet security infrastructure services to protect voice, video, and data interactions and transactions. She was recommended by two board members at VeriSign: Lou Simpson from MediaOne and Roger Moore, a board member at Western Digital. Ms. Cote is the sole female among eight directors. VeriSign chair Jim Bidzos welcomed Ms. Cote with these words: "Kath Cote has strong operational and governance experience in the technology industry, including guiding companies through transitions. VeriSign will benefit greatly from Kath's experience as we work to align our business around our core competency of offering scalable, reliable and secure Internet infrastructure."[6]

LESSONS LEARNED

Certainly the value Ms. Cote brings to her board roles is her strategic, operational, and financial experience. She transformed an essentially all-operational and manufacturing skill set into a broad-based expertise that today encompasses high technology, a global perspective, and investor-oriented insight drawn from some of the most tumultuous years of venture and technology ups and downs.

She is considered an independent director and a financial expert. Currently, she is chair of the audit committees at Asure Software and Workscape and is on the audit committee of the Western Digital and VeriSign corporate boards and the governance committee of Western Digital. She came to her board roles by climbing up the corporate technology ladder at CTI, MFE, Wang, and Prime/Computervision. She is tapped as one who occupied the CEO hot seat at two high-technology firms; boards know that she has personal insight into the challenges of taking the helm of a corporation into growth waters as well as bringing a company back home to a downsized, merged, or acquired entity. She has placed herself and her money on the line at start-up ventures while at Seagrass Partners and at Boston Commerce Ventures, so corporate boards can be confident that she brings a shareholder's perspective to their deliberations. She survived shareholder lawsuits, acquired and merged operations, closed down businesses, and sold them to others.

Ms. Cote gained her board roles through a range of opportunities: referrals came from executive search firms, former employees, former bosses, former colleagues, people she knew well, and even people who knew more of her than she knew of them. She has been involved in just a few community and academic efforts, principally as an extension of her corporate leadership positions, but also as an expression of her personal dedication to constant learning. "One of the things that drives me is learning. I'm a lifelong learner. I like to learn and I love to teach, which is why I believe in mentoring. Each of these experiences brought me some new learning dimension."

For Ms. Cote, nothing could be more important than learning what works well in business:

When the technology bubble was happening, I used to feel that I must be a dinosaur. All of the things that I believed in—about business models, profitability, and how you build a start-up into something of value—seemed to be no longer applicable. Businesses cropped up out of nowhere, there were no barriers to entry, and people threw good money after bad. It turns out that those times were the anomaly. We all learned the lesson that there are good reasons for fundamentals in business. Now, we're trying to get back to basics. We certainly relearned that the basic rules of good business still do apply. The rules really are there for a reason. Now, I don't feel so much like a dinosaur.

Ms. Cote did not seek out board roles as much as boards found her. Her experience demonstrates that boards want diversity and to add more women. "Nobody told me that diversity was part of the search criteria for many of the boards where I was selected. I just knew it. It was obvious to me."

Right now, I don't see a lot of women on corporate boards. My primary measure is that when I attend corporate director education programs at major universities or business schools, I don't see a lot of women there. It is still exceptional to see women in senior staff positions in technology; it is a little different in HR or in industries focused on women (such as apparel firms), where there are more women in line positions.

At Wang, I stopped what I was doing in order to take on that special high-profile project. I got the plant off the ground with a great team of people. You have to be willing to step out and take on these assignments that have a lot of visibility. You learn a lot, and you certainly get noticed when you succeed.

Ms. Cote suggests that women need to pursue opportunities to "take the helm"—to run a line organization—because she believes that P&L accountability is the key to achieving the top levels of leadership.

There are two guiding principles that I learned early in my career on corporate boards: the duty of care and the duty of loyalty. I believe that board members are now more attuned to these principles than in the past. At the same time, I believe there is more risk then ever before for a public company board member despite the Sarbanes-Oxley efforts. Corporate governance expectations continue to evolve every day.

8

CONCLUSION: QUO VADIS?

There's nothing quite like trying to walk in the shoes of the many outstanding women who currently serve on corporate boards of directors at public companies. These women were chosen to serve because their experience added value to their boards. Clearly, any woman can become competent, qualified, and capable of serving as a director. Some of the women we profiled came from small towns, low incomes, and hardship, while others grew up during an era when it was assumed that "good men would take care of us." Some of the women succeeded, failed, and succeeded again. They all became corporate directors. At the same time, it is clear that not every woman will become a director, nor should every woman become a director. A corporate board role is not an entitlement. It is an achievement.

The purpose of this journey was to extract, from the experiences of both the boards and the women, the lessons and advice that the next generation of women can use as they approach their careers and broach the following questions:

1. If you want to lead, what does leadership look like today?
2. If you want good corporate governance, what does it look like?
3. If you want more diversity in top companies, how does it happen?
4. If you want your company to grow and thrive, how might a company with outstanding women directors help make that happen?
5. If we want more women as leaders, where and how do women learn to be leaders?

WHAT BOARDS ARE NOT

The preceding chapters focused on the outstanding 114 women who serve on California-based *Fortune* 1000 companies, and on the lives of 15 exemplary women in particular. We live in a world where the popular and business media feed us stories about a host of other women: those who believe there are shortcuts into the boardroom, that they are entitled to a corporate director role, or that diversity stands alone as a measure of corporate success. It is essential that women start pushing back and challenging the stories ripped from the evening headlines about how women *don't...*, why women *can't...*, or why women *only....* The reason we examined myths about women directors in these pages was to substitute facts and to help readers develop a better understanding of what it truly takes for women to reach this top leadership position.

Companies with female directors on their boards selected those individuals, less and less today because of their gender, and more and more because the individual women represent the best-educated, the most experienced, and the most independently minded director candidates in the contemporary business marketplace. Corporations and their boards of directors do not succeed based on their ability to attract the attention of the evening news. They do not benefit from controversy about the gender makeup of their boards. In fact, smart boards—and the very savvy women directors there—avoid the news limelight to the best of their ability.

Effective boards succeed based on the quiet, intense deliberations that take place among a handful of highly competent people who dedicate themselves to providing direction, oversight, and a conscience for the company, its management, and its shareholders. Ineffective boards are the ones whose dirty laundry gets aired in the very public forum of news headlines. No one member of the board is the sole source of the success or the failure of the company: not one woman and not just one man. The headlines tell women today what some of their mothers have been trying to tell women who aspire to leadership roles: "If you want to play in the big leagues, honey, you better get ready to play by the rules of the game."

Sometimes the real world is not as pretty as our perfect households. If women want to be directors on the boards of today's corporations, they have to prepare themselves to deal with major issues like bankruptcies, the subprime mortgage crisis, executive compensation challenges, environmental regulations, overseas toy company fabrication, labor strife, and chemical risks in the food chain. The real world includes the challenges of salmonella, predatory lenders and brokers, and compensation consultants who behave like agents to Hollywood and sports superstars.

Women need to understand how business economies work if they want to take their place in the boardroom. Increasing the share of board seats held by women will not happen just because women wish it would be so. It won't happen if we rap businesses' knuckles with governance regulations, like a mommy ruler. If we want to see more women as directors at top corporate boards, women themselves have to accept that being a director today is a much tougher job than it ever was in the past; requires preparation, experience, education, and a certain toughness; and is a role for those who are willing to face business risks and tackle them to the floor in order to ensure the long-term success of the company, its management, its shareholders, and its stakeholders.

About 1,100 women today have accepted the challenge of serving on the top boards of directors of the nation's *Fortune* 1000 firms in one of the toughest, most competitive economies in the world. In 2009 alone, we could see another 300 women named to public corporate boards of directors on firms of that size or the tier just below it.

How do these women get onto boards of directors? They were *not* selected for a board because they attended a $1,000-a-plate fund-raising dinner where the speakers excoriated and embarrassed the men who built their corporations from a dream in a garage somewhere then organized a founder's board of directors to work together to grow the firm into a corporate powerhouse.

As we look at the backgrounds of the women who serve on top corporate boards, we see that they possess the same competence and skills as their male peers. And that is exactly why these women were chosen to be part of the corporate board of director team—because they have the competence to contribute in a world where headlines screamed on the outside. These are the women who could be counted on by their director peers during the quiet, intense, tough deliberations—away from the limelight—back in the boardroom, where they all were working together, trying to lead their company through some very tough times. These are the women, as Warren Buffet has said, who know how "to think like an intelligent owner."[1]

WHAT IS LEADERSHIP? WHAT IS A LEADER?

Women have to ask themselves what kind of leadership they want and therefore what kind of leaders they can aspire to become. Is a leader a television icon? A celebrity? A popular movie star? Someone who makes a lot of money or has great personal wealth? Is a leader simply someone who wins the attention of the press and news media? Is a leader some nice man or woman who makes people feel good or feel better about themselves? All these traits have been used to describe "leading women" and "women to watch."

Based on our examination of, and interviews with, the women directors of California corporations, we see leading women within the context of the steps each took to earn our respect and that of their professional peers. We are willing to turn over to them the keys to the boardroom of our major public shareholding corporations. What did they do to earn that trust and respect? Across all the career paths that they pursued, there are some things that they have in common:

1. They chose a worthy skill or endeavor that was of deep interest to them.
2. They refined that skill and enhanced and developed it through their personal efforts.
3. They connected with others who subscribed to goals and missions that complemented their primary area of interest; they recruited others and were recruited by others.
4. They delivered excellent results through delegation and synergies; they didn't try to do it all themselves.

5. They built organizations, institutions, and programs that could endure.
6. They demonstrated leadership, often in the face of challenge.

It's easier to point to leaders among men because they've been at this leadership thing longer. In business, leaders include W. Edwards Deming and Peter Drucker. In sports, the obvious leader would be coach John Wooden. In these pages, we have just met women who are the match of any male leader today. For the next generation of women who aspire to leadership, this is what we have learned from these incredibly outstanding women.

LESSONS LEARNED FROM OUTSTANDING WOMEN CORPORATE DIRECTORS

Engage in a Worthy Skill or Endeavor

First, a leader does something she perceives to be important, valuable, and very interesting. It's not enough simply to do the work that needs to be done. A leader is engaged in efforts that others in society recognize as valuable. Leaders engage in the best use of their intelligence and labors. They possess capabilities that they have refined and strengthened and skills that they have honed and improved. Leaders receive compensation and rewards for that investment of time, intelligence, and effort: they are paid, earn profits, achieve, compete, and garner awards and accolades for their accomplishments. Attention is not enough. Being the object of public adulation or paparazzi attention does not make a leader. A leader invests herself fully in comprehending the entire field in which she can excel: the subject of her chosen skill and all the complex interrelated issues. Each skill is highly valued by the business board on which she serves because the individual has established a clear, strong track record and because the skill complements or rounds out the competencies possessed by the other board members.

Enhance and Develop Your Chosen Skill Through Personal Effort

Second, a leader takes that skill to some higher, more refined level through the application of her own intellect. She brings unique insight to her skill set by further refinement, experimentation, and deliberation. She constantly improves the gift she's been given. Doing the same thing over and over leads to boredom. Doing something new and better enhances the skill and improves the skill holder. A leader is constantly learning about what her skill can become and what she can become through this process. She knows the strengths and weaknesses of the talent she possesses and can convey those insights to those who would benefit from knowing.

Recruit Like-Minded Individuals

Third, a leader is constantly looking for like-minded individuals who might be recruited to her mission of constantly enhancing this highly valued, worthy area of endeavor. She knows she cannot do as much alone as she could do in collaboration or partnership with other equally talented individuals. She is constantly on the lookout for the perfect match between the parts of the effort that can be broken into smaller, more manageable pieces and delegated to others and the talented, intelligent individuals in whose hands these parts would flourish.

Great leaders leverage their resources effectively. They spread success rather than keep it to themselves; they know their job is to foster the success of an entire team, a complete unit, or organization. Some of the best leaders say they look for people who are smarter than they are in the specific area of need that the leader is best at identifying. Outstanding women are not afraid of delegating and giving up control to others who can take her essential skill to the next level. Each woman we profiled was not content to stay in the middle, helping and supporting. Each one looked forward to bigger challenges, took them on one by one, and became known for more than a simple job or profession.

Deliver Excellent Results Through Synergies

Fourth, leaders are results driven. They know that success comes from the smooth operation of all the right parts working well together. Effort is not enough. A leader knows that synergies exist—that performance of the larger group can be greater than the effort of any one part alone. A symphony is stronger and more powerful than the sound of any individual instrument. Yet for a symphony to excel, each individual performer must know and perform her part with precision. The ability to manage that synergy and to move it toward the goal or mission is the leader's unique domain. Getting the right people performing their best role is half the challenge. Keeping them all moving in the same direction, in tune with each other, is the other half.

The individuals mentioned by the women profiled in the preceding chapters did not simply train or mentor the women, but rather they were equal partners in attaining results for the business entity. The women brought knowledge, abilities, a work ethic, and a willingness to learn and be challenged. They worked together toward the same goals, the same results, at the corporation or organization—not simply the success of one party or the other.

Create an Enduring Framework or Institution

Fifth, a leader creates an organization or an entity that will continue into the future. If a leader only functions within the short term, the value that she creates will end with her. For people to give their best, they need to believe that the results they produce will endure for longer than the moment and for the benefit of more than just themselves. People give their best for a mission they believe will prevail long after their immediate efforts. Even if the entity changes over time, as it inevitably will, those who invest in it need to have a reasonable expectation that it will prevail. The protection of creative ideas and rights—ensuring they will stand through time—is a critical factor in the success of business and of leadership. Outstanding women are not afraid of hierarchy or organizational structures that could house the value that they and their colleagues have established over the long term.

While most of the women profiled preferred to build growth-oriented businesses, they were not afraid to take on the downside of restructuring, merging, downsizing, or even closing the doors. They were not the type to simply hold onto the entity, control it, or rule over it. They were the types to seek out the greatest potential and try to make it happen.

Demonstrate Leadership

Sixth, leaders show others how to lead by their example. Some leaders do so over the course of a long career of accomplishments, demonstrating endurance and perseverance in their area of expertise. Others show a willingness to stand up, take on the difficult and unforeseen issues, and search for solutions and resolution through collaboration, negotiations, or decisiveness. Boards of directors need members who are willing to speak their minds and to make tough choices when called upon to do so. It is no wonder that when corporations see women who are able, willing, and ready to lead, they invite them into the boardroom to help address the strategic challenges of modern business.

These are simple guidelines, drawn from the collective wisdom and experience of 114 women corporate directors. This may be the first time that many readers encountered these talented leaders: they have not sought the media limelight as have our entertainment mavens, athletic superstars, or even industry titans. These outstanding women have been busy doing the jobs that we needed done. If we had the opportunity to read about and to learn from them throughout their lives, imagine how many more women and men might have been motivated to follow in their footsteps.

WHERE ARE WE GOING?

Women in leadership—those whom we had the honor to interview for this book—know that they are going forward: away from a past that might have limited them and their potential. They are ever alert for those marvelous opportunities just too good to resist. They have confidence in serendipity, knowing that many of the good things that have come their way were set in motion years ago, when they were just doing their very best. They are at ease with themselves, their lives, and their choices: they are comfortable in their own skin. These women in leadership recognize that there is no such thing as a six- or twelve-step plan that miraculously guarantees them a position on a board or career success. They do recognize that each woman charts her own path, chooses her own career, and adds her own value and insight to a boardroom where she has been invited to participate. Each woman makes her own progress and learns from her own mistakes.

The goal of this book is to demonstrate how very many possibilities have been tested successfully by the women in leadership at California-based *Fortune* 1000 firms. Take whatever you need from this array of exemplary role models. Learn from these women whatever will help you guide your own career path.

Look forward and be open to all the possibilities along the way. Look all around you to find other outstanding women and men in leadership whom you can respect and emulate. Do not look for the shortcuts, but look for the ways to go around, over, under, or through challenges that crop up—externally or internally. Do not look for the easy way *for a woman*, because that will forever mark you as an exception rather than exceptional. Never look back, either in time or in fear that someone else is on your heels. There will always be someone who runs either a faster race or a slower race than you, but there will never be anyone else who runs your race.

How does a woman find a corporate board role? She doesn't. She builds a career of achievement and leadership. When a board of directors needs her skills and competencies, it will find her. And she will recognize it as an opportunity too good to resist.

Appendix 1

FORTUNE 1000 COMPANIES BASED IN CALIFORNIA WITH WOMEN DIRECTORS, 2007

Company	Name
ABM Industries	Linda L. Chavez
ABM Industries*	Maryellen C. Herringer
Adobe Systems	Carol Mills
Adobe Systems*	Colleen Pouliot
Agilent Technologies	Heidi Kunz
AMD	H. Paulett Eberhart
Amgen	Judith C. Pelham
Applied Materials	Deborah Ann Coleman
Autodesk	Carol A. Bartz
Autodesk*	Mary Alice Taylor
Avery Dennison	Julia A. Stewart
Beckman Coulter	Risa Juanita Lavizzo-Mourey
Beckman Coulter*	Betty Woods
Broadcom	Maureen E. Grzelakowski
Broadcom*	Nancy H. Handel
Building Materials Holding	Sara L. Beckman
CB Richard Ellis	Patrice Marie Daniels
Charles Schwab	Nancy Hellman Bechtle
Charles Schwab*	Marjorie Magner
Charles Schwab*	Paula A. Sneed
Chevron Corporation	Linnet Frazier Deily

Company	Name
Cisco	Carol A. Bartz
Cisco*	M. Michele Burns
CKE Restaurants	Janet E. Kerr
Clorox	Jan L. Murley
Clorox*	Pamela Thomas-Graham
Clorox*	Carolyn M. Ticknor
Con-Way	Margaret G. Gill
Countrywide Financial	Kathleen Brown
DaVita	Nancy-Ann Min DeParle
Del Monte	Mary R. Henderson
DirecTV Group	Nancy S. Newcomb
eBay	Dawn G. Lepore
eBay*	Margaret C. Whitman
Edison International	France A. Córdova
Electronic Arts	Linda J. Srere
First American Corporation	Roslyn B. Payne
First American Corporation*	Virginia Mae Ueberroth
First American Corporation*	Mary Lee Widener
Fleetwood Enterprises	Margaret A. Dano
Franklin Resources	Laura Stein
Franklin Resources*	Anne M. Tatlock
Gap Inc.	Doris F. Fisher
Gap Inc.*	Penelope L. Hughes
Gateway	Janet Morrison Clarke
Gilead Sciences	Gayle Edlund Wilson
Google	Anne Mather
Google*	Shirley M. Tilghman
Granite Construction	Linda Griego
Granite Construction*	Rebecca Ann McDonald
Health Net	Gale S. Fitzgerald
Hewlett-Packard	Sari L. Baldauf
Hewlett-Packard*	Lucille S. Salhany
Hewlett-Packard*	Patricia C. Dunn
Hilton Hotels	Barbara Bell Coleman
Hilton Hotels*	Christine Garvey
Hilton Hotels*	Donna Frame Tuttle
Ingram Micro	Martha R. Ingram

Company	Name
Ingram Micro*	Linda Fayne Levinson
Intel	Charlene Barshevsky
Intel*	Jane E. Shaw
Intuit	Donna Dubinsky
Jack in the Box	Anne B. Gust
Jack in the Box*	Alice Bourke Hayes
Jack in the Box*	Linda A. Lang
Jacobs Engineering Inc.	Linda K. Jacobs
Jacobs Engineering Inc.*	Linda Fayne Levinson
KB Homes	Melissa Lora
KLA-Tencor	Lida Náprstek Urbánek
Lam Research	Catherine P. Lego
Levi Strauss & Co.	Angela Glover Blackwell
Levi Strauss & Co.*	Miriam L. Haas
Levi Strauss & Co.*	Patricia A. House
Levi Strauss & Co.*	Patricia Salas Pineda
Longs Drug Stores	Mary S. Metz
Longs Drug Stores*	Donna Tanoue
Mattel	Andrea L. Rich
Mattel*	Kathy Brittain White
McKesson	M. Christine Jacobs
McKesson*	Marie L. Knowles
McKesson*	Jane E. Shaw
Molina Healthcare	Sally K. Richardson
Molina Healthcare*	Ronna Romney
Network Appliance	Carol A. Bartz
New Century Financial Corporation	Marilyn A. Alexander
Northrop Grummond	Aulana L. Peters
Occidental Petroleum	Rosemary Tomich
Oracle Corporation	Safra Catz
Oracle Corporation*	Naomi O. Seligman
Pacific Life	Mariann Byerwalter
Pacific Life*	Jacqueline C. Morby
Pacific Life*	Susan Westerberg Prager
PG&E*	Maryellen C. Herringer
PG&E*	Mary S. Metz
PG&E*	Barbara L. Rambo

Company	Name
Petco	Sandra N. Bane
Qualcomm	Adelia A. Coffman
Qualcomm*	Diana Lady Dougan
Ross Stores	Sharon D. Garrett
Ryland Group	Leslie Myers Frécon
Ryland Group*	Charlotte St. Martin
Safeway	Janet E. Grove
Safeway*	Rebecca A. Stirn
SanDisk	Catherine P. Lego
Sanmina-Sci	Jacquelyn M. Ward
Science Applications Inc.	Anita K. Jones
Science Applications Inc.*	Claudine B. Malone
Solectron	H. Paulett Eberhart
Spansion	Patti S. Hart
Sun Microsystems	Patricia E. Mitchell
Sun Microsystems*	Naomi O. Seligman
URS	Betsy J. Bernard
VeriSign	Michelle Guthrie
Walt Disney	Judith L. Estrin
Walt Disney*	Monica C. Lozano
Watson Pharmaceuticals	Catherine M. Klema
Wells Fargo	Susan E. Engel
Wells Fargo*	Cynthia H. Milligan
Wells Fargo*	Judith M. Runstad
Wells Fargo*	Susan G. Swenson
Western Digital	Kathleen A. Cote
William-Sonoma	Jeanne P. Jackson
Xilinx	Elizabeth Vanderslice
Women-held board seats	123
Companies in *Fortune* 1000 in California (total)	102
Companies with women directors	74
Companies with zero women directors	27
Companies with more than one woman-held board seats	48

* = Companies with more than one woman-held board seat.

Appendix 2

WOMEN DIRECTORS ON *FORTUNE* 1000 COMPANIES BASED IN CALIFORNIA, 2007

Name	Company
Marilyn A. Alexander	New Century Financial Corporation
Sari L. Baldauf	Hewlett-Packard
Sandra N. Bane	Petco
Charlene Barshevsky	Intel
Carol A. Bartz	Autodesk
Carol A. Bartz*	Cisco
Carol A. Bartz*	Network Appliance
Nancy Hellman Bechtle	Charles Schwab
Sara L. Beckman	Building Materials Holding
Betsy J. Bernard	URS
Angela Glover Blackwell	Levi Strauss & Co.
Kathleen Brown	Countrywide Financial
M. Michele Burns	Cisco
Mariann Byerwalter	Pacific Life
Safra Catz	Oracle Corporation
Linda L. Chavez	ABM Industries
Janet Morrison Clarke	Gateway
Adelia A. Coffman	Qualcomm
Barbara Bell Coleman	Hilton Hotels
Debroah Ann Coleman	Applied Materials
France A. Córdova	Edison International

Name	Company
Kathleen A. Cote	Western Digital
Patrice Marie Daniels	CB Richard Ellis
Margaret A. Dano	Fleetwood Enterprises
Linnet Frazier Deily	Chevron Corporation
Nancy-Ann Min DeParle	DaVita
Diana Lady Dougan	Qualcomm
Donna Dubinsky	Intuit
Patricia C. Dunn	Hewlett-Packard
H. Paulett Eberhart	AMD
H. Paulett Eberhart*	Solectron
Susan E. Engel	Wells Fargo
Judith L. Estrin	Walt Disney
Doris F. Fisher	Gap Inc.
Gale S. Fitzgerald	Health Net
Leslie Myers Frécon	Ryland Group
Sharon D. Garrett	Ross Stores
Christine Garvey	Hilton Hotels
Margaret G. Gill	Con-Way
Linda Griego	Granite Construction
Janet E. Grove	Safeway
Maureen E. Grzelakowski	Broadcom
Anne B. Gust	Jack in the Box
Michelle Guthrie	VeriSign
Miriam L. Haas	Levi Strauss & Co.
Nancy H. Handel	Broadcom
Patti S. Hart	Spansion
Alice Bourke Hayes	Jack in the Box
Mary R. Henderson	Del Monte
Maryellen C. Herringer	ABM Industries
Maryellen C. Herringer*	PG&E
Patricia A. House	Levi Strauss & Co.
Penelope L. Hughes	Gap Inc.
Martha R. Ingram	Ingram Micro
Jeanne P. Jackson	William-Sonoma
Linda K. Jacobs	Jacobs Engineering Inc.
M. Christine Jacobs	McKesson

Name	Company
Anita K. Jones	Science Applications Inc.
Janet E. Kerr	CKE Restaurants
Catherine M. Klema	Watson Pharmaceuticals
Marie L. Knowles	McKesson
Heidi Kunz	Agilent Technologies
Linda A. Lang	Jack in the Box
Risa Juanita Lavizzo-Mourey	Beckman Coulter
Catherine P. Lego	Lam Research
Catherine P. Lego*	SanDisk
Dawn G. Lepore	eBay
Linda Fayne Levinson	Ingram Micro
Linda Fayne Levinson*	Jacobs Engineering Inc.
Melissa Lora	KB Homes
Monica C. Lozano	Walt Disney
Marjorie Magner	Charles Schwab
Claudine B. Malone	Science Applications Inc.
Anne Mather	Google
Rebecca Ann McDonald	Granite Construction
Mary S. Metz	Longs Drug Stores
Mary S. Metz*	PG&E
Cynthia H. Milligan	Wells Fargo
Carol Mills	Adobe Systems
Patricia E. Mitchell	Sun Microsystems
Jacqueline C. Morby	Pacific Life
Jan L. Murley	Clorox
Nancy S. Newcomb	DirecTV Group
Roslyn B. Payne	First American Corporation
Judith C. Pelham	Amgen
Aulana L. Peters	Northrop Grummond
Patricia Salas Pineda	Levi Strauss & Co.
Colleen Pouliot	Adobe Systems
Susan Westerberg Prager	Pacific Life
Barbara L. Rambo	PG&E
Andrea L. Rich	Mattel
Sally K. Richardson	Molina Healthcare
Ronna Romney	Molina Healthcare

Name	Company
Judith M. Runstad	Wells Fargo
Lucille S. Salhany	Hewlett-Packard
Naomi O. Seligman	Oracle Corporation
Naomi O. Seligman*	Sun Microsystems
Jane E. Shaw	Intel
Jane E. Shaw*	McKesson
Paula A. Sneed	Charles Schwab
Linda J. Srere	Electronic Arts
Charlotte St. Martin	Ryland Group
Laura Stein	Franklin Resources
Julia A. Stewart	Avery Dennison
Rebecca A. Stirn	Safeway
Susan G. Swenson	Wells Fargo
Donna Tanoue	Longs Drug Stores
Anne M. Tatlock	Franklin Resources
Mary Alice Taylor	Autodesk
Pamela Thomas-Graham	Clorox
Carolyn M. Ticknor	Clorox
Shirley M. Tilghman	Google
Rosemary Tomich	Occidental Petroleum
Donna Frame Tuttle	Hilton Hotels
Virgina Mae Ueberroth	First American Corporation
Lida Náprstek Urbánek	KLA-Tencor
Elizabeth Vanderslice	Xilinx
Jacquelyn M. Ward	Sanmina-Sci
Kathy Brittain White	Mattel
Margaret C. Whitman	eBay
Mary Lee Widener	First American Corporation
Gayle Edlund Wilson	Gilead Sciences
Betty Woods	Beckman Coulter
Woman-held seats	123
Women directors	114
Women on multiple boards	9

* = Women on multiple boards.

NOTES

CHAPTER 1: OVERVIEW

1. Irene Macauley, "Corporate Governance: Crown Charters to Dotcoms," *Stocks, Futures, and Options Magazine* (January 2003): 1, http://www.sfomag.com/article.aspx?ID=121&issueID=10 (accessed March 11, 2009).

2. National Women's Hall of Fame, "Patricia Roberts Harris: 1924–1985," http://www.greatwomen.org/women.php?action=viewone&id=200/ (accessed March 11, 2009).

3. Robert Clark, "Juanita Kreps: Profiles in Gerontology," *Contemporary Gerontology* (Winter 2002), http://www.econ.duke.edu/dje/2004/JUANITA%20KREPS.pdf (accessed March 11, 2009).

4. "Shirley M. Hufstedler," *Attorneys & Professionals,* Morrison Foerster, http://www.mofo.com/attorneys/3771/summary.html (accessed March 11, 2009).

5. Pamela Wilson, "It All Adds Up: Mary Lanigar '38 Blazed a Trail to Corporate Success for Women," *Mills Quarterly* (Spring 2008): 40.

6. Vita of Leslie L. Luttgens.

7. "A Current Glance of Women in the Law: 2007," American Bar Association, http://www.abanet.org/women/CurrentGlanceStatistics2007.pdf (accessed March 11, 2009).

8. American Medical Association, *Physician Characteristics and Distribution in the U.S., 2008* (Chicago: American Medical Association, 2008), http://www.ama-assn.org/ama/pub/about-ama/our-people/member-groups-sections/women-physicians-congress/statistics-history.shtml (accessed March 16, 2009).

9. Bureau of Labor Statistics, "Occupational Employment Statistics: May 2007" (Washington, DC: U.S. Department of Labor, 2007), http://www.bls.gov/oes/current/oes111011.htm#nat (accessed March 11, 2009).

10. Center for Women's Business Research, *The Leading Edge: Women-Owned Million Dollar Firms* (Washington, DC: Center for Women's Business Research, 2004).

11. U.S. Census Bureau, "Survey of Business Owners—Women-Owned Firms: 2002," (Washington, DC: U.S. Census Bureau, August 2006), http://www.census.gov/csd/sbo/women2002.htm (accessed March 11, 2009).

12. Catalyst Inc., University of Michigan Business School and the Center for the Education of Women, "Women and the MBA: Gateway to Opportunity" (New York: Catalyst, 2000), 2.

13. Alice Clark Ronce, "Views from Women on Fortune 500 Boards," *DataLine* 1, no. 9, (Cyberwerks.com, March 1992), http://web.archive.org/web/20070212084032/cyberwerks. com/dataline/mapping/womenonf.html (DataLine originally accessed June 14, 2007).

14. Catalyst Inc., "Women and the MBA."

CHAPTER 2: MOTHERS TERESA

1. Mary Maxwell Gates (1929–1994) served 18 years (1975–1993) on the board of regents of the University of Washington (her alma mater, where she led the effort to divest university holdings in South Africa as a protest of apartheid). She was a director at First Interstate Bank of Washington, Unigard Security Insurance Group, Pacific Northwest Bell Telephone Company (later U.S. West Communications), and KIRO Incorporated.

2. "About CEO," Center for Equal Opportunity, http://www.ceousa.org/content/view/ 40/52/ (accessed March 11, 2009).

3. "The C200 Business Leadership Index 2005: Annual Report on Women's Clout in Business," (Chicago: Committee of 200, 2005).

4. Chicago Network, "Women Mean Business" (Chicago: Chicago Network, 2007).

DIRECTOR PROFILE: GAYLE EDLUND WILSON

1. Gail Sheehy, *Passages: Predictable Crises of Adult Life* (New York: Bantam Books, 1976).

2. "Our Mission," *About AJLI,* The American Junior League International. http://www. ajli.org/?nd=about_about (accessed March 11, 2009).

3. "The History of CEE," *About Us,* The Center for Excellence in Education, http://www. cee.org/about/history (accessed March 11, 2009).

4. "Gayle Wilson Elected to Caltech Board of Trustees," Caltech press release, March 27, 1995.

5. "College Access Foundation of California Adopts New Name—Reflects Mission of College Access for All," College Access Foundation press release, April 3, 2007.

6. "Corporate Responsibility," Gilead Sciences Inc. http://www.gilead.com/corporate_ responsibility (accessed March 11, 2009).

7. "Carla A. Hills Joins Gilead Sciences' Board of Directors," Gilead press release, January 23, 2007.

DIRECTOR PROFILE: ANDREA L. RICH

1. Suzanne Muchnic, "New LACMA President: A Woman of Possibilities," *Los Angeles Times,* July 7, 1995, F1, 48.

2. Stephen Bainbridge, "The Hammer Museum Backstory," *The Law Blog,* October 6, 2007, http://209.85.173.132/search?q=cache:fCFk_MdTXaUJ:www.businessassociationsblog. com/lawandbusiness/comments/the_hammer_museum_backstory/+Stephen+Bainbridge, +Hammer+Museum+Backstory&hl=en&gl=us&strip=1 (accessed March 11, 2009).

3. Larry Gordon and Marina Dundjerski, "Protesters Attack UCLA Faculty Center," *Los Angeles Times,* May 12, 1993, B1.

4. Joye Mercer, "UCLA Adjusts to Painful Budget Surgery," *Chronicle of Higher Education* 40, no. 33 (April 20, 1994): 36–37, 41.

5. Muchnic, "New LACMA President."

6. "LACMA Acquires One of World's Finest Collections of Islamic Art," LACMA press release, 2002.

7. "Andrea Rich Elected to Mattel Board of Directors," Mattel Inc. press release, November 5, 1998.

CHAPTER 3: POLITICIANS

1. Center for American Women in Politics, Rutgers University, *Women in Elective Office 2009,* http://www.cawp.rutgers.edu/fast_facts/levels_of_office/documents/elective.pdf (accessed March 6, 2009).

2. Ronna Romney with Beppie Harrison, *Momentum: Women in American Politics Now* (New York: Crown, 1988).

DIRECTOR PROFILE: LINNET FRAZIER DEILY

1. Carla Anderson Hills, "The Stakes of Doha," *Foreign Affairs* 84, no. 7 (2005): 1, http://www.foreignaffairs.org/20051201faessay84703/carla-a-hills/the-stakes-of-doha.html (accessed March 11, 2009).

2. "Former Deputy U.S. Trade Representative Linnet Deily Joins Board of Lucent Technologies," Alcatel-Lucent press release, November 10, 2005.

3. "Honeywell Board of Directors Nominates Former Deputy U.S. Trade Representative Linnet F. Deily to Stand for Election as a Director at 2006 Annual Meeting," Honeywell press release, March 13, 2006.

DIRECTOR PROFILE: LINDA GRIEGO

1. "Linda Griego Named to City National's Boards of Directors," City National Bank press release October 26, 2006.

2. Shari Redstone, Sumner Redstone's daughter, is not considered independent under the Securities and Exchange Commission definitions.

DIRECTOR PROFILE: SALLY K. RICHARDSON

1. "Director's Message," West Virginia University, Institute for Health Policy Research, http://www.hsc.wvu.edu/wvhealthpolicy/message.html (accessed March 11, 2009).

CHAPTER 4: LES BELLES LETTRES

1. Douglas Branson, *No Seat at the Table: How Corporate Governance and Law Keep Women out of the Boardroom* (New York: New York University Press, 2006).

2. Martha S. West and John W. Curtis, "Organizing Around Gender Equity: AAUP Faculty Gender Equity Indicators 2006" (Washington, DC: American Association of University Professors, 2006), 8.

3. "Katharine Malone Prizes for Academic Excellence," Wellesley College press release, October 6, 1996.

4. "Nina Henderson/CoMAD and Baiada Center Business Plan Competitions. 2008," Drexel University CoMAD press release, winter 2008.

5. American Council on Education, *The American College President, 2007 Edition* (Washington, DC: American Council on Education, 2007).

DIRECTOR PROFILE: ALICE BOURKE HAYES

1. Dr. Hayes's honorary degrees are from Loyola University Chicago (science, 1994); Fontbonne College in St. Louis, Missouri (humane letters, 1994); Mount St. Mary's College in Los Angeles (humane letters, 1998); Saint Louis University (law, 2002); Providence College (education, 2004); and University of San Francisco (education, 2006).

2. Alice Hayes, "The New Presence of Women Leaders," *Journal of Leadership Studies* 6, no. 1/2 (1999): 115–21.

3. Dr. Hayes was a member of the Chicago Network, the Missouri Women's Forum, and the Council of 100.

4. Marguerite Rigoglioso, "Diverse Backgrounds and Personalities Can Strengthen Groups," *Stanford Graduate School of Business News,* August 2006, http://www.gsb.stanford.edu/news/research/hr_neale_groupdiversity.shtml (accessed March 11, 2009).

5. Alice Hayes, "The Lion King and Women Leaders," *Society of Women Engineers* 43 (1997): 29.

DIRECTOR PROFILE: MARY S. METZ

1. Dr. Metz was elected to Furman's Gamma chapter of Phi Beta Kappa in 1980 as an honored alumna (there was no chapter when she was an undergraduate).

2. Dr. Metz authored three books on French instruction: *Reflets du monde français* (New York: McGraw-Hill, 1971); *Le français à vivre* (New York: McGraw-Hill, 1978); and *Le français à découvrir* with Jo Helstrom (New York: McGraw-Hill, 1972).

3. She has been honored with an LHD in humanities from Furman College in Greenville, South Carolina, in 1984; an LLD from Chapman University in Orange, California, in 1985; and a PhD in literature from Converse College in Spartanburg, South Carolina, in 1988.

4. Susan Tifft, "Dollars, Scholars and Gender," *Time,* May 21, 1990.

5. Tifft, "Dollars, Scholars and Gender."

6. Tom Petruno, "UnionBanCal Accepts Sweetened Buyout Bid from Mitsubishi UFJ," *Los Angeles Times,* August 19, 2008, C3.

7. Alice K. Boatwright, "Dean Mary Metz to Retire from UC Berkeley Extension," *Berkeleyan,* June 10, 1998.

8. "University of California Berkeley Opens Online School," UC Berkeley press release, June 27, 1996.

9. Boatwright, "Dean Mary Metz."

10. "Mission," S.H.Cowell Foundation, http://www.shcowell.org/sections/whoweare/wwa_mission.php (accessed March 11, 2009).

11. Mary S. Metz. "Inside the Audit Committee," *Internal Auditor,* October 1993.

CHAPTER 5: ANGELS AND VENTURES

1. Candida Brush, Nancy Carter, Elizabeth Gatewood, Patricia Greene, and Myra Hart, *Gatekeepers of Venture Growth: A Diana Project Report on the Role and Participation of Women in the Venture Capital Industry* (Kansas City, MO: Kauffman Foundation, 2004).

2. "MoneyTree™ Report, Data: Thomson Reuters: Total U.S. Investments by Year Q1 1995–Q4 2008," National Aggregate Data (Arlington, VA: National Venture Capital Association: 2008), https://www.pwcmoneytree.com/MTPublic/ns/nav.jsp?page=notice&iden=B (accessed March 4, 2009).

3. Claire Cain Miller, "Where Are the Women Venture Capitalists?" *Forbes,* January 25, 2007, http://www.forbes.com/2007/01/25/07midas-powerful-women-tech-cz_ccm_0125wo men.html (accessed March 4, 2009).

4. Geraldine Fabrikant, "Corner of Finance Where Women Are Climbing," *New York Times,* March 22, 2008, C1.

5. Brian Perry, "US Center for Venture Research 2006 Report," *The Angel Investor Magazine,* March 19, 2007, http://www.theangelinvestor.com/article/100039;jsessionid=8FC0B B1FDBAB106952000FFE1A85CB88/US-Center-For-Venture-Research-2006-Report/ (accessed March 11, 2009).

6. John R. Becker-Blease and Jeffrey E. Sohl, "Do Women-Owned Businesses Have Equal Access to Angel Capital?" *Journal of Business Venturing* 22, no. 4 (2007): 517.

DIRECTOR PROFILE: LESLIE MYERS FRÉCON

1. "Ryland Elects Leslie Frecon to Board of Directors," Ryland press release, July 28, 1998.

2. Center for Women's Business Research, *The Leading Edge: Women-Owned Million Dollar Firms* (Washington, DC: Center for Women's Business Research, 2004).

3. Candida Brush, Nancy Carter, Elizabeth Gatewood, Patricia Greene, and Myra Hart, *Gatekeepers of Venture Growth: A Diana Project Report on the Role and Participation of Women in the Venture Capital Industry* (Kansas City, MO: Kauffman Foundation, 2004).

4. Ibid.

5. "About Springboard," Springboard Enterprises, https://www.springboardenterprises. org/about (accessed March 4, 2009).

DIRECTOR PROFILE: DONNA FRAME TUTTLE

1. In October 2007 Hilton Hotels Corp. was merged into The Blackstone Group, a global manager of investment funds.

DIRECTOR PROFILE: DEBORAH ANN COLEMAN

1. Mary Pat McCarthy was the vice chair of KPMG LLP in 1997 and was the first woman to serve on their management committee. With Keyur Patel she coauthored *Digital Transformation: The Essentials of e-Business Leadership* (New York: McGraw-Hill, 2000).

2. "Deborah Coleman Added to Synopsys Board," Synopsys press release, November 7, 1995.

3. "Applied Materials Names Merix CEO Debi Coleman to Board of Directors," Applied Materials Inc. press release, March 20, 1997.

4. SBIC (Small Business Investment Corporation) is a private venture capital fund overseen by the U.S. Small Business Administration.

CHAPTER 6: HAN SOLOS

1. Laurent Bouzereau, *Star Wars: The Annotated Screenplays* (New York: Del Rey, 1997), 8.
2. Jason Clifton and James G. Clawson, "The Life and Career of a High-Tech Entrepreneur (A) and (B)" (Darden Business Publishing Ref. UVA-OB-0843 and 0844, University of Virginia, 2005).
3. Patricia Greene, Candida Brush, Myra Hart, and Patrick Saparito, "An Exploration of the Venture Capital Industry: Is Gender an Issue?" *Frontiers of Entrepreneurship Research: 1999* (Wellesley, MA: Babson College, 1999), 1, http://www.babson.edu/entrep/fer/papers99/IV/IV_A/IVA.html (accessed March 11, 2009).
4. Candida Brush, Nancy Carter, Patricia Greene, Myra Hart, and Elizabeth Gatewood, *Women and Equity Capital: An Exploration of Factors Affecting Capital Access* (Wellesley, MA: Babson College, 2000). See the final report: Candida Brush, Nancy Carter, Elizabeth Gatewood, Patricia Greene, and Myra Hart, *An Investigation of Women-Led Firms and Venture Capital Investment: Final Report* (Duxbury, MA: CB Associates, 2001).
5. U.S. Small Business Administration, *Women in Business: A Demographic Review of Women's Business Ownership* (Washington, DC: U.S. Small Business Administration, 2006).
6. Ibid.
7. Center for Women's Business Research, *The Leading Edge: Women-Owned Million Dollar Firms* (Washington, DC: Center for Women's Business Research, 2004).

DIRECTOR PROFILE: JUDITH L. ESTRIN

1. Vinton Cerf, as told to Bernard Aboba, "How The Internet Came to Be," *The Online User's Encyclopedia* (New York: Addison-Wesley, 1993), http://www.netvalley.com/archives/mirrors/cerf-how-inet.html (accessed March 11, 2009).
2. Tekla S. Perry, "Planting Seeds of Technology," *IEEE Spectrum: People* (July 2001): 68–73.
3. "Cisco Systems Appoints Judith Estrin as Chief Technology Officer," Cisco Systems press release, March 11, 1998.
4. The dot-com bubble burst at the turn of the century: the NASDAQ peaked at 5048 in March 2000 and then fell to a low of 1148 in October 2002. Venture capital investments also reached a peak in the first quarter of 2000 and then fell for the next 11 quarters, bottoming out in the beginning of 2003.
5. Mr. Carrico and Ms. Estrin divorced in 2005.

DIRECTOR PROFILE: LUCILLE S. SALHANY

1. Bernard F. Dick, *Engulfed: The Death of Paramount Pictures and the Birth of Corporate Hollywood* (Lawrence: University Press of Kentucky, 2001).
2. "Scholarship to Be Created in Honor of Lucille Salhany," *Expression*, Winter 2003, 29.

CHAPTER 7: LADDER CLIMBERS: THE CORPORATE PATH

1. Reena Aggarwal, Isil Eerel, René Stulz, and Rohan Williamson, "Do U.S. Firms Have the Best Corporate Governance? A Cross-Country Examination of the Relations Between

Corporate Governance and Shareholder Wealth," working paper, Fisher College of Business, Ohio State University, 2006.

DIRECTOR PROFILE: JANET MORRISON CLARKE

1. Ms. Clarke created the Clarke Littlefield name by combining her name with that of a New England entrepreneur whom she admired, Edmund Littlefield, to convey a professional and inspirational image. Ms. Clarke is the 12th generation of the family that sprang from Edmund Littlefield, who came from England to Exeter, New Hampshire, in 1636 and then relocated to Wells, Maine, where he became a successful entrepreneur, founding taverns, grist mills, and lumber yards.

2. Ms. Clarke currently serves on board of the privatized parent company, Forbes Media LLC.

3. "Asbury Automotive Group Appoints New Directors to Board," Asbury Automotive Group press release, March 16, 2005.

4. "Ted Waitt Retires from Gateway Board of Directors: Former President and Long-Time Director Richard Snyder Elected Chairman of Gateway Board," Gateway press release, May 19, 2005.

5. David A. Garvin and Artemis March, "R. R. Donnelley & Sons: The Digital Division," Harvard Business School Case No. 9-396-154, January 12, 1996; Shona L. Brown and Kathleen M. Eisenhardt, "Training Manual and Teaching Guide," *Competing on the Edge: Strategy as Structured Chaos* (Boston: Harvard Business School Press, 1998), http://www.channel501.com/education/chaos21.html (accessed March 16, 2009).

6. "Mimeo.com Announces the Appointment of Janet Clarke to Its Board of Directors; Print Industry Veteran Joins Expanded Board," Mimeo.com press release, June 29, 2006.

DIRECTOR PROFILE: JUDITH M. RUNSTAD

1. Ms. Runstad was a member of the Governor's State Environmental Policy Act Commission (1983–1984), the Governor's Puget Sound Water Quality Authority (1985–1987), the Governor's Washington State Growth Strategies Commission (1990–1991), and the Governor's High Speed Ground Transportation Commission (1991–1992). She was co-chair of Governor Locke's Washington Competitiveness Council (2001–2004) and of Governor Gregoire's Global Competitiveness Council (2005–2006).

2. Ms. Runstad was on the board of directors of the Seattle branch of the San Francisco Federal Reserve Bank until 1991 and was chair from 1990 to 1991. From 1992 to 1997, she was a director at the San Francisco Federal Reserve Bank and was its chair from 1995 to 1997.

3. "About the Alliance: Our History," The Alliance for Education, http://www.alliance4ed.org/about/history.htm (accessed March 2, 2009).

DIRECTOR PROFILE: KATHLEEN A. COTE

1. Ms. Cote was the public face of Wang in many Holyoke community positions. She was a director of Babson College's Women's Initiative for Technology Leadership, the Boston chapter of the National Urban League, the Massachusetts Private Industry Council, and the Council for Women in Technology (co-sponsored by the Department of Labor and the University of Massachusetts), and the Massachusetts High Technology Council and vice chair of the Massachusetts Council for Advanced Technology Transfer in Manufacturing. In 1997, she was awarded the University of Massachusetts, Amherst, Chancellor's Medal in

recognition of her achievements as an alumna and in May 2003 she received an honorary doctorate of humane letters from the University of Massachusetts, Amherst.

2. "WorldPort Names Kathleen Cote as Chief Executive Officer; Heisley Remains Chairman of the Board," WorldPort Communications Inc. press release, May 24, 2001.

3. "Kathleen A. Cote Elected to Western Digital Board," Western Digital press release, January 31, 2001.

4. "RadView Shuffles Board," by boston.internet.com staff, InternetNews.com (April 27, 2001), http://www.internetnews.com/bus-news/article.php/754231 (accessed October 17, 2008).

5. "Workscape Appoints Kathleen Cote to Board of Directors," Workscape press release, January 30, 2006.

6. "Technology Industry Veteran Kathleen Cote Joins VeriSign Board of Directors," VeriSign press release, February 25, 2008.

CHAPTER 8: CONCLUSION: QUO VADIS?

1. "To the Shareholders of Berkshire Hathaway Inc." from Warren E. Buffet (February 28, 2007), http://www.berkshirehathaway.com/letters/2006ltr.pdf (accessed March 12, 2009).

Selected Bibliography

Aboba, Bernard. *The Online User's Encyclopedia.* New York: Addison-Wesley, 1993.

Aggarwal, Reena, Isil Erel, René Stulz, and Rohan Williamson. "Do U.S. Firms Have the Best Corporate Governance? A Cross-Country Examination of the Relations Between Corporate Governance and Shareholder Wealth." Working paper. Fisher College of Business, Ohio State University, 2006.

American Council on Education. *The American College President, 2007 Edition.* Washington, DC: American Council on Education, 2007.

American Medical Association. *Physician Characteristics and Distribution in the U.S., 2008.* Chicago: American Medical Association, 2008.

Becker-Blease, John R., and Jeffrey E. Sohl, "Do Women-Owned Businesses Have Equal Access to Angel Capital?" *Journal of Business Venturing* 22, no. 4 (2007): 503–521.

Bouzereau, Laurent. *Star Wars: The Annotated Screenplays.* New York: Del Rey, 1997.

Branson, Douglas. *No Seat at the Table: How Corporate Governance and Law Keep Women out of the Boardroom.* New York: New York University Press, 2006.

Bratton, William W., and Margaret M. Blair. "Restoring Trust in America's Business Institutions, Panel III: The Changing Role of Corporate Directors." Working Paper No. 05-25, Law & Economics Working Paper Series, Vanderbilt University Law School, November 2003.

Brown, Shona L., and Kathleen M. Eisenhardt. *Competing on the Edge: Strategy as Structured Chaos.* Boston: Harvard Business School Press, 1998.

Brush, Candida, Nancy Carter, Elizabeth Gatewood, Patricia Greene, and Myra Hart. *Gatekeepers of Venture Growth: A Diana Project Report on the Role and Participation of Women in the Venture Capital Industry.* Kansas City, MO: Kauffman Foundation, 2004.

Brush, Candida, Nancy Carter, Elizabeth Gatewood, Patricia Greene, and Myra Hart. *An Investigation of Women-Led Firms and Venture Capital Investment: Final Report.* Duxbury, MA: CB Associates, 2001.

Brush, Candida, Nancy Carter, Patricia Greene, Myra Hart, and Elizabeth Gatewood. *Women and Equity Capital: An Exploration of Factors Affecting Capital Access.* Wellesley, MA: Babson College, 2000.

Bureau of Labor Statistics. "Occupational Employment Statistics: May 2007." Washington, DC: U.S. Department of Labor, 2007.

Catalyst Inc., University of Michigan Business School and the Center for the Education of Women. "Women and the MBA: Gateway to Opportunity." New York: Catalyst, 2000.

Center for Women's Business Research. *The Leading Edge: Women-Owned Million Dollar Firms.* Washington, DC: Center for Women's Business Research, 2004.

Clifton, Jason, and James G. Clawson. "The Life and Career of a High-Tech Entrepreneur (A)." Darden Business Publishing Ref. UVA-OB-0843, University of Virginia, 2005.

Clifton, Jason, and James G. Clawson. "The Life and Career of a High-Tech Entrepreneur (B)." Darden Business Publishing Ref. UVA-OB-0844, University of Virginia, 2005.

Dick, Bernard F. *Engulfed: The Death of Paramount Pictures and the Birth of Corporate Hollywood.* Lawrence: University Press of Kentucky, 2001.

Garvin, David A., and Artemis March. "R. R. Donnelley & Sons: The Digital Division." Harvard Business School Case No. 9-396-154, January 12, 1996.

Gentile, Mary, and Todd D. Jick. "Debi Coleman and Apple Computer, Inc." Harvard Business School Case No. 9-488-024, March 17, 1988.

Gentile, Mary, and Todd D. Jick. "Donna Dubinsky and Apple Computer, Inc. (A)." Harvard Business School Case No. 9-486-083. February 21, 1986.

Gentile, Mary, and Todd D. Jick. "Donna Dubinsky and Apple Computer, Inc. (B)." Harvard Business School Case No. 9-486-084. February 21, 1986.

Gentile, Mary, and Todd D. Jick. "Donna Dubinsky and Apple Computer, Inc. (C)." Harvard Business School Case No. 9-486-085. February 21, 1986.

Greene, Patricia G., Candida Brush, Myra Hart, and Patrick Saparito. "An Exploration of the Venture Capital Industry: Is Gender an Issue?" In *Frontiers of Entrepreneurship Research.* Ed. W. Bygrave, N. Carter, C. Maxon, D. Meyer, S. Manigart, and K. Shaver. Wellesley, MA: Babson College, 1998.

Grunig, Larissa A., Linda Childers Hon, and Elizabeth Lance Toth. *Women in Public Relations: How Gender Influences Practice.* New York: Guilford Press, 2001.

Hayes, Alice. "The Lion King and Women Leaders." *Society of Women Engineers* 43 (1997): 26–29.

Hayes, Alice. "The New Presence of Women Leaders." *Journal of Leadership Studies* 6, no. 1/2 (1999): 115–21.

Lorsch, Jay William, and Elizabeth MacIver. *Pawns or Potentates: The Reality of America's Corporate Boards.* Boston: Harvard Business School Press, 1989.

Lublin, Joann S. "Management: How One Woman Manages in Male Boardroom World." *Wall Street Journal,* November 28, 1997.

McGarvie, Blythe. *Fit in, Stand Out: Mastering the FISO FACTOR—the Key to Leadership Effectiveness in Business and Life.* New York: McGraw-Hill, 2006.

Metz, Mary S. "Inside the Audit Committee." *Internal Auditor,* October 1993.

National Foundation for Women Business Owners and Wells Fargo. "1999 Facts on Women-Owned Businesses: Trends in the Top 50 Metropolitan Areas." Washington, DC: National Foundation for Women Business Owners and Wells Fargo, 1999.

Patel, Keyur, and Mary Pat McCarthy. *Digital Transformation: The Essentials of e-Business Leadership.* New York: McGraw-Hill, 2000.

Romney, Ronna, with Beppie Harrison. *Momentum: Women in American Politics Now.* New York: Crown, 1988.

Schwartzman, Edward. *Political Campaign Craftsmanship: A Professional's Guide to Campaigning for Public Office.* New Brunswick, NJ: Transaction Publishers, 1989.

Sheehy, Gail. *Passages: Predictable Crises of Adult Life.* New York: Bantam Books, 1976.

U.S. Census Bureau. "Survey of Business Owners—Women-Owned Firms: 2002." Washington, DC: U.S. Census Bureau, 2006.

U.S. Small Business Administration. *Women in Business: A Demographic Review of Women's Business Ownership.* Washington, DC: U.S. Small Business Administration, 2006.

West, Martha S., and John W. Curtis. "Organizing Around Gender Equity: AAUP Faculty Gender Equity Indicators 2006." Washington, DC: American Association of University Professors, 2006.

Index

About the Author

ELIZABETH GHAFFARI is president and CEO of Technology Place Inc., a technology advisory firm. With a background in corporate bank computer operations, economics, and project management in the United States and abroad, in 2004 she began analyzing the changes arising as a result of federal laws mandating greater transparency and accountability in U.S. publicly held companies. Her *Surveys of Women on Boards of Directors at California-Based Fortune 1000 Firms* provided the biographical and research foundation for *Outstanding in Their Field*. Ms. Ghaffari is the author of articles appearing in the *Corporate Board* and *Personal Wealth Journal* and a contributor to *Information Systems Management in Practice* by Barbara C. McNurlin and Ralph H. Sprague, Jr. (1993).